In Gratitude

Tom Tanner

ATLA Monograph Series
edited by Dr. Kenneth E. Rowe

1. Ronald L. Grimes. *The Divine Imagination: William Blake's Major Prophetic Visions.* 1972.
2. George D. Kelsey. *Social Ethics Among Southern Baptists, 1917–1969.* 1973.
3. Hilda Adam Kring. *The Harmonists: A Folk-Cultural Approach.* 1973.
4. J. Steven O'Malley. *Pilgrimage of Faith: The Legacy of the Otterbeins.* 1973.
5. Charles Edwin Jones. *Perfectionist Persuasion: The Holiness Movement and American Methodism. 1867–1936.* 1974.
6. Donald E. Byrne, Jr. *No Foot of Land: Folklore of American Methodist Itinerants.* 1975.
7. Milton C. Sernett. *Black Religion and American Evangelicalism: White Protestants, Plantation Missions, and the Flowering of Negro Christianity, 1787–1865.* 1975.
8. Eva Fleischner. *Judaism in German Christian Theology Since 1945: Christianity and Israel Considered in Terms of Mission.* 1975.
9. Walter James Lowe. *Mystery & The Unconscious: A Study in the Thought of Paul Ricoeur.* 1977.
10. Norris Magnuson. *Salvation in the Slums: Evangelical Social Work, 1865–1920.* 1977.
11. William Sherman Minor. *Creativity in Henry Nelson Wieman.* 1977.
12. Thomas Virgil Peterson. *Ham and Japheth: The Mythic World of Whites in the Antebellum South.* 1978.
13. Randall K. Burkett. *Garveyism as a Religious Movement: The Institutionalization of a Black Civil Religion.* 1978.
14. Roger G. Betsworth. *The Radical Movement of the 1960's.* 1980.
15. Alice Cowan Cochran. *Miners, Merchants, and Missionaries: The Roles of Missionaries and Pioneer Churches in the Colorado Gold Rush and Its Aftermath, 1858–1870.* 1980.
16. Irene Lawrence. *Linguistics and Theology: The Significance of Noam Chomsky for Theological Construction.* 1980.

17. Richard E. Williams. *Called and Chosen: The Story of Mother Rebecca Jackson and the Philadelphia Shakers.* 1981.
18. Arthur C. Repp, Sr. *Luther's Catechism Comes to America: Theological Effects on the Issues of the Small Catechism Prepared In or For America Prior to 1850.* 1982.
19. Lewis V. Baldwin. *"Invisible" Strands in African Methodism.* 1983.
20. David W. Gill. *The Word of God in the Ethics of Jacques Ellul.* 1984.
21. Robert Booth Fowler. *Religion and Politics in America.* 1985.
22. Page Putnam Miller. *A Claim to New Roles.* 1985.
23. C. Howard Smith. *Scandinavian Hymnody from the Reformation to the Present.* 1987.
24. Bernard T. Adeney. *Just War, Political Realism, and Faith.* 1988.
25. Paul Wesley Chilcote. *John Wesley and the Women Preachers of Early Methodism.* 1991.
26. Samuel J. Rogal. *A General Introduction of Hymnody and Congregational Song.* 1991.
27. Howard A. Barnes. *Horace Bushnell and the Virtuous Republic.* 1991.
28. Sondra A. O'Neale. *Jupiter Hammon and the Biblical Beginnings of African-American Literature.* 1993.
29. Kathleen P. Deignan. *Christ Spirit: The Eschatology of Shaker Christianity.* 1992.
30. D. Elwood Dunn. *A History of the Episcopal Church in Liberia, 1821–1980.* 1992.
31. Terrance L. Tiessen. *Irenaeus on the Salvation of the Unevangelized.* 1993.
32. James E. McGoldrick. *Baptist Successionism: A Crucial Question in Baptist History.* 1994.
33. Murray A. Rubinstein. *The Origins of the Anglo-American Missionary Enterprise in China, 1807–1840.* 1994.
34. Thomas M. Tanner. *What Ministers Know: A Qualitative Study of Pastors as Information Professionals.* 1994.

WHAT MINISTERS KNOW
A Qualitative Study of Pastors as Information Professionals

by
THOMAS M. TANNER

ATLA Monograph Series, No. 34

The American Theological Library Association
and
The Scarecrow Press, Inc.
Metuchen, N.J., & London
1994

This book is based on the author's thesis, "The Pastor as Information Professional: An Exploratory Study of How the Ministers of One Midwestern Community Gather and Disseminate Information," accepted as partial fulfillment of the requirements for the degree of Doctor of Philosophy in Library and Information Science, University of Illinois at Urbana-Champaign, Urbana, Illinois, 1992.

British Library Cataloguing-in-Publication data available

Library of Congress Cataloging-in-Publication Data

Tanner, Thomas M. (Thomas Michael), 1951-
  What ministers know : a qualitative study of pastors as
information professionals / by Thomas M. Tanner.
    p. cm. -- (ATLA monograph series ; no. 34)
  Based on the author's thesis (doctoral), University of Illinois at
Urbana-Champaign, 1992, originally presented under the title: The
pastor as information professional.
  Includes bibliographical references and index.
  ISBN 0-8108-2916-9 (alk. paper)
  1. Pastoral theology--United States--Case studies. 2. Clergy--
United States--Intellectual life. 3. Information science--United
States--Case studies. I. Title. II. Series.
  BV4011.7.T36 1994
  253--dc20   94-16609

TABLE OF CONTENTS

LIST OF TABLES AND FIGURE vii

EDITOR'S FOREWORD ix

ACKNOWLEDGMENTS xi

PREFACE xiii

1. INTRODUCTION 1

The Cultural Context 1
The Historical Context 5
The Ministerial Context 6
The Approach of This Study 8
The Methodological Framework 11
The Clergy Chosen 16
The Presentation of Findings 19

2. THE PASTOR AS INFORMATION
    PROFESSIONAL 21

The Professional Image of the Pastor 23
      1. The Generalist: The Pastor
         as Public Librarian 33

iii

88797

2. The Expert: The Pastor
   as Academic Librarian   38
3. The Equipper: The Pastor
   as Reference Librarian   43
4. The Wounded Healer:
   The Pastor as Activist Librarian   48
5. The Interpreter: The Pastor
   as Special Librarian   54
Summary of the Five Images   65
The Professional Authority of the Pastor   65
   Educational Authority   70
   Institutional Authority   79
   Personal Authority   85
   Divine Authority   90
The Professional Knowledge of the Pastor   98
   Spiritual Knowledge   99
   Three Kinds of Knowledge   100
      Factual Knowledge   101
      Relational Knowledge   101
      Limited Knowledge   106
Summary   109

3. THE PASTOR AS INFORMATION
   GATHERER   110

Ministerial Needs for Information   110
   Origin of Needs   111
   Utilitarian Needs   117
   Current Awareness Needs   121
   Information Overload   124
Ministerial Channels of Information   127
   Formal Channels   130
      Books: The Bible   130
      Books: Non-Biblical   141
      Periodicals and Newspapers   154

Audiovisuals 168
Computer Databases 176
Personal Libraries 182
Institutional Libraries 186
Informal Channels 191
Professional Conferences 193
Ministerial Associations 198
Personal Networks 201
Summary 206

4.   THE PASTOR AS INFORMATION
     DISSEMINATOR 208

The Influence of Media in Ministers'
Dissemination of Information 209
Print Media 211
Electronic Media 216
Oral Media 225
The Minister's Two Major Roles
as Information Disseminator 230
The Pastor as Healer 233
The Tension over Care and Counseling . . 234
The Questions Being Asked 238
The Answers Being Given 245
The Answers Not Being Given 251
Summary 257
The Pastor as Herald 258
The Purpose of the Sermon 262
The Role of the Messenger 264
The Information in the Message 269
The Choice of Topics 269
The Use of Sources 277
The Styles of Delivery 296
Summary 299

The Minister's Other Roles as
Information Disseminator 299
    The Pastor as Teacher 300
    The Pastor as Writer 302
    The Pastor as Media Personality 304
    The Pastor as Community Spokesperson 307

5.   CONCLUSION 309

Overview of Findings 309
    The Research Questions 309
    The Pastor as Information Professional 312
    The Pastor as Information Gatherer 317
    The Pastor as Information Disseminator 318
Summary of Major Findings 322
Limitations 323
Areas for Further Study 325
Implications of This Study 326

APPENDIX: A BIBLIOGRAPHIC ESSAY
ON INFORMATION USE 329

A Review of the Literature on "Information" 329
A Review of User Studies in General 334
A Review of User Studies Among the Clergy 338

ENDNOTES 347

LIST OF SOURCES CITED 361

INDEX 382

ABOUT THE AUTHOR 388

LIST OF TABLES AND FIGURE

TABLE

1. Educational Background of the
   Ministers in This Study   72

2. Importance of Information Sources
   for Ministry 128

3. Importance of Books as Information Sources 146

4. The 15 Most-Cited Serials Read by Clergy 155

5. Importance of Audiovisuals as
   Information Sources 168

6. An Overview of the Seven Case-Study
   Churches 260

7. Categories of Sermon Topics Preached 271

8. Frequency of the Sources Used
   in the 48 Sermons 278

FIGURE

1. Two Kinds of Knowledge 105

EDITOR'S FOREWORD

Since 1972 the American Theological Library Association has undertaken responsibility for a modest monograph series in the field of religious studies. Guidelines for projects and selections for publication are made by the Publications Section of ATLA in consultation with the editor. Titles are selected from studies in a wide range of religious and theological disciplines. We are pleased to publish Thomas M. Tanner's *What Ministers Know: A Qualitative Study of Pastors as Information Professionals* as number 34 in the ATLA Monograph Series.

Following undergraduate studies at Lincoln Christian College, Thomas Tanner took a Master of Divinity degree at Lincoln Christian Seminary. In addition, Dr. Tanner holds two master's degrees from the University of Illinois: an M.A. in Classical Philology and a Master's degree in Library Science, along with a Ph.D. in Library and Information Science. He is the author of "A History of Early Christian Libraries from Jesus to Jerome" (*Journal of Library History*, Fall 1979), "Bring the Books" (*Journal of Religious & Theological Information*, Winter 1993), and *A Manual of Style for Bible College and Seminary Students*, 4th edition (Lincoln Christian College Press, 1994). Dr. Tanner currently serves as Library Director for Lincoln Christian College and Seminary in Lincoln, Illinois.

Kenneth E. Rowe, Series Editor
Drew University Library
Madison, NJ 07940 USA

ACKNOWLEDGMENTS

Many people had a hand in the dissertation research that led to this book, and to them I owe a great deal. To my dissertation committee, especially Brett Sutton, I am grateful. His analysis and insight were constant and creative. I am also indebted to my colleagues at Lincoln Christian College and Seminary, especially Dean Shaw and Drs. Lowery, Strauss, Castelein, and Sackett. My thanks also to the trustees and administrators who granted me a sabbatical for this project, especially President McNeely, Don Green, and Mark Searby. I am particularly grateful to Phyllis Bussmann, Ann Spellman, and Nancy Olson, who filled the gaps in my absence.

The ministers in this study, however, are the ones to whom I owe the biggest debt. It was they who opened up their hearts to me and allowed me to hear their dreams and also see their nightmares. They are professionals in the best sense of that word, serving for the sheer joy of helping people and praising their God. Several--I wish I could name their names--were particularly invaluable to me in this research project, and on them I invoke God's richest blessing.

Finally, to my family and to my friends I say thank you, especially Mom, Randy, Mark, and Rod. To Deb and Melissa, I can only say that I dedicate this book with deepest love to you both. Only you know the pain, and only you know the gain. I thank my God in my every remembrance of you...with joy.

PREFACE

In 1934 a poet from St. Louis wrote a play to help some churches in London, where he was then residing. In looking at how pastors use information, one must not forget the larger questions raised by that poet T.S. Eliot in his play *The Rock*.

The endless cycle of idea and action,
Endless invention, endless experiment,
Brings knowledge of motion, but not of stillness;
Knowledge of speech, but not of silence;
Knowledge of words, and ignorance of the Word.

All our knowledge brings us nearer to our ignorance,
All our ignorance brings us nearer to death,
But nearness to death no nearer to God.

Where is the Life we have lost in living?
Where is the wisdom we have lost in knowledge?
Where is the knowledge we have lost in information?
. . . .
Silence! and preserve respectful distance.
For I perceive approaching
The Rock. Who will perhaps answer our doubtings.
The Rock. The Watcher. The Stranger.
He who has seen what has happened.
And who sees what is to happen.
The Witness. The Critic. The Stranger.
The God-shaken, in whom is the truth inborn.

1. INTRODUCTION

The Cultural Context

"Ministers Rated Highly as Community
Advice and Information Sources"

So read the headline in the May 1990 issue of *Emerging Trends*, a monthly newsletter published by the Princeton Religion Research Center. This publication reports new developments in the field of religion and society as determined by periodic Gallup polls researching these aspects of American life. The article under the headline described the results of a national telephone poll of 1,012 American adults over the age of 18 conducted by The Gallup Organization in February of 1990.[1] Fully 70% of those surveyed rated ministers as important sources of information and advice in the community, virtually tied with pharmacists (71%) and second only to physicians (84%). Further down on the list of those ranked as important community information sources were such professionals as lawyers (60%), bankers (55%), and librarians (40%).[2]

These findings are not overly surprising when one considers how much the clergy and the church permeate contemporary culture in this country. In quantitative terms, seven out of ten Americans claim church membership.[3] Six out of ten attend services at least monthly, and four in ten once a week. Attitudinally, over half (55%) of all American adults say that religion is very important in their lives, and 61% believe that religion can answer all or most of today's problems.[4] Even in those regions of the United States where the influence of religion is not as strong, citizen surveys in California and New England indicate that nearly 10% use religious leaders as information resources--a ranking similar to that given to libraries.[5]

These findings indicate that in modern American society, the clergy still occupy an important role in the flow of information. The primary purpose of this study is to consider in what ways the pastor does and does not function as an information professional, focusing particularly upon the pastor as an information gatherer and an information disseminator. Put in simpler terms, this study is concerned with what pastors know and how they communicate that information to their American parish. Why, as The Gallup Poll results suggest, are pastors rated so highly as information providers?

This research is intended to bring more understanding to the study of information use, a field that has been selected by the United States Department of Education's Office of Library Programs' planning document, "Issues in Library Research--An Agenda for the 1990s," as one of the major research fronts in the library and information science profession (see Mathews, 1991). Grover and Greer (1991) listed the study of information use and information users as two of the four major areas that "comprise the theoretical foundation for the education and research required for the maintenance and advancement of the profession" (p. 110).

Other professions outside of library and information science are also recognizing the importance of research in how people use information, including the study of clergy as information users and providers. The American Association for the Advancement of Science, for example, is currently conducting an "AAAS Black Churches Project," which, among other efforts, seeks to "train ministers to be advocates for quality math, science, and technology education; and introduce science into church-sponsored scout and preschool programs."[6] Results of an AAAS-sponsored survey of a sampling of the estimated 65,000 black churches in America suggest that ministers and churches serving the black community are actively engaged in providing information through educational programs to children and that these programs are as likely to serve children in the neighborhood as children within the congregation.[7]

Similar research projects that recognize the important informational role that ministers occupy, especially in ethnic communities, have been conducted in the last few years in other fields. Shields (1988), working within the discipline of social work, studied the gatekeeper role of black ministers in AIDS education in California communities, surveying 46 black clergy in Los Angeles County by means of a questionnaire. The results she obtained from the 20 ministers who responded (44%) indicated that "black ministers have a strong desire for information on AIDS" (Shields, 1988, p. 51) and most (94%) "felt that AIDS education had a place in the church" (p. 41), though only 42% had ever preached a sermon on the topic (p. 48).

Bratcher-Porter (1987), following the lead of earlier research by Scarlett (1970), Bruder (1971), Anderson (1975), Askey et al. (1983), and Roberson (1985), investigated the role of black ministers in providing health care information, particularly their role in disseminating cancer information. As part of her research in health sciences, Bratcher-Porter surveyed by mail 200 black clergy serving the city of Dallas, Texas. The responses from the 55 returned questionnaires indicated that "a majority of subjects were knowledgeable about cancer" (Bratcher-Porter, 1987, p. 62), that they were open to learning more, and that these ministers thought their congregations should know more as well about cancer prevention.[8]

In addition to the interest in this research area shown by various academic disciplines, societal demands for an informed clergy are also evident in another arena of contemporary American culture--the courtroom. Within the last six years clergy malpractice has become, according to Postell (1985, p. 91), "an emerging field of law" in this country.[9] In 1986 a major monograph on the topic by Malony, Needham, and Southard was published, the first ever devoted exclusively to this growing legal issue for pastors. Though much of this litigation centers around professional misconduct of a moral nature and some, no doubt, is due to the general rise in litigation in American society, the information role of the modern minister is still very much an issue in this recent trend.

For example, in the most publicized case to date, *Nally v. Grace Community Church* (157 Cal. App. 3d 912, 204 Cal. Rptr. 303 [1984]), a California couple brought a wrongful death suit against a church and its pastors alleging that their son's suicide was due to the failure of one of the pastors counseling him to exercise "the standard of care that a clergyman of his ... training ..." should exercise (English and Dibert, 1988). While this case was eventually dismissed, questions regarding the authoritativeness and accuracy of the information that ministers disseminate are still being raised.

The "value-added" role that clergy occupy as information disseminators is also evident in several other recent legal cases. In *Moroni v. Holy Spirit Association for Unification of World Christianity*, for example, the church started by the Rev. Sun Myung Moon was sued for "subjecting the decedent to an intensive indoctrination program" (598 F. Supp. 126 [D.D.C. 1984]) that went beyond the bounds of normal catechetical instruction. In *Redecki v. Schuckardt* (600 F. Supp. 757 [D.D.C. 1984]) two husbands alleged that a bishop "alienated the affections of their wives by promoting the belief that his followers should leave their spouses if the spouse interfered with his religious teachings" (summarized by English and Dibert, 1988, p. 8). Improper counseling was the basis for *Destefano v. The*

Diocese of Colorado Springs (Civ. Act. No. 84CVO773 [July 1984]), in which the court dismissed claims that a priest had violated professional ethics by engaging in an intimate relationship with a counselee.

Citing an article from *Case and Comment*, Postell (1985) observed that "the day when the clergy were the only learned members of the community and were considered to be the ultimate authorities on both civil and church matters has long since passed" (p. 91). A brief look at American history indicates how much the situation has changed in the last few hundred years.

The Historical Context

The issue of an informed clergy who function as information professionals in the community is not a new development in American society. For two centuries in this nation's history, the American colonies and the country they formed claimed for the church's leadership a major portion of America's brightest and best. The great educational institutions of Harvard, Yale, Princeton, and dozens like them were all founded to produce informed pastors. Indeed, one of the founding purposes of Harvard was "to advance Learning and perpetuate it to Posterity; dreading to leave an illiterate Ministry [sic] to the Churches, when our present Ministers shall lie in the Dust."[10]

In colonial New England ministers dispensed not only spiritual advice, but many of them were the sole source of medical information in the community as well. Watson's (1987, abstract) research into these Puritan preacher-physicians notes that their provision of health care was seen as "an extension of their intellectual prowess and profound hegemony in New England society."

Stout (1986) has also noted the primacy of the colonial

clergy in terms of the information dissemination role that they played. He observed that "the average weekly churchgoer in New England (and there were far more churchgoers than church members) listened to something like seven thousand sermons in a lifetime, totaling somewhere around fifteen thousand hours of concentrated listening" (p. 4). This investment is comparable to the time a typical college student spends in class during a modern four-year undergraduate degree. Stout concluded that in colonial America "the sermon was the only regular voice of authority" (p. 4).[11]

That colonial clergy were held in such high regard as a central community information source was a natural consequence in many ways of their educational training. According to May (1934, 2:24), from 1640 to 1740 more than half of all college graduates in the United States became clergymen and from 1740 to 1840 nearly a third did so. In the last 150 years the percentage has plummeted to less than five.

The Ministerial Context

In the last half of the twentieth century, however, the theological world has tried to recoup some of its former stature in terms of producing an informed clergy. In 1969, when the Association of Theological Schools in the United States and Canada began systematically gathering enrollment data and reporting it in its *Fact Book on Theological Education*, there were only 25,950 seminarians preparing for ministry. By 1990, the last year for which figures are available, the number had more than doubled to 59,033.

The numbers are even more striking in the area of continuing education for ministers in the field. To address the problem of keeping current in the profession of ministry after the initial Master of Divinity degree, many theological schools began adopting a Doctor of Ministry program in the mid 1960s for resident ministers to continue their studies. In 1969 there were only 325 persons in seven such programs; by 1990 there were 6,738 in ninety-one programs.[12]

In their landmark sociological study of contemporary clergy, *Ministry in America*, Schuller, Strommen, and Brekke (1980) provided some insight into the role of the modern minister as an information professional. Working under the auspices of the Association of Theological Schools, these three editors (one a social research scientist) reported the results of an "in-depth survey of [3,124 clergy and 1,871 laity in] 47 denominations in the United States and Canada" (p. 1).

The survey, which employed a critical-incident technique, asked clergy and laity to evaluate 444 characteristics in terms of how important they were for ministers to possess. These 444 traits were grouped into 64 "core clusters," and through factor analysis the researchers were able to identify nine major ministerial themes that were rated as "quite important." Interestingly, three of these nine themes relate to the minister's knowledge, information base, and understanding of community problems.

Among the 64 "core clusters" of clergy characteristics that were measured in this massive sociological study of ministers, 36 (56%) emphasized in one way or another the importance of a well-informed ministry that takes its information role seriously. For example, "core cluster 30" measured ministers' "use of broad knowledge." Such characteristics as "teaches and preaches from a broad base of knowledge," "reflects an awareness of current affairs reported in newspapers and periodicals," and "speaks knowledgeably about subjects outside theology without being a bore" were all rated above the mean by pastors and parishioners.

Regarding the minister's ability to "apply learning from books," the respondents uniformly agreed that the inability to do so was viewed as a "major hindrance to ministry." Even more highly rated were these information-related traits: "gives evidence of continued and thorough study of the Scriptures," "demonstrates knowledge of Scripture," "increases own theological competence through research and study," and "continues theological education through reading professional books and journals." Another "cluster" of desirable clergy traits that rated above the mean dealt with knowledge of a church's particular denominational history and polity.

Two other items, however, that measured ministers' use of a broad range of information resources indicated that the responding ministers and church members did have some hesitations about what sources were "appropriate." For example, within the "cluster" of traits related to interest in new ideas, the habit of regularly attending the theater and cinema was rated negatively as a "minor hindrance in ministry." Buying and reading a wide range of popular books and magazines was ranked as an asset in ministry, but only a "minor" one (p. 158). Still, the overall impression one is left with from Schuller, Strommen, and Brekke's 1980 sociological study of the modern American ministry is that people on both sides of the pulpit take seriously the information role of the clergy.

The Approach of This Study

This study examines more closely the informational role that ministers occupy in American society. The approach taken here, however, is to examine the clergy, not the community to whom they minister. Since these professionals are rated so highly as information sources, it seems appropriate to ask what is happening within the profession itself. This study addresses how and why ministers gather and disseminate information relative to the performance of their professional tasks. The purpose of this study is not to judge whether the community trust is justified in its high view of ministers as information sources; rather, the objective is to shed more light on how this group of professionals functions as information professionals.

The "light" metaphor is, perhaps, an apt one, given the complex nature of information and how people use it in modern society. It is tempting to take a focused "flashlight" approach and concentrate on only one or two variables associated with this topic (e.g. number of books read or educational level) or to look closely at a single aspect of the issue (e.g. information-seeking behavior), but current theory (see, for example, Dervin and Nilan, 1986) suggests that the topic of information use and users is much more diffuse. The approach taken in this study is more reminiscent, therefore, of the prism than the penlight. The goal is to utilize more naturalistic methods, particularly personal interviews, to illuminate how information is used by ministers, focusing on the pastors in one particular American community.

In this study, there were three basic research questions that guided the project:

1) To what extent do pastors function as information professionals?

2) Why and how do pastors gather information as part of their professional duties?

3) In what ways do pastors disseminate the information that they gather as part of their professional duties?

These three questions served as the umbrella issues that limited the range of questions asked during the interviews with the pastors in this one community. In addition to the interview method and in order to delve more deeply into these larger questions of why and how the pastoral profession uses information, a case study approach was also utilized. Here the researcher functioned as a participant-observer analyzing scores of sermons from a smaller group of clergy as they were preached to a variety of congregations. The purpose of these case studies was to provide a more in-depth analysis of how these ministers gathered and disseminated information. A particular focus was on the preaching event, the most public and regular task that they performed as pastors. The case study approach permitted more detailed data to be collected than would have been possible using only the personal interview method.

From a library and information science perspective, the present research topic is part of the well-plowed field of user studies. A review of the literature in this field is provided in the Appendix. This review yields three basic research areas relevant to the present study: 1) studies of the topic of information itself, 2) user studies in general, and 3) specific studies of clergy as information users. The body of literature on the last topic is considerably less prolific than the other two areas despite the important role that ministers seem to occupy in the information network of American adults.

What distinguishes the present study from much previous research is the emphasis that is placed upon how these pastors actually used information, not simply on where they gathered it. The distinction is comparable to the oft-cited input/output measures problem in evaluating public libraries. Past user studies, like traditional evaluation measures, have focused on what comes in (education, number of books read, etc.), rather than upon the output that is produced by users as they process information. This study, in keeping with more recent studies in the field, does not assume that ministers are merely hollow tubes or empty conduits through which information passes intact. The "value-added" dimension of pastors as information professionals is a key component of the present study, as shown in Chapter 2.

The Methodological Framework

The primary means chosen to investigate the three basic research questions guiding the present study was the personal interview method, supplemented with case studies. This methodology was pursued mostly within a naturalistic framework, in keeping with Dervin and Nilan's (1986) call for a new paradigm for user studies. The population interviewed was a group of some 70 ministers serving a mid-sized community of nearly 100,000 people in the Midwestern United States.

The naturalistic framework chosen for this study and its reliance upon interpretive methods (e.g. personal interviews and case studies involving participant-observation) was useful in three ways. First, interpretive methods, particularly the case study, allow for a greater depth of detail, an important consideration when investigating the complex nature of information use in contemporary society.

Second, there is also an inherent power in the case study and naturalistic interview approaches to reveal unexpected relationships, which was of particular value in an exploratory study such as this one. For example, asking an open-ended question about counseling provided an opportunity for many pastors to talk about the tension they felt over pastoral care versus pastoral counseling, an issue that was not anticipated at the beginning of this project (see Chapter 4).

Third, the interpretive methods common to naturalistic inquiry emphasize the importance of context and framework, useful in examining what Dervin and Nilan (1986) termed "systematic individuality." The intent was to maintain as much as possible the unique power of individuality, while delicately balancing that focus with group-based findings. Consequently, many of the data presented in the findings are the individual comments by specific pastors, but these data are supplemented, where appropriate, by aggregated data that provide the responses of these pastors as a group.

As stated above, the primary methodological approach was to ask questions of ministers concerning their use of information. The goal of this study has not been to generate broad generalizations about this topic, but to develop an idiographic body of knowledge that may be transferable from context to context, recognizing that differences are often as important as similarities (see, as an example of this kind of qualitative research, Wilson, 1981).

In general and as much as possible, interviewees were encouraged to use their own words, with structured questions kept to a minimum. This approach of "captur[ing] what people have to say in their own words" (Patton, 1980, p. 22) provides what the anthropologist Geertz calls "thick description" (1973, p. 6). These descriptions, as in this study, tend to be lengthy ones, enabling the researcher to provide a "vicarious experience" of the research setting (Guba and Lincoln, 1988, p. 85). The resulting findings beget what Natoli (1982, p. 167) called "knowledge through description--accurate detailed description."

One of the difficulties with this newer approach, utilizing the assumptions of the naturalistic paradigm, is the problem of the "trustworthiness" of the data and the consequent findings (see the discussion by Guba and Lincoln, 1988). Attempts to enhance the trustworthiness of the data collected in this study included prolonged observation (in the case studies), referential documentation (which included the audiotaping of interviews), cross-checks of observations and data with other members of the group under study (which were done anonymously), and peer debriefing (two professors of ministry were consulted throughout this project about the data being collected and possible interpretations).

In addition, triangulation was employed in this study. This included the use of more than one source (69 different individuals were interviewed for an average of 50 minutes each, some more than once) and the use of more than one method (interviews, case studies, document analysis, and participant-observation).

Attempts to preserve the naturalistic framework of the interview process in this study included the use of natural surroundings (interviews were conducted in the pastor's office), the emphasis upon understanding and dealing with respondents on an individual basis rather than merely recording mechanical responses (an interview schedule was followed but only as a guide, not slavishly), and the recording and use of the interviewee's own words (relying on both copious field notes and nearly 1,000 pages of transcriptions from the 82 interviews that were tape-recorded; two were not recorded due to equipment failure).

The questions asked during the personal interviews with pastors revolved around these four topics:

1. How did you go about preparing the last sermon you preached? How did you choose the topic you did? What sources did you use? How did you use them?

2. What kinds of questions are being asked of you as a minister? What is the most commonly asked question you hear? What was the most unusual question you have been asked? Do you get many questions from people outside your congregation?

3. Do you do much counseling? What are the topics you are dealing with? What percentage of your time do you spend in counseling? Do you ever refer people to other agencies? On what basis?

4. Do you read any magazines regularly? Are you currently reading any books? Do you use any of the libraries in the area? Can you think of a recent instance where you did? Do you regularly watch television, listen to the radio, or attend the theatre? Are there any other sources that you rely on? Do you attend professional conferences? Are you a member of any ministerial groups?

The first set of questions employed the critical-incident technique in an effort to discover how these ministers gathered and disseminated information in their preaching. The second set of questions was intended to probe informants to consider the wide range of their information needs, not just their use of information relative to preaching. These questions also allowed the researcher to examine the minister's intermediary role as an agent serving the information needs of others, much as a librarian might do.

The third set of questions examined the counseling role of the modern minister. An earlier pilot project (Tanner, 1991) indicated that counseling was second only to preaching in the information demands that it placed upon the minister, and this was also confirmed in the present study. Counseling is also an area of information provision in which modern society is beginning to hold ministers more accountable, as is evidenced by the rise in religious litigation (see pp. 4-5).

The last set of questions dealt with the various sources

of information that these ministers utilized, both formal and informal. The interview data here was supplemented with the responses from a written questionnaire concerning the importance of various sources for ministry. The questionnaire was given to every minister at the conclusion of the interviews so as not to "prejudice" the open-ended nature of the interview questions. While this approach was considerably more structured than were the interview questions, it helped provide a more quantitatively oriented means of cross-checking responses given to the more open-ended questions. The particular categories listed on the questionnaire were suggested by both Porcella (1973) and Tanner (1989) in their research into ministers' use of information sources.

In an effort to explore in more detail how these ministers gathered and disseminated information, as well as to provide a triangulation of methods, a series of case studies at seven different churches was conducted. A convenient summary and discussion of these seven churches is provided in Chapter 4 under the section on the pastor as preacher (herald). The "case" to be studied was the minister as an oral disseminator of information in the pulpit.

The case study approach allowed for the use of a variety of relevant data, not just personal interviews, to discover how ministers disseminated information publicly in the pulpit. The number of visits at each of these seven churches ranged from a maximum of seven to a minimum of two, with the total number of visits being twenty-nine and the average per church being four. Two of the churches were chosen because their pastors spoke regularly either on local television or on local radio, providing an opportunity to explore more fully how these two media were used in the public dissemination of information by pastors.

The purpose of the case study approach was to allow the

researcher to function as a participant-observer in the one event
that made the most information demands upon the minister, the
weekly sermon. Since the sermon is an oral, communal event
with extemporaneous characteristics, an analysis of a manuscript
would not have achieved the same results, though written sermon
notes were also examined as part of this approach. Additionally,
tape recordings of most of the sermons observed were obtained
in order to provide an archival reference for analyzing the data.
Supplemental data were also obtained by attending the Sunday
services of thirteen other churches in the community.

The Clergy Chosen

The clergy chosen for this research project was a group
of full-time, preaching ministers serving a mid-sized, Midwestern community, which is also home to two universities, four
colleges, and a number of other information providers, e.g. a
public library, a pastoral counseling center, and an information
referral agency.   The choice of locale was due in part to
Porcella's (1973) suggestion that future research on this topic
should involve a university town.

This study is limited to preaching ministers (including
campus ministers who preach regularly), since the preaching
event is a particular, though certainly not the only, focus of this
study. Unlike most earlier research, every attempt was made to
interview ministers of all Christian sects, not just Protestant or
mainline denominations. Religious leaders of other faiths (e.g.
Judaism, Buddhism, Islam, etc.), however, were not interviewed
given the considerably different nature of their role relative to
the preaching task.

Of the 21 different religious groups represented in this
community, 18 had churches with full-time pastors. Of these 18
religious groups, 17 (94%) participated in this study, suggesting

broad religious representation. Among the 64 churches with current, full-time preaching pastors, 58 (91%) participated in this study, including six of eight campus ministers in the community. The reasons for not participating given by the six pastors who declined were either their lack of time (in the case of four) or their poor health (in the case of two).

Among the 58 churches represented in this study, 62 pastors were interviewed. The other four pastors were associate ministers who regularly preached for their congregations. Nearly half (30) of the 62 pastors in this study were the sole pastor on staff. Among all 62 pastors interviewed, there were 58 men and 4 women, the latter number representing all but one of the female clergy in this community. Three of the 62 pastors interviewed in this study were black, representing all but one of the full-time black pastors. Three other pastors served congregations that could be described as racially mixed. In order to preserve the anonymity of the pastors in this study, specific details regarding age, gender, race, and religious affiliation have frequently been deleted or altered slightly (where such alteration was both possible and appropriate) in presenting the findings.

The age range of the 62 pastors interviewed was 27 to 80, with 42.4 being the average age (40.5 was the median). The pastors had averaged 16.4 years in ministry (15.0 was the median), including an average of 6.5 years ministering in the community under study (the median was 4.0). One of the implications of these last two statistics is that the ministers interviewed here were rarely first-time pastors. Most had served other congregations before coming to their present church. The average weekly attendance for these churches was 350, with a median of 150.

The population of the community under study was nearly 100,000, including nearly 30,000 students who attended one of two universities and four colleges in the immediate vicinity. The median age of the residents, exclusive of college students, was just over 30 years. The socioeconomic status of the community was estimated by local census researchers to be at the 68th percentile nationally, indicating that the community was mostly upper middle class. Just over 6% of the non-student population were black and another 3% were of other races, mostly Hispanic.[13]

The major occupations were white collar in nature, with the area colleges and universities and two or three major corporations accounting for the largest number of workers. According to a local Chamber of Commerce publication, the unemployment rate during the year of this study was just over 4%, providing further evidence of the economic stability of the area. Nearly 40% of the workforce were college graduates, and over half had taken some college courses. The presence of a large state university and smaller private post-secondary schools no doubt contributed to this high level of education in the community. More than 57% of the jobs held by residents were white collar; only 19% were traditional blue-collar occupations.

These facts, coupled with the 68 percentile score regarding socioeconomic status, indicates that this community was not necessarily a "typical" American community. However, a recent article in a major demographic journal had listed this community as being among the twenty most "representative" communities in the country in terms of several key demographic variables, e.g. age, gender, race, mobility, and income.

The community had three libraries accessible to clergy, two associated with universities and a public library. Together these collections numbered nearly two million items, with the public library having an annual circulation count of nearly one million. In addition, a widely used information referral agency operated in the community, whose outreach and use is described briefly in Chapter 4 under the section on the pastor as healer (counselor). Finally, a large pastoral counseling center, staffed mostly by pastors or former pastors and owned by the churches in the area, provided another range of counseling-related information services to the local residents.

In order to provide a broader context for the data gleaned from interviews with ministers and from the case studies at several churches, interviews were also conducted with professionals at other community agencies involved in providing information. These persons included two administrators of the pastoral counseling center, two directors of the information referral agency, and two public librarians. Additionally, the manager of a well-used bookstore located in one of the seven case-study churches was also interviewed.

The Presentation of Findings

The findings from the present study are presented in Chapters 2, 3, and 4. Chapter 2 focuses upon the pastor as information professional, looking at three key issues: the pastor's professional image, the pastor's professional authority, and the pastor's professional knowledge. Chapter 3 examines the information needs of pastors, as well as the formal and informal channels that pastors use in meeting those needs. Chapter 4 presents findings relative to the pastor's roles as information disseminator, particularly the twin roles of counseling and preaching, including a brief overview of how the use of print, electronic, and oral media influence these roles.

Chapter 5 concludes the study by summarizing the findings from this research project, noting the limitations of this kind of research, suggesting areas for further study, and discussing several implications that arise from this type of user study. This research has implications not only for the field of user studies, but also for public libraries in terms of identifying and utilizing community information gatekeepers. The findings presented here also have significant implications for theological librarians as well, especially regarding the pedagogical methods they employ in teaching prospective ministers how to function most effectively as information professionals in American society.

2. THE PASTOR AS INFORMATION PROFESSIONAL

The dual roles of the pastor as information gatherer (Chapter 3) and the pastor as information disseminator (Chapter 4) are both based on the pastor's foundational role as information professional. Admittedly, "information professional" is a term that more commonly conjures up images of librarians, corporate information specialists, database indexers and abstractors, and others whose primary occupational role is providing information.[14] What does the modern minister have to do with these kinds of occupations? Certainly, I would not want to argue that a pastor and a librarian are simply variations on the same theme. There are, as shall be pointed out shortly, some significant differences.

Yet, the comparison is not totally new nor unique to this study. In his classic economic analysis of the knowledge industry in this country, Machlup (1962), for example, listed the church as one of nine educationally based, knowledge-producing industries in America. He even ranked the knowledge or information provided by the church well ahead of such traditional information providers as academic and public libraries in terms of their economic impact, citing 1958 expenditures of $2.4 billion by the church versus $.11 billion and $.14 billion respectively by academic and public libraries (p. 83 and pp. 104-105).

In updating Machlup's original study, Rubin and Huber (1986) noted an even larger role for the church in providing information as compared to academic and public libraries. They listed 1980 expenditures of $17.7 billion for the church in its educational role of information provider versus expenditures of $1.63 billion for academic and $1.96 billion for public libraries (p. 27 and p. 61).

The comparison of the pastor to such traditional information professionals as librarians, however, is important in this study not for economic or historical reasons, but because of both the similarities and the differences in these occupations. In studying a profession such as the pastorate that on the surface seems so foreign to the field of library and information science, it is this initial comparison between the two that allows the subsequent contrasts to be detailed and discussed in a more meaningful manner. The comparison serves also to remind the reader that the focus in this study is upon the pastor's use of information, not upon everything that the pastor does.

This chapter on the pastor as information professional is intended to answer the first research question cited in Chapter 1: To what extent do pastors function as information professionals? The answer to this question provides a framework for discussing how the pastors in this study gathered and disseminated information, the topics of Chapters 3 and 4.

The issue is not simply how many books pastors read, or what use they made of computers, or whether they preferred to provide information orally rather than through printed means. The underlying issue is how these pastors viewed their role as information users and providers, especially providers. What do they have in common with traditional information professionals who also provide information? How do they differ? Therefore, it seems altogether appropriate to look first at the foundational issue of the pastor as information professional, before examining the details of how ministers gathered and disseminated information.

In this chapter on the pastor as information professional, three specific issues will be discussed: the professional image of the pastor, the professional authority of the pastor, and the professional knowledge of the pastor. The image issue is important because it provides the specific conceptual framework for studying how these pastors viewed their roles as information providers. In this study five such images were cited by pastors. The topic of authority is also important to this study, partly because it helps define how a professional functions in a social context and partly because it clearly shows both the similarities and the differences in how these pastors and traditional information professionals provide information. The professional knowledge of the pastor is likewise central to this discussion because it helps set the boundaries for the ways in which the pastor does and does not function as an information professional, particularly concerning the issue of limited knowledge.

The Professional Image of the Pastor

The first issue, that of image, provides the foundation for understanding how contemporary clergy--at least those in this study--view their role as information providers. What were the verbal images, the descriptive nouns, that these ministers themselves used to explain how they interacted with information? What pictures did they paint of themselves as "information professionals"? How do those images compare and contrast with such traditional fillers of that role as librarians? Before examining the differences between pastors and traditional information professionals, it should be pointed out that there are at least two significant similarities.

First, both of these information providers function as

professionals. For example, the pastorate displays the same characteristics of a profession that Asheim (1978) described in his article, "Librarians as Professionals." Borrowing from the classic studies on professionalism by Flexner (1910) in medicine, Brandeis (1914) in business, and Williamson (1923) in librarianship, Asheim listed five defining criteria for professionals, which apply equally well to ministers and librarians.[15]

Both the pastor and the information professional have a certain intellectual training, typically a three-year Master of Divinity degree for the former and a one- or two-year Master of Library Science for the latter. Both pursue their profession primarily for others not for self, with each vocation looked upon as a service profession. Both professions measure success in other than monetary terms, particularly when one considers that the average salaries for both these occupations in the United States is only in the $30,000 range (see Berkley, 1992, and Lynch, 1991). Both display a degree of autonomy in a mostly self-policing profession, though certainly not to the extent that the medical and legal professions do with their stringent credentialing policies. This autonomy is based in part on the professional knowledge which each possesses and which draws clients or patrons to them for information. Finally, both the pastor and the information professional have some sense of authority in what they do, an authority that is granted to them for a variety of reasons, as shall be pointed out later in this chapter.

Second, both professions are concerned with information, at least in terms of how that concept has been described in this study (see Appendix). While it can easily be argued that the traditional information professional--both in educational training and in vocational emphasis--is much more focused on providing information, still in the public's eye the difference may not be that great. In fact, the results of the Gallup Poll cited in Chapter 1 suggest that the American public is more inclined to seek information from ministers than they are from librarians. The public's perception of the pastor as an information professional is even more pronounced in the black community, where by tradition in this country such ministers have been viewed as primary sources of information (see pp. 2-3 above and Niles, 1984, p. 43). The importance of considering the public's perception of the information profession is underscored by Estabrook and Horak's (1992) recent study on the differences between public and professional opinions of libraries.

However, despite these two similarities in these professions, there are at least three significant differences between how pastors provide information and how traditional information professionals, such as librarians, do so. Two of these three distinctions will be examined later in this chapter--those dealing with the authority and the knowledge that are characteristic of each profession. A third distinction concerns the "value-added" role that contemporary pastors fulfill in their provision of information.

To be sure, the ministers in this study did not use the term "value-added" in describing their roles nor would it likely be a model or perspective they would consciously appropriate--at least in any negative sense. Still, "value-added" does appear to be a helpful rubric for describing the variety of ways in which these pastors "added value" to the information they acquired and passed on to others. This label also underscores the fact that these pastors' pronounced non-neutrality denies them any "empty conduit" role in the information transfer process. This value-added aspect of information provision among the ministers in this study was evident in at least three areas.

First, these pastors made no claim to "neutrality" in the way they disseminated information--at least not in the librarian's usual understanding of that concept. For example, the "Intellectual Freedom Statement," which, though no longer binding as a policy statement of the American Library Association, is still viewed as "a position paper applicable exclusively to library service and the library professional" (*Intellectual Freedom Manual*, 1989, p. 96), espouses an intentional "value neutral" position for librarians in their role as information providers. Note its prohibition against "employ[ing] our own political, moral, or esthetic views," a prohibition that most pastors would not likely accept.

Quite the contrary, many of the pastors in this study candidly admitted that they were driven by the values they espoused, and they interjected them freely and purposefully into their professional role as information provider. Typical of this nonneutral approach to how pastors dispensed information is the following brief episode. One Baptist pastor recounted how he had answered the question of a young girl in his high school youth group who wanted to know what Episcopalians believed, since she knew a boy who was one.

> I gave her a copy of some materials in my library. It was a one-page bulletin put out by our denomination on what Episcopalians believe and how that contrasts and compares with our church. It has a bibliography for further reading too. I gave her a copy of that and went over it briefly with her. I touched on a couple of points there and assured her that they were a Christian organization. But, of course, I told her she would need to ask him about his particular salvation experience.

On the surface, this pastor did what any self-respecting reference librarian might do. He provided her with printed information that appeared to answer her factually oriented question.

Yet, at a deeper level, it seems apparent that the minister

was primarily interested in giving her only one perspective on the issue ("put out by our denomination") and on making sure ("but, of course") she gathered intensely private information ("about his particular salvation experience") that would be well beyond the scope of anything that most information professionals would provide. He went on to reveal that this girl was currently dating an Episcopalian so he wanted to make sure they were "spiritually compatible" before things "got too serious," a decidedly non-neutral concern.

Second, the value-added role that these ministers filled in their use of information was also evident not just in why they chose the sources they did, but in how they used any source. Even supposedly "neutral" sources of information were frequently used in a very "value-laden" manner.

For example, one pastor with a doctorate from an Ivy League seminary mentioned that he not only read the *Wall Street Journal*, but also watched MTV. Why? Because "they both look at values," values which he "need[ed] to understand" so he could preach and teach effectively to the people espousing those values in his congregation. The point he was making was that he did not read the *Journal* nor watch MTV merely to acquire bits of information, but to understand and critique value systems in the society, whether they belonged to Wall Street yuppies or musically motivated youth. He used "neutral" sources in order to change the values of his parishioners by critiquing the supposed neutrality of these sources.

The pastor went on to explain this approach by distinguishing between what a Sunday-morning preacher does as opposed to a full-time pastor. "Well, a preacher [is] more concerned with the proclamation of Scripture, but the pastor has got to be concerned as well with the hearts [i.e. values] of the people."

Third, the pastor's value-added role evidenced in this study is not merely a non-neutral expression of intellectual bias towards a particular viewpoint. It also has to do with the purposive nature of how and why these pastors provided information. Many pastors alluded to this motivational aspect of their use of information in the course of the interview process. They were particularly open about this issue when discussing their preaching. One of the more succinct summaries of this aspect of the clergy's value-added role was provided by the following graphic line from the pastor of a large church: "I preach for the jugular. I teach to inform, but I preach for decisions." Representative of this decision-making model of information is this preacher's comment:

> I feel a little empty if I get to the end of a message and I have not challenged anybody. If all I've done is disseminate information... I feel certainly that information can challenge, but I always have a goal in my preaching that there be some urgent request for change.

He went on to point out that he always put the initials "U.S.E." at the top of all of his written sermon notes. They stood for urgent, sincere, and eye contact. It was his way of reminding himself every time he stepped into the pulpit that he was not simply delivering a lecture or dispensing information orally. His motivation for providing information was behavioral change. Another example of how pastors frequently subordinated information to a higher value is found in this preacher's comment:

> Knowledge is not my primary objective in my preaching. [Nor is it] the transference of the dogma or the Christian creed from my mind to theirs, but showing them how this creed has affected my life and can change theirs as well. My primary objective is not to communicate

truth intellectually or the transference of knowledge. What I'm attempting to do is to allow them to leave with a changed behavior.

One of the more visible manifestations of this aspect of value-added information was apparent among the more theologically conservative churches in the community, many of whom were openly involved in local political issues. Here was how the pastor of one such church explained his professional role:

> We are always trying to be value driven.... We don't want you to be the same when you leave as when you came in. I want you to think differently, feel differently, perceive differently, expect differently, have a better understanding when you leave, be challenged when you leave.

He went on in the interview to give examples of what he meant by wanting his parishioners to think and feel "differently" and what he meant by being "challenged." "It needs to come down to the local level [in the community]. When there is an opportunity to do something against abortion, do it. When there is an opportunity to do something against pornography, do that." This congregation, like several others in the community, often had members sign petitions and attend rallies against certain social "problems"--all based on information provided by the pastor. It is hard to imagine a public librarian, for example, disseminating information with such intentionality as a driving force.

To be sure, there were some pastors and some churches in this community who objected to such intentionality in information dissemination. As the pastor of one of the more theologically liberal churches explained:

> My piety and my particular way of living out the faith [is that] I understand my sinfulness. The

part of that that touches me is that I have no right to tell the members of my congregation that this is what the faith is like and this is how you have to live it out. I am absolutely offended that the people at [a nearby church] are asked to sign pro-life documents or political things about whether they approve of gambling or not.

The purpose of the church is that faithful people may in their conversations debate, argue, and decide. When the church becomes a political instrument for any party, I don't care if it is our own church... My understanding is that when you come into these walls there is no flag of any nation nor any political opinion that will be expressed here as being "the faithful thing to do." In fact, faithful people gather together in a form where from their own limited and sinful perspective they say, "This is what I believe God is calling me to do." We debate, we argue, but then we individually decide.... As the church, we are supposed to be the place to provide refuge, freedom, open discourse of faith, and to let people argue and decide.

Of course, this pastor too was very value driven in his provision of information to others in that the paradigm that controlled his view of knowledge and information was decidedly Christian. It is just that he drew the line in his answers to "faith questions" at certain significant points, one of which was on political issues.

Nevertheless, despite these differences, contemporary clergy and today's information professionals do exhibit similarities relative to their informational role as professionals. To be sure, very few ministers would compare themselves professionally to librarians. They are much more likely to use such images as preacher, teacher, counselor, or even administrator.[16] Yet the comparison is appropriate here since the focus of this study is on the information role pastors occupy, not on everything that they do.

In particular there are five images that seem appropriate when looking at the professional persona that the pastor displays to the community relative to his or her information role. Several observations may be made at this point. First of all, these images are all drawn from the pastors' own words spoken during the course of the interviews. Given the naturalistic framework that guides this study, the decision to use the informants' own words as much as possible was both intentional and desirable. At no point, however, did I ask pastors any questions about their perceived "image as an information professional." The conceptual framework of these images is my own. The pastors' answers came in response to general inquiries regarding their "philosophy of ministry" or their "approach to preaching" or were simply volunteered in the process of answering other questions.

Another important observation is that these five images are not meant to be exhaustive of all that a pastor does or is. In fact, ministers mentioned many more images that they saw themselves portraying--father figure, prophet, intercessor, manager, fundraiser, friend, pilgrim. The particular five (listed below) were chosen because they represent the range of roles that the ministers under study saw themselves filling in that portion of their profession that deals with providing information. The choice of the term "image" is also intentional in that it is meant to be suggestive, not precise. Certainly, these five images are not intended as simplistic labels that are definitively descriptive. The pastors in this project are too diverse to be susceptible to easy categorizations. In fact, these five images are designed to help capture and reinforce that diversity, not deny it.

Also, these five images (except perhaps for the first one) attest to the increasing specialization that is overtaking the pastoral profession, as has happened in many professional fields, including the field of library and information science. This trend is most apparent in the educational training of ministers, which will be discussed later in more detail. Suffice it to say at this point that the highly specialized Doctor of Ministry degree, which is offered with as many as a dozen specializations, has begun in the last decade to supplant the Master of Divinity's generalist program as the desired terminal degree for pastors.

In discussing the five images of the pastor as information provider, it is useful to compare and contrast these pastoral images with analogous roles that librarians fill as a further means of explaining and illustrating how ministers function--whether well or poorly--as information professionals. It needs to be stressed at this point that the analogies drawn from the library profession are intended to be for illustrative purposes only.

For example, my findings strongly indicate that one image that frames how pastors use information is the image of the pastor as wounded healer. The related analogy to the activist librarian is meant only as one point of comparison to the otherwise foreign field of library science. The analogy suffers-- or at least differs--at many points, and the image can stand on its own without the analogy. The analogy is merely my attempt to find at least some common ground in these two otherwise disparate professions, while at the same time clearly indicating how they differ.

In addition, I am not trying to be exhaustive in the use of these analogies. For example, in referring to the pastor as an expert, the accompanying analogy to the academic subject specialist librarian is not meant to include everything that academic librarians do, only their role as "expert" is at issue.

With these caveats in mind, the five images, with their closest library counterparts, are listed here and discussed below:

1. The Generalist: The Pastor as Public Librarian
2. The Expert: The Pastor as Academic Librarian
3. The Equipper: The Pastor as Reference Librarian
4. The Wounded Healer: The Pastor as Activist Librarian
5. The Interpreter: The Pastor as Special Librarian

One final observation is in order. These five images are not mutually exclusive in terms of how these pastors provided information. A pastor, for example, may function as an interpreter in the pulpit, but as a wounded healer in a counseling encounter. The five categories are meant to demonstrate the range and diversity of the pastor as an information provider; they are not meant to be neat little divisions unique to themselves.

1. The Generalist:
The Pastor as Public Librarian

Even in an age of increasing specialization for the pastoral profession, there is still a strong sense among some pastors that they are primarily generalists. Like public librarians, they must appeal to a variety of patron interests-- everything from speaking at the local Kiwanis club to teaching children to supervising remodeling projects. In a conversation with one pastor, who noted the wide variety of responsibilities he held--teaching, preaching, counseling, administrating, speaking for civic groups--I asked him what he considered his overall role to be. His response:

I'm a generalist. I was a liberal arts major in college so I have been educated as a generalist. I learned to understand and have some aware- ness of a wide range of issues. Even though my seminary degree is a specialized master's in ministry, it is based on my undergraduate liberal arts program. So when I minister, I can explain Scripture, for example, to a wide range of people in a very general, but professional, sort of way.

The results of interviews with several other pastors indicate that the generalist image was not uncommon. The interview data also suggest that while this approach to ministry is helpful in dealing with the variety of ministry tasks, there is a point at which the generalist image of pastors as information providers reaches a decided limit. Among clergy, the counseling task is the area least amenable to generalists. For example, when asked if he ever referred people to other agencies, such as a local counseling center, for specialized help, one minister quickly responded:

> Oh, yeah. Most of the time. I refer them to the agencies that are professionals in those areas. I stay away from there. They call us jacks of all trades and masters of none. We have to be wise enough to know that in this day and time there is a lot of suing going on.

Though his motivation may have been financial, his opinion is representative of those pastors who perceived themselves to be "jack of all trades, and master of none." Again, in the context of the counseling role and these pastors' ready willingness to defer to specialists, another pastor used the following analogy:

> I refer to [a local professional counseling agency] often.... I say to people, "Hey, I work on sermons, they counsel, for eight hours a day." I wouldn't want to send my child to a heart specialist. I would send him to a pedia-

trician. I'm a general practitioner. I realized
early my limitations.

The medical model was even more pronounced in the following
generalist's view of the ministry. When asked about his strong
policy regarding the frequent referral of counselees in light of
the fact that his pastoral staff included some highly educated
people in that area, he responded quite pointedly:

> Our policy here is very explicit. You may only
> have three counseling sessions with a pastor.
> Then, you must be triaged out. Why? We're
> not a counseling center. We are a church. Now
> our people are very gifted. We're good counsel-
> ors, but that's not what they are called to do.
> As senior pastor I said very specifically the first
> few months I was here, "I will not allow anyone
> on my staff to counsel anyone more than three
> times. It's not because we don't love you. It's
> because we do. And love means getting you the
> best person we can." Your general practitioner
> would not say, "Gee, you have a brain tumor.
> I think I'll do it because I care so much about
> you." No, instead he'd refer them to the spe-
> cialist who can do it best. That's how we
> operate.

The image of the pastor as public librarian--at least
relative to some things that public librarians do--was made clear
by the following interchange with a pastor who had entered
ministry later in life. When asked toward the end of the
interview a "routine" question about his use of the local public
library, he paused to reflect and then responded:

> Pastor: Yes, sometimes I go to browse. I mean
> I was a librarian in my previous life.... I got

my MLS at [a nearby university] and then went
back to [a midwestern state], which is where I'm
from, and was librarian in a small town public
library for three years. [There were] about
10,000 people and a 30 to 35,000 volume collection. Little old Carnegie building. [He
paused as if to say more but didn't, so I pursued.]

Interviewer: Do you see any comparisons in the
two professions of pastor and public librarian?

Pastor: Yes, there are some similarities, partly
maybe because of the kind of librarian I was and
maybe being in the small town.... I'm pretty
introverted, but I am also people oriented. And
I did pastoral ministry in some ways in that
library, you know, when I think about it. I can
remember doing things like--this family lived on
the wrong side of the tracks, but used the library
a lot. Their son got sent off to juvenile jail for
awhile, and I wrote him letters and took books
over to them when his mother fell and broke her
leg. I can remember talking to people, almost
like counseling instead, at the circulation desk.
That was a library that had had old lady librarians....

Interviewer: The typical stereotype?

Pastor: Yes. They didn't want anybody messing
up their library. Now, while I like order a lot,
I think when I left there, it was a so much more
hospitable place. So it was kind of a ministry of
hospitality.... I mean there was probably some
theological significance, which sometimes I've

wondered about. You know, as a pastor now I try to convince people that they have a ministry in the world, that they don't have to go to seminary. I've wondered sometimes if I was already doing ministry in the library, maybe unreflectively, maybe not thinking about why I was doing what I was doing. Gee, pastoral librarian--a whole new category and a whole new course in the MLS.

As a former public librarian, it was not difficult for this pastor to draw ready analogies between the two professions based on the fact that both perform as service-oriented generalists who do everything from taking books to needy families to talking to patrons at the front desk to just being people minded.

Two other ministers in this community had also worked in libraries before entering the ministry, but one had done so only as a student employee in an academic library and her only reflection on that experience was, "I like libraries," and a seven-minute denunciation of that school's firing of the library director, her former boss. The other pastor, who had served as a professional librarian in England before entering the ministry, had just recently arrived in the community as part of an exchange program. His only point of comparison between the pastor and the public librarian was that "I suppose we both like to read books."

Though the analogy between pastor and public librarian suffers at many points, the intent of the comparison here is to underscore how the pastor frequently functions as a generalist in terms of the range of information needs that he or she is required to meet on a regular basis. Like the small-town public librarian, many of the clergy in this community used information in tasks ranging from administration to public speaking, from answering a diversity of "reference" questions to working personally with individuals.

2. The Expert:
The Pastor as Academic Librarian

If some pastors saw themselves as generalists in the same vein as the traditional public librarian, others were much more open to the image of "expert." The use of quotation marks is meant to qualify this term in the following regard. As an academic librarian is frequently a subject specialist who has "expertise" in a certain area, so also some clergy identified with this image of the pastor in their role as information provider. To be sure, very few, if any, pastors pushed the image of "expert" very far. Nor would I want to push the analogy with academic librarians to any great extent. The major point of contact here is that both the subject-specialist academic librarian and the "expert" pastor claim a certain territory of expertise in which they dispense information with some degree of confidence.

The image of the academic expert is hard to shake in this community where more than half of the work force had some college education and more than a third were college graduates. It is likely that the image of the pastor as expert is more visible in this community than it would be, for example, in an agricultural or industrial setting.

In fact, a pastor who had recently relocated from a blue-collar community complained, "Here...you are dealing more with educated, intellectual people who, though they have as many problems as blue-collar workers, are sometimes even harder to work with because they think they have it all together." Another pastor who had been in the community for a long time, after describing his congregation as "very professional," offered the following insight into what he viewed as his particular area of expertise.

I don't think I have to be an expert in every-

> thing, but... You know the thing I think I have
> to be an expert in? How to relate Biblical truth
> to [these people] in an applicable fashion. I
> have to be a professional when it comes to Bib-
> lical information. That's what they are looking
> for. I don't have to be an expert about comput-
> ers. I don't have to be a professional about
> building trades. I mean I want to be able to talk
> about it intelligently so we can converse, but I
> don't have to be an expert in it. But I do have
> to know enough about it that I can bring Biblical
> truth to bear upon those particular cultural set-
> tings. But it is intimidating from time to time
> because this is a highly educated community,
> and I don't have a Ph.D. I never did finish a
> master's program even.

While this pastor claimed expertise for other than educational
reasons, the educational connection was not ignored either in this
community, where one-fifth of the ministers interviewed had or
were pursuing a professional doctorate. One pastor, who mentioned at some length his eight years of post-secondary education
and three degrees, related the following incident concerning a
professional exchange he had had with a local neurologist.

> I was on the hospital floor the other day and
> [named the surgeon], a gifted young woman who
> is the brain surgeon here and is a member of
> this congregation--you know, she feels perfectly
> comfortable saying, "I'm just absolutely stymied
> by what to do with this patient. What do you
> think?" So I suggested that some of the people
> in the congregation pray for her, and then, here
> are some other things to do.... Now, I suggest
> that that doesn't happen in many places, but I
> think it's because we are authentic here, and

people know that we don't play religious games. They also know that they are free to talk about their own concerns without losing their professional credentialing where they are.... As a brain surgeon, it is okay to say to the pastor, "I am really worried about my patient Sarah, and I don't know what to do next? Can you help?"

This same minister stressed the high degree of specialization that was evidenced among his pastoral staff due to their various areas of expertise. Just as many large research libraries hire academic specialists who preside over certain subject areas, so too do some pastors of large churches follow a similar model. One senior minister elaborated on the "team ministry" that existed at his large congregation, an approach based on the hiring of experts with certain specializations:

Lyle Schaller [a nationally recognized church growth expert among American churches] has been a good friend of mine over the years. He says that one of the emerging things that he sees in large congregations is the "team/specialist" model. That's the model we use here. I don't call the other pastors on my staff associates. We are a team of specialists. There are five pastors on staff...and in [this denomination] you're probably aware that that's eight years of education--four years undergraduate and four years graduate--even to be ordained. But the custom in [this denomination] has been that there are assistant pastors and that the senior pastor is boss and they assist him. Now that's partly still true here. The difference is that the pastors here were brought in from across the country because of their specialty and ability in specific areas.

He then went on to enumerate the specialties that each one brought to this church. These areas of expertise included international work for the World Council of Churches, national experience as a staff member at the denomination's headquarters, consulting for nationally recognized churches such as Robert Schuller's Crystal Cathedral, seminary teaching experience, and the writing of several published works in church growth and work with youth.

This level of expertise was not encountered at any other church in the study, but it does illustrate the extent to which the "expert" model governs some pastors' professional image, particularly as it relates to information. Illustrative of this pastor's emphasis on specialized expertise was his answer to a question about the magazines that he read. After listing some rather unusual titles (e.g. *Vanity Fair*, *GQ*, *Dance America*), I asked if he read any of a ministerial nature. He replied:

> Oh, a number of technical journals and so forth, but I just figured you'd assume that. I'm not sure, but I have a hunch that the other people you talk to read all of those. If they aren't, they are missing a wide range of important information in their preaching.

His pastoral team often took turns preaching through a popular book (e.g. Covey's *Seven Habits of Highly Effective People*) in a series of sermons. His rationale for using such sources was consistent with the image of the expert: "Because you are dealing with experts who are finding creative ways of saying things...and if somebody says, 'I really need to know more about that,' here it is in the book." Such a sentiment would also be characteristic of the academic librarian.

Other ministers dealt with the pastor's, and the community's, "expert" image in other ways. The minister of a university church, after noting he'd "never had a congregation with so many Ph.D.s," stated his role in the following terms:

> I think my primary task is to lead in the Christian faith this body of people at a level that they can understand. It is not too low a level for those who are highly educated. It's not too high for those who don't have that much education. Frankly, a lot of the university people may be highly trained in a particular area, but they might not be very well advanced in their understanding of the Bible, or the Christian faith, or church history, or things like that. You know, I just don't ever assume that kind of knowledge for most of them.

Overall, however, the image of the pastor as expert was an infrequent one among these ministers, even in this highly educated community. My observation was that the expert image was probably just too uncomfortable for these pastors, who appeared to value more highly the ability to be both unassuming and humble. For example, one pastor with an earned doctorate, after mentioning that his congregation included not only university presidents, professors, and deans, but "28 attorneys" as well, declined to describe himself as an expert in any sense.

> I don't try to come across as being an authority or an expert. I certainly don't intend to do that. If I do it is unintentional. No, I come along as one who is in the same search. We are on the same journey, and maybe I have uncovered a few rocks that will help explain the rock you come to. So I don't think of myself as an expert or authority.

The preacher of a church replete with professionals of

various sorts (company presidents, university professors, corporate executives) summarized this attitude as follows. Confessing that it "used to worry me when I came here" to stand every Sunday morning and look out at such a display of expertise, he continued:

> But I guess I see myself more now as one sharing my faith and seeing how it relates to theirs, how my story interconnects with their story. I try to be a facilitator for them, and not an expert. I don't have all the answers. I'm on the jury too.

Unlike the academic librarian who takes pride in his or her subject expertise, these pastors were reticent to express pride of any sort. Perhaps, that is one reason why the image of the pastor as expert was not more pronounced in this community.

3. The Equipper:
The Pastor as Reference Librarian

The term "facilitator" in the previously cited pastor's comment points to the third image that these pastors painted of themselves in their role as information professionals, that of equipper. The image of the pastor as an equipper was one of the most common themes echoed by the ministers in this study, with nearly half of them using the term "equip" at least once during the interview process to describe what it was that they did. As one pastor explained at the very beginning of his interview:

> My model of ministry is pretty much equipping. I see my role as to equip the body [the church] to minister.... I really discourage people from seeing me as the source of information.... My goal is to train leaders and people who can

respond to those kinds of questions. I do not
encourage people to look to me as the source of
information, the source of ministry.

Based on these comments, one might wonder if the analogy of
the information science educator as "equipper" might be more
appropriate than that of reference librarian: teaching others to
provide information, not being the front-line distributor. But
upon further inquiry, it became clear that even for this pastor his
informational role was similar to what reference librarians do.

I just had a call the other day from somebody
who had been working with [a counseling case]
that was over her head. She called and wanted
to know how to deal with it. I gave her guidelines on what her role should be. [pause] When
it comes right down to it, I do try to work
directly with people and give them the information they ask.... I try to steer them to the right
sources, to get help in that way. My goal is to
steer people toward....

"Steering people toward" is a fair summary of what
reference librarians do as they try to equip people with the
information they need so that they can do whatever it was that
led to the information need in the first place. It is also a fair
summary of what pastors often do. When asked what kinds of
questions he was asked as a pastor, one minister answered: "I
get a lot of questions that I can't answer right away...and I
always tell them, 'I'm not sure but let me check and I'll let you
know.'" The distinguishing difference here, of course, was that
he added, "And, of course, I always say, 'Let me pray with you
about that too.'"

The pastor may parallel part of what the reference librarian does, but not in terms of being value-neutral. Some

ministers even bring the reference desk into the pulpit. For example, one preacher related how he always listed "recommended readings" at the bottom of his sermon outline that he included in the Sunday bulletin so people would know where to find out more information about his sermon topic. One church even had its own bookstore, with a separate section for books recommended from the pulpit. Another had a retired university reference librarian who arranged similar displays in the church library that she directed on a volunteer basis.

The point of reference, however, was not always to books or printed sources. One pastor, a self-proclaimed "information junkie" with over 10,000 books in his personal library and subscriptions to 101 magazines and journals (he gave me a typed list), had altered his equipper image over the years, at least in terms of downplaying his ready reference to printed sources.

In the past that was often my tendency, to pass on reading materials because I am obviously a reader and a lover of books. But I have found over the years that people aren't as responsive to that. They experience that more as, "Here, read about it. Get out of my life. I don't want to talk about it. I don't want to listen to you talk about it." So, more recently I am more or less inclined to be more hesitant about doing something like that. I might say now, "Well, I remember reading such and such." And if they say, "Where was that?" I can say, "Well, it was here if you want to see that." But not to say, "I just read about that. Here, you read this." That is not what they want to do. They are more interested in having somebody else hear their pain and at least talk about it and care, not read about it.

The personal nature of many of the questions that these pastors were asked by information seekers did color their image as an equipper. The human touch was quite pronounced. Unlike most reference librarians, the pastors in this community did make house calls. Even when the search for information by parishioners came secondhand, the information that pastors provided reflected this personal involvement.

For example, the friends of one young woman who wanted to seek treatment for a history of suicidal tendencies contacted the preacher of a small church by phone. His response, after he determined there was not any immediate danger to her life, was to contact a number of professional counseling and medical agencies in the area, and gather information on each one (including brochures describing their services). He then set up an appointment with the woman, went over to her house, and sat down with her at length to discuss what he had found for her so that he could "basically just give her all those options and let her decide." While the last sentiment is certainly expressive of what reference librarians do, the house call seems more than a little uncharacteristic.

Another minister related two incidents that typified the pastor's personal involvement in the "steering people toward" approach to providing information.

> I am seen as one who often does referrals. In fact, one elderly man in this church was about ready to throw in the towel and did not know where to turn, so his wife called me up to come over. I came right over and he was emotionally distraught. I was able to get him in touch that afternoon with the local council on aging, and that opened up a lot of doors for him.

> Oh, yeah, there was another case. I had a man

that I thought was a transient, but it turned out that he was a man whose family had attended here some time ago and had dropped out. He came in needing help to avoid a pending divorce. I just picked up the phone and called one of the new counselors with [a local counseling agency] who had just joined our church. I called up and said, "Are you open for a new client?" That turned out to be a wonderful move. The family got reconciled. They're still working on issues, but they started coming to church here. I'm very quick to do referrals like that.

Admittedly, reference librarians rarely have "converts," but these incidents do underscore the similarities as well as the differences in how these two professionals handle information. The common thread is their emphasis on helping others find the information that they need. Like reference librarians, the "need" is often determined by means of a "reference interview" that helps establish more carefully what the person wants to know.

The example cited earlier of the high school girl who wanted to know what Episcopalians believed illustrates this point. The pastor's conversation with this person revealed that the need was not simply for factual information. She was dating an Episcopalian, and the pastor felt that he had to ask the questions that would lead him to "equip" her with the information that was needed for that specific situation: Are you serious? Is he "saved"? Are you spiritually compatible? Based on this "reference interview," he directed her to the information he thought most appropriate for her particular context.

This incident also highlights the importance of context that Dervin and Nilan (1986) emphasized in their analysis of information user studies and their call for greater sensitivity to the "systematic individuality" inherent in the way people use information.   Note also the overt personal involvement in how these pastors answered reference questions in contradistinction to how reference librarians are typically trained to do so.

For example, the issue of personal involvement by reference librarians was discussed in a recent edition of the series, "How Do You Manage?" in *Library Journal* (Anderson, 1992).   This management case study presented for critique a situation in which a reference librarian appeared to become overly involved with a patron.   One library professional, speaking out against such involvement, even made the comment, "While there is nothing inherently wrong about offering one's given name when meeting a patron, it is not done by most reference librarians" (McGrath, 1992).   Here the pastor and the reference librarian part company.

4. The Wounded Healer:
The Pastor as Activist Librarian

The personal involvement that ministers exhibit in their provision of information is most notable in the image of the pastor as "wounded healer."   The term, reminiscent of such Biblical phrases as "suffering servant," was popularized by the Roman Catholic theologian Henri Nouwen in his 1972 book, *The Wounded Healer.*   He saw ministers as the epitome of incarnational theology in the way in which they involved themselves personally and experientially with their parishioners.

The emphasis in this image is upon the pastor as one who provides answers to questions out of his or her own personal context, often in answer to counseling-related questions. "I have been wounded like you, and I want to help heal you as I was healed."   It is also the image of the involved pastor who "incarnates" the informational role in both personal and professional life. It is the image of the pastor as activist librarian, information professionals whose private experiences and personal interests intertwine with their professional careers. The focus is on the empathetic professional (cf. Mason, 1990, on this point).

At the demonstrative end of the activist scale, the "wounded healer" pastors in this study have little in common with the activist librarian whose personal involvement is mostly manifested in marching, protesting, and boycotting. But at the other end of the scale, pastors who identified with this image are very much like the dyslexic librarian who collects literacy materials for dyslexic patrons, or the sexually assaulted librarian who organizes a rape crisis center in the library, or the librarian from Appalachia who brings books to the rural poor. The activist pastors in this community were much more likely to express their activism in quiet ways. Said one middle-aged pastor:

> Henri Nouwen. He's my model for ministry, incarnational theology. I am able to allow people to feel open and free enough with me to ask questions, to share themselves because I'm a vulnerable kind of guy anyway. But I share with others my journey of faith, where it is that I've come from. That has allowed people to see me, not as a distant relic or a distant pillar, unmoved and unfeeling, but somebody who is down with them. Not down, so much as one who is in the midst of life, experiencing what they are.

The theme of "experiencing what they are," of the vulnerability that comes from openness about one's own personal pain that this pastor expressed, is a common component of the image of wounded healer. To some it is a *sine qua non* of ministry, just as the activist librarian must act on his or her personal experiences and interests. A senior minister of a very large

congregation explained why he still made pastoral calls on the
sick by recounting this true story:

> Years ago, I had a seminary professor named
> [named the professor]. He was pastor at First
> [named the church], which was a big church,
> probably 3,000 members. They hired him there
> to be the preacher only. They said, "We want
> you to go into this room, shut the door, work 40
> hours a week, and we want you to set us on end
> on Sunday morning." He said, "Whoa! This is
> a preacher's dream, surrounded by books, and
> doing my craft." Well, the first sermon he
> preached there he said was the best one he had
> ever preached and the best one he had ever
> heard. He said, "I had it well illustrated. It
> was so well prepared that I could just go into
> that sanctuary and spin it off my lips like gold."
> And the next week he said he did the same
> thing, but by the time he got to the third or
> fourth week he ran out. He said, "I don't know
> these people so I can't preach to them."
>
> And I remember him telling us that story. If a
> preacher is not in contact with the congregation,
> he is speaking in generalities. This week I held
> a woman's hand who is on a dialysis machine.
> I held a woman who has had a stroke. I was
> with a man recently who asked me, "After 71
> years of life, dying of cancer, did I live well
> enough to go to heaven?" My own wife is fac-
> ing a mastectomy. I know the pain.

This note of empathy was also sounded by a pastor who
described his church as "the recovery church." He went on to
explain that a previous pastor had been a recovering person and

that he himself had been divorced and remarried. When he looked out on his congregation on Sunday morning from the pulpit, this pastor explained what he felt thus: "By and large, these people hurt a lot. I'm not here to beat them up. I'm here as God's spokesperson during that hour to share encouragement."

As noted above, the image of the wounded healer was even more prominent in the counseling context than in the pulpit. During the course of one interview, the minister recounted in rather general terms the kinds of counseling cases he had and how he dealt with them. In an effort to probe more deeply into the nature of these information transfer situations, I asked him about one in particular.

> Interviewer: What kinds of questions are people asking you and how are you attempting to answer them?

> Pastor: Well, this is a mostly unchurched congregation in that we're a new church, a church plant. I hear all kinds: sexual immorality, chemical dependency, dysfunctional families.... I'm seeing a tremendous amount of sexual abuse among children, even among Christians.

> Interviewer: Let's take one of those cases as an example. When you get a question, say, concerning sexual abuse, how do you handle it? What do you say?

> Pastor: Well... [He glanced at the tape recorder on the desk, but did not ask to turn it off. His eyes began to tear, and he spoke in very measured tones.] I start from a very practical, experiential kind of viewpoint. My daughter

was sexually abused. This is still kind of recent so it still kind of hurts to talk about it. It was done by a teenager in our church, and he just served jail time for doing it. And so that... You know, there's a price to pay in the ministry. I'm convinced that God... A.W. Tozer said--good lines--he said, "God can't use a man mightily until He's hurt him deeply." And I understand those kinds of things.

Interviewer: If you'd rather not...

Pastor: No. My ministry has not been without those kinds of wounds, but that has built a bridge of understanding. And God has seemingly brought people across my path that I can minister to because I do have that understanding firsthand. So, my counseling, like my preaching, takes on a very personal flavor. I'm not a theologian, although I love to study the Word of God. I am not some kind of pie-in-the-sky, ivory tower counselor. I have to be able to feel what they are feeling. So, when those kinds of things come across my path, God, for some reason, has allowed me or my wife to experience those kinds of things. So we're able to build a bridge very quickly there.

One of his concluding comments was, "There is a lot of pain in the pastorate." The wounds that this pastor felt were not unusual among the pastors in this study.

For example, one pastor disclosed that she served as a volunteer police chaplain and was often brought in to help counsel in rape cases since, "I am a former rape victim and have done a lot of reading in that area." Another was preaching a series of sermons on "Healing the Wounds that Hurt Us" at the time of the interview. He had just completed a sermon on child abuse, during which he told the congregation for the first time that he had been an abused child. Afterwards, several parishioners confessed the same experience and asked to confer with him about how to deal with it. One pastor, who had called from the hospital to reschedule an interview because of a third heart attack, noted that whenever he made hospital calls on the cardiac floor he always had an instant rapport with the heart patients because of their shared experiences.

Two of the pastors interviewed emphasized that their personal experiences as adult children of alcoholics were key elements of their ministry. One, a campus minister, had organized a university group of "ACOA's," as she called them, and had written her doctoral project on the issue. Another pastor noted how strongly her image as "wounded healer" influenced not only her philosophy of preaching, but her call to ministry:

> I had originally planned on being a pastoral counselor, and so I started seminary that way.... I remember one seminary professor telling me I should preach. I said, "But I hate it.... I'm too much of a people person to like the time I have to spend by myself working on the sermon. I'd much rather be out there *with the people* [emphasis mine] than by myself reading, and searching, and studying.

> Actually, a lot of my preaching comes from my own personal experience. When I don't like a Scriptural text or I am struggling with the lectionary, then that's part of my sermon. I just tell them that I've got this text, and I hate it. But it's more. I feel that I'm really sharing

myself. One Sunday I mentioned in a sermon that I am an adult child of an alcoholic. By laying that out I had more people call me that week and say, "I am an alcoholic." Or "I grew up with an alcoholic, and I'm a dysfunctional child." And so by my saying, "This is who I am, and there's nothing to be ashamed of. You know, one in ten people are alcoholics. So look around you in the pews. Some of you here today probably are." So by my bringing it up from the pulpit to say it was okay to talk about these things, people now feel that they can talk about it to me.

The phrase "with the people" captures the essence of how such pastors differ from the traditional information professional, though not from the activist librarian who displays a similar need to be "with the people." Zweizig (1979) observed that in library and information science "one of the damaging assumptions of the field has been that our primary professional attention must be directed to the information store and not to the clients" (cited by Dervin and Dewdney, 1986, p. 511).

Of course, it is not surprising that the image of wounded healer is so pronounced in the pastorate. People expect the human touch when they talk to clergy. On the other hand, such vulnerability does not come without a price tag, as will be pointed out in Chapter 4 when the clergy malpractice issue is discussed. Patrons expect the pastoral information professional to be involved, but also to retain his or her professional detachment. They want a wounded healer, not a healed wounder.

5. The Interpreter:
The Pastor as Special Librarian

In the public arena, the pastor's most visible image is probably that of the interpreter of sacred text, particularly in the Sunday morning message. Like the special librarian in the corporate setting who deciphers arcane data and synthesizes a multitude of materials in order to present to constituents relevant, decision-oriented information, so too the pastor "interprets" key sources in order to facilitate change.

"My role in ministry is to open the text so my people can apply it to their lives," was how one pastor put it. The term "text" was frequently used in the interviews by clergy without any qualifying phrases. To Christian clergy there is only one *text*, the Bible. Though this text comes with a host of supporting materials ranging from lectionaries to commentaries, they all serve to shed light on *the* text. These pastors even used a number of "code" words in describing the text they interpreted, as this pastor did:

> To apply the Scriptures to our lives is what being a pastor is all about. I mean you've got to know other disciplines, be acquainted with them, but it is taking the Word and applying it. Otherwise, I'd be a psychologist or something.

The image of the interpreter was a decisive one for many pastors. Though the term carries several religious connotations, ranging from mediator to one who deciphers ecstatic languages, it is used here in reference to one of the original meanings for the word "pastor," a transliteration of the Latin Vulgate term for "shepherd" or "feeder of the flock." The "food" that these pastors provided was their interpretation of Scripture. This became clear in one minister's statement of his philosophy of preaching:

> When I preach that is a feeding for them.... I heard an illustration one time that the minister's

> preaching is that the church has chosen that
> person to spend intentional time in studying and
> reflecting on the Word and then running into the
> pulpit on Sunday and saying, "Hey, look what I
> found this week to share with you!" That's kind
> of what I try to do, say, "Hey, look what I
> found this week!"

The goal of the pastor as interpreter, like the goal of the special
librarian, is to be able to run into the sanctuary--or the board
room--and say, "Hey, look what I found." Though the interpretive task is often lonely, sitting and sifting through mounds of
materials, the end goal is to offer the interpretation to an
audience.

In ministerial jargon, the difference is between *exegesis*,
based on a Greek word for interpretation, and *exposition*, where
the findings of the interpretive task are proclaimed in an oral
message, usually from the pulpit. Only one pastor confided that
he preferred exegesis to exposition, admitting that the reason he
became a pastor was "I like to study the Word of God. I could
sit here for hours at my desk with my Greek and Hebrew text
and if the phone never rings or no one ever comes in, I couldn't
be happier." More typical, however, is the following candid
comment by a pastor that illustrates how much emphasis these
pastors placed on the expositional end of the interpretive task:

> Where else in the world do you get the privilege
> of talking uninterrupted for thirty to forty
> minutes every week, giving your point of view,
> which is hopefully God's point of view, without
> anyone interrupting, without anyone challenging,
> and then accepting it as truth? I mean, what a
> privilege and opportunity we pastors have.

The image of the interpreter was quite strong among

many of the pastors interviewed in this study. In a somewhat emotional vein, a middle-aged minister explained why, in the thirteen years since his ordination, he had never re-preached a sermon even once.

> Maybe it's arrogance [small laugh]. I dislike canned sermons. It irks me [voice rising] when you get people from headquarters who come out to an installation service, and they bring along "Installation Sermon #5" and just put different names in the blanks. I think one of the chief reasons the ordained ministry exists is that the pastor is the one who is allowed the privilege to have the time to exegete the text, to prepare a message, and then to proclaim it to the people. We follow the lectionary so every three years I could use the same text and the same sermon, but the world will be different, I will be different, and my exegesis had better be different. Maybe it is my arrogance, but I've been trained to do this so I'm going to do it.

The seriousness with which this minister approached his interpretive task was evident in the detailed approach he took to sermon preparation. He always followed a two- to three-page "exegetical guide" that included translation of the Scriptural text from the Greek or Hebrew, textual criticism in which he looked for variant textual readings, word studies of significant words in Greek or Hebrew lexicons, grammatical analysis of the passage in the original language, and commentary studies. He also prepared his exposition to the point that he preached for twenty to thirty minutes every Sunday without ever using a single note.

The comparison of the interpreter/pastor to the special librarian should not be pushed too far. There are just too many shades of meaning to the term "interpreter" in the ministry. The pastor as interpreter is a complex image that has been discussed for some time and at some length in the technical literature of this profession. An entire theological journal, *Interpretation*, has been devoted to this one issue.

In recent years, the particular focus has been on the preaching event as interpretation. This is especially true in the inductive approach to preaching championed by Fred Craddock, former professor of preaching at Duke University's Candler School of Theology. Craddock, frequently referred to as the most influential homiletical theoretician on the current American scene, outlined this approach in *As One Without Authority* (1979) and *Preaching* (1985).[17] Inductive preaching, unlike the traditional deductive style, encourages the interpreter to withhold "the explanation" until the end of the message so that the audience can be involved in the interpretive process as well. In one of a series of articles in the *Christian Century* debating the validity of this approach to preaching, Shepherd (1990, p. 822) pointed out the weakness of the older approach and the benefits of the inductive method:

> In our typical sermon, a "theme sentence" is announced and illustrated with a myriad of disconnected images. This statement of "what the gospel is all about" is treated as a starting point rather than a goal: this is what the Bible means, take my word for it, no sense in getting into the details--let's talk about how Uncle Harry learned this lesson. The congregation is not led to see how the message was derived from the text and applied to the church.... The inductive sermon recreates the process of discovering the meaning in the text.

One of the more concrete examples of how current clergy are opening up the interpretive process to include the congregation even before the sermon is delivered was found in the approach of one downtown pastor whose congregation included a number of educators and other professionals. At the time of the interview, he was in the process of writing his Doctor of Ministry project on "interpretation as dialog," using the hermeneutical writings of philosopher Hans-Georg Gadamer. This minister, like most in the study, followed the lectionary, which is an ecumenical publication in various forms that assigns certain Biblical passages to every Sunday over a three-year cycle.

His approach to interpreting these Biblical passages was to meet with a small, adult Bible study group every Wednesday evening to go over the text that the lectionary had "assigned" him to preach on in two weeks. His goal in these meetings was to "ask open questions about the text and try to get them to explore and then use that as a basis to inform my dealing with the text." He despised commentaries because "very few succeed in opening up the text; most of them succeed in destroying any kind of creativity... they're just too cut-and-dried, too canned." His desire in this "group exegesis" was to engage his people in dialog with the text, to "open up the text and ask it questions and then to be silent and let it ask questions of us." His purpose in this interpretive method was, to paraphrase current homiletical theory, "to preach *for* people and not just preach *to* them."

The dialogical nature of the interpretive task between pastor and parishioners is quite unlike the task of the special librarian. Though dialog certainly occurs in the corporate setting between the special librarian and his or her employer, it is of a distinctly different nature. This difference is especially pronounced when considering black pastors. The interpretive interaction between minister and members has a long tradition in the black church.

Twenty-two years ago Holt's analysis of black preaching

in "Stylin' Outta the Black Pulpit," presaged this current emphasis in homiletical theory. "[T]he black ministerial figure (pastor, preacher, reverend, or leader) does not deliver a message *to* his audience; he involves his audience in the message" (Holt, 1972, p. 200). Sometimes, she pointed out, the "intensity and volume of audience response signals the preacher that he is...telling the truth" (p. 192). At other times, it is the content of the responses themselves that attest to the nature of the dialog. Comments such as "hunh?" from the preacher (meaning, "Am I right in this?") or such verbal interjections from the congregation as "Amen" ("That's right!") or "He's on the road now!" or "Tell the truth. Tell it. Talk!" are all intended to involve both parties in the interpretive task (p. 197). Of course, such interchanges also attest to the highly oral nature of the interpretive event of preaching, as shall be pointed out in Chapter 4.

An example of this orality was found in a visit to one black congregation. Prior to the Sunday service, I asked the pastor what he had preached on the previous Sunday. He responded that he could not tell me because "when I get done with the sermon, it's gone." My later observation of his preaching was that the message was so dialogical in expression that even a copy of his sermon notes, which he always used, would have been only a small part of the message. As Niles (1984) accurately observed, one of the reasons why analytical study or rhetorical criticism of black sermons via the manuscript method is so difficult is that "most black sermons are in dialogue form, [and] manuscripts may not satisfactorily represent what actually took place in church" (p. 44).

Even among non-ethnic congregations, the interchange between pastor and parishioner is often so intertwined in contemporary preaching that isolating the preacher's interpretive role is difficult. It does not always take an overtly dialogical stance. Sometimes, the interpretive partnership is much more indirect.

The librarian-turned-minister mentioned earlier stressed how his interpretive task was to make the connection between a first-century book and a twentieth-century people so that they could "see their story in light of the Scriptural story," to help them make for themselves the connections between "the Biblical narrative and their own narratives." It is a view of information dissemination that cares less about the content than it does about the recipient. As one pastor explained:

> I hope [my preaching] can be a point of discussion for them. I guess I see my sermon more as a stepping stone for their own search, their search in the community, and their search with God. I remember being taught in seminary class that if you see somebody daydreaming, it does not necessarily mean that they're bored. You may have clicked a memory in them that--it might not be the theme of the sermon--but you might have talked about an old Sunday School teacher and that's where they are now. And that's okay too because you are putting them in touch with the purpose of God or a memory-- though sometimes people may be just sleepy. I guess what I want to do is share the journey with others, to give them a place to think, a little piece of meat to chew on, and hopefully to have them talk to others about what they are thinking.

This role of the pastor as interpretive catalyst raises another important difference between ministers and special librarians. Librarians working in special settings typically limit their interpretive task to the documents they have retrieved. Pastors are just as concerned, if not more so, with the Word behind the words, as this pastor explained regarding the purpose of his interpretive task:

> [I want] to facilitate the experience of the
> presence of Christ and Christ's Word through
> the moment of the preaching event, when the
> sermon manages to create an atmosphere where
> the living Word behind the written Word clicks
> with the living experience of the people. I guess
> I see myself as a catalyst for that.

His explanation makes it clear that the pastor, unlike the special librarian, views the interpretive task as more than mere explanation of printed text. Many of the pastors in this study noted the importance of distinguishing between animate ("living Word") and inanimate ("written Word") text. The interpretive task for these pastors was not merely an oral exposition of a written document. They treated the Scriptures qualitatively differently than any other text. The sense of the sacred was very pronounced, and this feeling was typically expressed in one of two almost opposite ways.

At one extreme were those pastors who viewed *the* text as the very words of God. Their task was to "just preach the Word of God." The meaning of the text was obvious for all to see. They merely announced that meaning to others. They did not see themselves as "interpreters" at all. As one stated bluntly, "They know what the Bible says. I'm not going to put my interpretation on it. I'm just going to let the Word speak for itself." In one sense, this attitude of "honoring the text" is very much like what a librarian does: retrieve the document for the patron and let it speak for itself. In reality, however, this is not what those pastors who claim to follow this model actually do. The most vivid example of this claim to "honor the text" was given by this minister when asked his view of preaching:

> I just give them the message the Lord done give
> me. I deliver the message the Lord done give.
> That's all I'm trying to do.... When it comes

time for to deliver the message, I'm the newsman. I report the news, and I tell them that if
they've got anyone they want to get angry at,
get angry at God, because I am just the newsman. I just report the news. I don't make it.
I report it.

Further inquiry, however, indicated that this pastor was actually
very much involved in the interpretive process, from choosing
the particular texts to "share" with his audience to using
exegetical tools to help him explain that text to his congregation.
He had "thousands of books" in his library, especially commentaries, and was "always reading" because "you have to build [the
sermon] according to Scripture and you have to build that according to what other scholars who have written on these same
Scriptures on the same theme, you know, have said."

The difference was that his mental image of his interpretive role was that of God's spokesperson, not interpreter, even
though he was quite involved in the interpretive task. It was a
matter of authority for him, as will be pointed out later in this
chapter when that critical issue is raised. The issue of authority
in interpretation was also noted by a Roman Catholic priest, who
complained that his parishioners were reading the Bible much
more than when he first entered the priesthood. "The problem,"
he said, "is that they interpret it for themselves in so many
different ways, and...they come up with some outlandish interpretations... that can help justify some position they have."

At the other end of the interpretive process were those
pastors who openly and willingly interpreted the Scriptures as
human words, but not just human. They were familiar with
higher criticism and knew all about the "JEPD theory of the
Pentateuch and the Q source underlying the Gospel narratives,"
as one said. They were neither literalists nor fundamentalists,
but still *the* text was different than any other. This pastor's

understanding of Scripture and his interpretive role are illustrative of this approach.

> You have to remember that the tradition I come
> out of is a very orthodox one...which is not
> fundamentalist Christian. You know, Luther
> used the Christmas image. He said that the
> Scriptures are not the Word of God. He said
> that no person who understands what the Word
> itself says about who Jesus Christ is--John's
> Gospel begins, "The Word was made flesh."
> He said clearly that the early Christian tradition
> was that the Word was made flesh in Jesus. It's
> no longer a book, but the book is the manger
> that holds the Christ Child.

> We treat the Scriptures probably--as Protestants
> would say--with less regard than they do. But I
> think in terms of the whole tradition of the
> Church, we would say that we treat the Scrip-
> tures authentically in that we are very clear to
> say that even the Scriptures, just as the Church
> does at its best, point to Jesus Christ as the
> "capital W" Word of God.... Luther said the
> canon's never been closed on Scripture. Luther
> said the Epistle of James is an epistle of straw
> and that I recommend you not read it.

While such pastors do not share any of the Puritan image
of "the book as totem" (cf. Cressy, 1986), they still sense the
sacredness. This sensation, of course, is one of the critical
distinctions between the pastor and the special librarian in terms
of their respective roles as interpreters for their constituents.
The pastor's focus in interpretation is not on the container nor
even necessarily on the content, but perhaps more accurately, on
discovering the *animus* that permeates the printed page of the

text they interpret. "My philosophy of preaching," summarized one minister, "is basically to interpret the witness of Scripture, so that people have some encounter with the living Word as opposed to the printed text.... For me Scripture points to the Word; it is not equated with it."

Summary of the Five Images

The pastors in this study mentioned five images that conceptualize and control their role as information providers. These images are that of the generalist, the expert, the equipper, the wounded healer, and the interpreter. These images have been compared with the analogous roles that librarians fill by way of illustrating to what extent pastors are similar to and different from traditional information professionals.

While these five images are an important framework for examining how pastors function as information professionals, there are two other issues that are also significant in this discussion. One of these is the professional authority of the pastor, and the other is his or her professional knowledge. No matter what image of information provision the pastorate portrays, the issues of authority and knowledge are still central.

The Professional Authority of the Pastor

One of the defining characteristics of a professional is authority, as mentioned at the outset of this chapter in the study by Asheim (1978). A discussion of this topic is especially relevant when one considers that one of the more troublesome issues for librarians as information professionals is the problem of authority. As Asheim pointed out, the library information professional has, since the end of World War I, increasingly downplayed authority in favor of freedom of access. In perhaps overly melodramatic tones, Goode (cited by Asheim, p. 232) lamented that this increasing lack of authority in the library profession has resulted in a situation where "the librarian is a gatekeeper who can exclude almost no one.... At present, the librarian has little power [i.e. influence or authority] over his clients."

In a larger sense, the granting of authority to any professional in American society--whether librarians or clergy--is becoming more difficult, partly because of the current culture's concentration on freedom at the expense of authority, as Bellah and his associates have observed in their penetrating analysis of contemporary American society, *Habits of the Heart: Individualism and Commitment in American Life* (1986).

In the ministerial field, one of the more intriguing discussions on authority is by Theiss, who argued in "Preaching for Public Life" (1991) that clergy find it difficult today to address such issues of "the public good" as literacy and world hunger because parishioners are so involved in individual freedom that they cannot hear legitimate authority.[18]

Before proceeding too far, it might be helpful to attempt to define what is meant here by authority.[19] One of the more useful definitions is found in Wilson's *Second-Hand Knowledge: An Inquiry into Cognitive Authority* (1983). He suggested very simply that authority is the influence that one person has over another (p. 13). More particularly, person A has authority over person B if what A says in a certain sphere carries weight with or has influence over B.

This definition includes three elements useful for this discussion. First, authority involves at least two people. One can be an expert in isolation and without recognition, but one can only be an authority in relationship to other people. Second, authority must be granted by the other party; it cannot be unilaterally claimed. The basis for this granting varies, but often two issues are involved: trust and competence. Third, authority is usually granted to a person relative to a specific domain. One can be an authority in one subject, but not in another.

The implications of these elements of authority are important for pastors in considering their role as information professionals. First, the authority that a pastor carries is tied very much to a personal context. Perhaps that is one of the reasons why the image of the pastor as "expert" is not very pronounced in this community. The picture of the lonely, ivory-tower scholar, detached from the people and dispensing advice at a distance, was quite foreign to most of the clergy inter-viewed. My observation of these pastors was that the need for human interaction was deeply embedded in what could be termed the pastoral psyche. Their sense of authority seemed bound to human-to-human encounters. Their need for feedback in what they were saying was often immediate.

For example, one pastor protested when asked to preach on the radio, "I have to see the congregation. I can't preach to a microphone." As will be discussed in Chapter 4, this need for social intercourse may also help explain why so few of these pastors were writers. The published article meant for anony-mous readers did not appear to offer these pastors the same sense of whether their authority was being accepted as did the oral delivery to a sea of faces. As one put it, "I just can't preach unless I see some eyeballs."

The second element present in Wilson's definition of authority concerns the granting of that authority by one person to another individual. Authority cannot simply be claimed in isolation; it must be granted in a social context. It does not necessarily have to be earned, in the sense that one has to meet some universally accepted criteria (e.g. passing the bar exam or acquiring a Ph.D. degree), but it does have to be granted.

Among traditional information professionals, such authority is typically granted on the basis of technical competence. A reference librarian is asked a reference question because he or she is presumed by the patron to be competent to provide an acceptable (i.e. authoritative) answer (but see the discussion on "Institutional Authority" below). Corporate information specialists are able to influence company policy because their supervisors judge them to be technically competent to provide accurate and useful data relevant to decision making.

For the pastor, the bases for being granted authority by the public or the parish are slightly more complex. The issue of trust is just as important, if not more so, than technical competence. As Wilson observed: "The point about cognitive authority is that it is trusted for substantive judgment and specific advice, not for recital of information [technical competence] relevant to making judgments" (1983, p. 181).

A self-proclaimed "information addict" with several university degrees brought the significance of the trust issue to my attention very early on in the interview process. After relating how he "had a problem with information" in that he was always trying to get more--whether by reading or attending conferences or listening to the radio, he offered this insight into the trust component in information:

> My whole thinking on information changed after
> I went to a right-wing, anti-abortion conference.
> You know, I'm not into that right-wing stuff. I
> mean I'm against abortion like most evangeli-
> cals, but I don't go in for that right-wing stuff.
> Anyway, I went and I was prepared to not
> listen. I had my mind made up. But then this
> guy started talking and his whole demeanor...
> I mean his face lit up, and I found myself really
> listening. Not because of all his facts, but

because I found myself starting to really like him as a person. That's what it's all about. Not information, but can I trust this guy who is up saying all this stuff to me? Do I know him? Do I like him? Can I trust him to tell me what's right? What I need to know?

I mean look at Jesus. Who was this guy? He didn't have a problem with information overload. His message was very simple. But 15 or 20,000 people just got up and followed Him one day into the wilderness just to hear Him speak. And two days later, they all looked around and said, "Hey, we don't have anything to eat." That's what we need to capture. Not all this information stuff. I need to concentrate on myself, not my message. I have enough information in my head to last a lifetime, even if I never read another book. I mean I'm not just trying to put down information. I'm an information addict. But that's not what people need. They need to know they can trust you.

The issue of trust is a fundamental one for pastors in terms of the authority that they exercise in their roles as information providers (cf. the "fiduciary relationship" noted by Mason, 1990, for information professionals). In this study, four bases for granting authority were uncovered in the course of the interviews, two based on trust and two based on competence. The four foundations for authority are these: educational authority, institutional authority, personal authority, and divine authority. Each of these will be explored in turn below as a means of examining how and why these ministers were granted authority by their publics.

It should be pointed out here that since this study was

limited to interviews with pastors, not parishioners, the "granting" of authority is discussed on the basis of what pastors reported or what I observed to be occurring and on the basis of data presented in the literature, not on the basis of what church members said. Such a study would also be useful, but is outside the scope of this project.

The third element present in Wilson's (1983) definition of authority concerns the limits to authoritative knowledge. This aspect will be discussed in the last section of this chapter.

Educational Authority

Authority for the information professional is typically based on technical competence, which in turn is often educationally derived. For the professional librarian in this country, a one- to two-year degree from a Master of Library Science program that is accredited by the American Library Association provides the educational authority that enables a person both to be and to be judged (i.e. by employers, peers, and sometimes the public) technically competent. Certainly, technical competence and the resulting authority can be gained through means other than this professional degree, but that is not the professional standard.

Among American ministers of most mainline denominations, the standard professional degree is the three-year Master of Divinity degree accredited by the Association of Theological Schools in the United States and Canada. The qualification "most mainline denominations" is necessary because there are many religious groups that do not require the Master of Divinity degree--or any degree, for that matter--for ordination, the most common of three ways of being legally recognized as a minister.

For example, the largest Protestant fellowship in this

country, the Southern Baptist, does not require this professional degree for ordination, although they strongly encourage it (the two largest seminaries in the world, in fact, are Southern Baptist). Many locally autonomous religious groups, such as the independent Christian Churches and Churches of Christ, require neither professional education nor ordination, but 95% have an undergraduate degree in ministries from a Bible college and an additional 35% have a Master of Divinity degree (Tanner, 1989).

On the other hand, many denominations are encouraging ministers to pursue a professional doctorate, the Doctor of Ministry degree. This advanced degree for practicing pastors was first offered in 1964 by the Divinity School of the University of Chicago and was followed shortly by seminaries at Claremont in California, Vanderbilt in Tennessee, and Princeton in New Jersey (Carroll and Wheeler, 1987). The degree has been accredited by the Association of Theological Schools since 1970 and has grown more than tenfold in the last two decades, from a nationwide enrollment of only 688 students in 1971 to 7,274 students in 1992, the last year for which figures are available (*ATS Factbook*, 1993).

The Doctor of Ministry degree, which requires as prerequisites a Master of Divinity and at least three years of professional experience in ministry, has a decided professional focus with the equivalent of three years of classroom work offered in one-week or two-week formats, followed by a written "project" that addresses the nature and practice of some issue in ministry. It is also a degree that allows pastors to specialize in as many as a dozen different areas, from counseling to urban ministries. One minister summarized the value of the Doctor of Ministry degree for the pastoral profession in these terms:

> I had originally thought of a ministry of teaching, thinking of a Doctor of Philosophy degree, and went into the parish as a very temporal

commitment. As that commitment got firmed up
and then as family responsibilities came along,
the Doctor of Ministry just seemed to me, after
being out of seminary roughly ten years, to be
the right kind of experience. I needed to get
back into the academic setting and reflect on
what I was doing and have the kind of practical
orientation that that degree has, which is far
more beneficial for parish ministers than a Ph.D.

The diversity of educational experience among American
ministers--ranging from no college education to the professional
doctorate--was also evident in this study. One-fifth (21%) of the
sixty-two ministers interviewed already had or were currently
working on a Doctor of Ministry degree, while three (5%) had
less than a bachelor's. Table 1 below provides a summary of the
educational background of all sixty-two ministers.

Table 1
Educational Background
of the Ministers in This Study

Highest Earned Degree	Number of Ministers	Percentage of Total	Cumul. Percent
Doctor of Ministry	13	21%	21%
Master of Divinity	28	45%	66%
Other Master	7	11%	77%
Bachelor	11	18%	95%
Associate/Diploma	3	5%	100%
TOTAL:	62	100%	

The thirteen ministers who are listed in the "Doctor of
Ministry" category in Table 1 above include four pastors who
were currently enrolled in the program at the time of the study,

the other nine having already completed their degrees. Except for one Master of Divinity student, these four were the only pastors in the community who were still in seminary. The 21% figure for the percentage of pastors with the professional doctorate is also somewhat misleading in that only Master of Divinity graduates with at least three year's ministry experience are allowed to enter the Doctor of Ministry program. When these two conditions are factored in, the percentage of eligible ministers who either had or were earning the professional doctorate in ministry jumps from 21% to 50% (thirteen of twenty-six).

No published comparative data are available, but it appears that the percentage of pastors in this community with ministerial doctorates is probably higher than in the country at large. The fact that this was a highly educated community and that the parishes in this town were rarely first-time ministries for pastors helps explain this high percentage.

The educational emphasis in this community that is home to four colleges and two universities may also help explain why unearned or unaccredited doctorates were also relatively popular among these pastors. Seven (11%) of the sixty-two ministers in this study either had honorary doctorates (three did) or unaccredited, correspondence-school "doctorates" (two did and two were pursuing them). These unearned degrees are not noted in Table 1 above. Of the three pastors with honorary doctorates, two used the title prominently in their church publications. The other pastor, who had only a bachelor's degree and was fairly new to the community, offered this view of his "doctorate":

> I've got an honorary doctorate, but I don't tell anyone about it. I told some guys at the ministers' meeting the other day. I mean, I told them because it's a joke really. Oh, it's serious in that they [the college] seriously gave it to me, but I could seriously care less.

Of the four pastors with unaccredited doctorates, two had "Ph.D." degrees in counseling and Biblical studies from a correspondence school in the Midwest, one had a "Th.D." degree in theology from a similar diploma school in the South, and one had a "Doctor of Divinity" degree from a traditionally black seminary, also in the South. The correspondence approach to educational degrees is evidently quite common among many black pastors, including two of the three interviewed in this study. As one explained, "You learn yourself."

The desire for educational credentialing of this sort among black clergy may also be due in part to the "dual composition" of the highly educated and the not-so-highly educated membership of many black churches discussed by Holt (1972). In these situations, Holt argued that the black preacher often preaches two sermons. First, he delivers a message "devoted to reason and intellect" and then, "after getting warmed up with reason...proceeds to symbolically take off his frock (often physically doing so) and 'gets with it,' embracing all the myths, superstitions, and irrational assumptions of fundamentalist religion" (pp. 194-195). A similar phenomenon (even to the point of the removal of his robe halfway through the sermon) was observed in the preaching of one of the black preachers in this study who had secured a doctorate via correspondence, but seemed ambivalent about it. In fact, all four of these pastors with unaccredited doctoral degrees appeared somewhat uncomfortable in discussing them.

The numerical analysis of the educational backgrounds of the pastors in this study, however, is only part of the picture. The various ways in which these ministers viewed their "educational authority" is more revealing. At one end of the spectrum was the paradoxical position of those pastors who had considerable education, but who down-played any such references in discussing ministerial authority. One such pastor, who had four earned degrees (a bachelor's and a master's in history from a prestigious university, as well as a Master of Divinity and a Doctor of Ministry from an Ivy League seminary), explained this perspective on authority in these terms:

> If I have any authority, it is because of ordina-
> tion, not because of education. The only thing
> you see hanging in this room, although I have a
> doctorate--the only thing that hangs in this room
> is my ordination [certificate]. That is where I
> get my authority. I feel called of God to do
> what I am doing, and my authority is through
> the ordination and through the Bible that I was
> given authority to preach.

Ironically, several pastors in this study who had had little formal education were not at all hesitant about displaying prominently their "diplomas of achievement" in their offices or talking proudly about receiving educational certificates that "required me to read all of these books on this shelf." More typical, however, was the attitude of this pastor, who had no formal, seminary education in ministry.

> At [named his church] we see a big difference
> between education and training. So many min-
> isters in seminary say, "I'm here to get edu-
> cated." But when they get out there in the
> churches, they don't know what to do. They got
> all this knowledge from books, but they haven't
> been trained how to minister. So we try to
> train. You know, a lot of our pastors [in this
> religious fellowship] are seminary graduates, but
> I'm not sure they have the training, you know,
> to administrate and counsel and how to do all
> that kind of stuff.

In essence, this pastor was raising the issue of education as experience, an almost apprenticeship view of education (a point made by Mason, 1990, in his discussion of the educational experiences needed by information professionals). However, these somewhat negative views of education were unusual.

At the other end of the spectrum were those pastors who stressed the importance of the "educational authority" that ministers have. These positive attitudes were much more common than those who eschewed education. Contrast the just-cited minister's emphasis on practical experience over seminary study with this pastor's explanation of why he became a minister:

> I went to seminary primarily to study. I didn't know what I wanted to do.... I just knew I wanted to study. I had a passion to learn the Scriptures, and that is what still drives me. I don't have a real strong vocational inclination to be a "clergyman." It is more of a pursuit of knowledge and learning. It's having the knowledge of God and imparting that.

The importance of seminary education was stressed frequently by pastors. At the very beginning of one interview in response to a question about his sermon topic for the previous Sunday, a pastor whose congregation had many highly educated members responded at some length instead about the considerable number of years of seminary study he and his pastoral staff had had, so that I would understand in any discussion about ministry at this church how "academically well trained to begin with" the pastors were.

Even among ministers without seminary master's degrees, the issue of educational authority was not ignored. In describing the nature of his ministry in this professional community, one pastor, who began a seminary degree years ago but never finished, confessed:

> It is intimidating from time to time because this
> is a highly educated community, and I don't
> have a Ph.D. I never did finish a master's
> program even.

This same individual compensated for his lack of formal educational training by reading, rather extensively, authors who were "cutting-edge experts in ministry." Acknowledging his earlier lack of interest in education, this pastor admitted:

> Reading is hard work for me. I was not a good
> student when I was in school. Not because I
> couldn't have been. I obviously just chose not
> to do that. So, embarrassingly, life has been a
> continuous catch-up ballgame for me.

His current "catch-up" in reading he felt was necessary in order to give him the technical "competence" that educational authority begets. For many ministers, educational authority was a motivational factor in their regular involvement in continuing education. For them, continuing education was not only desirable, but also often required by the denomination. Some religious groups required their clergy to submit an annual form for continued clerical "standing" on which the minister was to list not only what continuing education classes he or she had completed, but also what books had been read that year.

Several of the ministers in this study mentioned their participation in formal continuing education opportunities, citing such things as "Skill Schools" and "Colleges of Ministry" that their denomination offered. Others, however, weren't so impressed with their own denominational offerings, and made such comments about their quality as "useless," "impotent," "yuck," "out of touch with current ministry," and "overly political."

In contrast, seminars and workshops provided in the region by several well-known seminaries (e.g. Fuller Theological Seminary of California) were often cited by pastors in the interview process as exceedingly helpful continuing education forums for them. Overall, continuing education appeared to be highly prized by most of the ministers in this study (only 6 of the 62 pastors interviewed mentioned no such experiences in the last year or two). The following pastor's rationale is representative of many ministers: "I get two weeks a year as continuing education time as part of my position description, and I use all of that and more. I'm a lifelong student."

What is not so clear in this study is how the educational authority of ministers is viewed by the "grantors" of that authority, i.e. parishioners and others who come to pastors for information. Since the research design, as was noted above, focused almost exclusively on pastors, there were few opportunities to explore this issue beyond the pastoral perspective.

One small piece of evidence that such pastoral authority was taken seriously by non-pastors were the comments by two professional counselors in the community who were also interviewed in this study. One of these, the clinical director of a local counseling center who had a Ph.D. in psychology from a well-known research university, commented on how well trained he felt that the local pastors were "by and large" when it came to issues of pastoral counseling. The other, the administrative head of the same agency, noted that he had hired several of the local clergy as professional counselors based on their Master of Divinity training and pastoral experience. This same agency also offered a Doctor of Ministry degree in counseling in cooperation with three seminaries in the region and had had nearly one hundred graduates in the decade of its existence, many of whom were local pastors.

In summary, educational authority was a significant issue

for the pastors in this study. For some, professional education was important, but only as it confirmed or prepared one for ordination. For others, educational authority was particularly pronounced in this intellectually oriented community (note here the earlier discussion of the pastor as expert). And for still others, the bases for authority were to be found in areas other than educational. One of these was the institution of the church itself.

Institutional Authority

One could argue that information professionals, such as academic librarians, have authority, not because of their educational training, but because they work in an institution from which they derive their authority. Library patrons, so the argument goes, do not grant academic librarians their authority, at least not initially, because of their technical competence (educational authority), but simply because they work in an academic institution known as a library. Their authority comes not because of any individual criteria or expertise that they possess, which is often not even known to the patron, but because they work in an institution which the patron assumes to represent a certain range of authoritativeness.

The assumption by many library patrons that anyone who works in a library is a librarian is indicative of this view. These professionals are an authority not because of what they know, but because of where they work. Competence is still central to their authority, however, because the extended assumption is that the institution hired them for their professional expertise.

This same perspective applies also to some extent to the pastor as an information professional. Wilson (1983), in fact, devoted an entire chapter to the issue of institutional authority, arguing that both librarians and ministers wield this kind of in-

fluence. In modern society, Wilson contended, "the prime locus
of institutional cognitive authority is the scientific community,
the social institution of science" (p. 82). However, the church
is also an organization that "may have cognitive authority independent of the particular individuals occupying [its] offices" (p.
81). The power of the pastor's institutional authority was
demonstrated in a variety of ways in this study.

Several pastors made reference in the course of the interviews to the institutional authority that was granted to them by
virtue of their office, an authority that was sometimes in conflict
with their personal views. One young minister who had recently
served in a campus ministry and was now pastoring in a mostly
unchurched part of town where "immorality was rampant" acknowledged this dilemma in the following interchange:

> Interviewer: How do you answer some of the
> questions you get about drugs or premarital sex
> when you are dealing with young people who
> are not members and don't share your church's
> views?

> Pastor: From two perspectives. I always tell
> them, "I wear two hats," and I try to be as real
> as I possibly can from both of those perspec-
> tives. One perspective is that I do represent the
> institutional church, and there is an institutional
> church or Biblical perspective that I do have to
> represent. Now sometimes that perspective may
> not be my personal perspective. Therefore, I
> give both: my personal and my institutional per-
> spective. Most of the time, I like to try to think
> that they are on the same wavelength with one
> another, but if they are not, I'm honest with
> them about that and how I would reconcile not
> being on the same wavelength as the institution.

Interviewer: How do you reconcile those two perspectives?

Pastor: First of all, I don't see my role as one of judge. Only God has that power and, therefore, my role is to lift up the tenets of the Scriptures, but not for me to be the judge. And I am really uncomfortable with those in the church who attempt to judge others. While I do not condone various lifestyles... Like I don't condone homosexuality, but I don't put the person who is homosexual outside the means of God's grace. That's not my role. If I have an opportunity to extend that grace at any time, I think that is what I should be doing and that is what this church should be doing. And God will judge them in the end.

This pastor's comments point out not only the possible tension over institutional authority from the pastor's own perspective, but also the problem of differentiating in the public's mind between legitimate institutional authority (what the church officially teaches) and the distorted view that perceives only what certain members of the church portray as *the* church's position. Some pastors, for example, were quick to quote from official church policy manuals that they had handy on their desks when answering certain questions, as if to underscore the need to refer to legitimate institutional authority.

This deference to institutional authority is something that even the pastors demonstrated. During one case study I noticed, for example, that the pastor presented a very formal persona while speaking at the altar--stiff posture, always standing, raised hands, never humorous--but was much more informal during his sermon--sat on stool, frequently joked, spoke in conversational tones. His response was that while standing at the altar, he was

"presiding at the liturgy of the church" and that these were "not
my words but the words passed on in the history of the church."
His authority at this point was institutional, and he treated his
role as "information provider" in this social context as an institutional, not a personal, one.

Another pastor, whom I had heard preach several times
prior to this particular interview, stressed this same institutional
authority during his sermons. In response to my devil's advo-
cate question, "What right do you have to stand in the pulpit
every Sunday morning and tell these people what to do?" he
responded:

> Only insofar as I represent the church. You
> may have noticed that I always pray before I
> preach.... I always run the danger that my
> words will be self-serving...[that] I will be
> extremely tempted to say, "I believe, therefore
> you must." Instead, I will say, "We believe."
> I'll use the words of the creed. Everything I
> preach, I think, is credal in nature. It reflects
> the traditions of the church. I am extremely
> conservative on that point.

His choice of the word "conservative" was significant in that
whatever information he disseminated on Sunday morning was
intended to "conserve" the traditions, the language, the authority
of the church. Although he never mentioned the phrase "institutional authority," it was clear that this was the basis for his
preaching to the parish.

The pastor's institutional authority among the ministers
in this study was also evident externally in how some dealt with
community and political issues. When asked if he served on any
local boards or organizations as a means of helping provide
religious information to the community, one long-term minister

shook his head no and then explained:

> I still make my voice known. Rather than do it
> before any local board, I do it with a board
> member, one on one, you know. The mayor
> and I are very good friends, and if I have a
> problem, I go directly to him. If I need to talk
> with the police chief, I go directly to him. If
> there is a problem at school, I will talk to the
> superintendent of the school or the principal. I
> go directly to them, you know. I always believe
> in going direct. And I always tell them, "If you
> don't listen, there is always Monday coming."
> Monday is election day, you know. Because
> you see when I look out on Sunday morning, I
> can see 200 or 300 people and they each know
> ten other people, and they know ten others.
> And they all vote. So I get my point across.
> These officials know the ballot box has a place
> in our church.

This pastor's authority was noticeable in this community because of the church's influence in local elections. Not coincidentally, this church was also the only one in town during the time of this study to have the two highest officials running against each other in a local primary address the congregation during Sunday morning worship services prior to the election.

Ironically, the institutional authority that pastors enjoyed by virtue of their organizational affiliation did not always extend to the denomination that they represented. Three of the thirteen times that pastors noticed the tape recorder were occasioned by their reference to dissatisfaction with "denominational headquarters." Institutional authority for them was limited to the "church universal," not to their particular brand of it.

Even among parishioners, this hesitancy to accept "official" authority as represented by the denomination was noted by several pastors. One Catholic priest "complained" that his congregation was becoming more Biblically literate because they were now less likely to accept the Catholic Church's interpretation of any given Scriptural text or doctrine. In order to pursue this issue in greater detail, I asked another veteran priest his perspective on the role of religious authority and whether it was increasing or decreasing. He responded:

> I think it's as great now as it always has been, but the nature of that authority is different because people are less inclined to take what somebody says because he says it or because some religious authority says it. They're inclined to say, "Why?" But that's okay with me because any good moral position should be defensible on rational grounds. Now, we're not talking here about the three persons of the trinity or about issues of divinity. I'm talking about things that have to do with human life, with morality. It should be defensible on grounds of reason, but that does not deny in any way that our reason is clouded.

This increasing questioning of religious institutional authority was not unique to Catholic priests in this study. However, such questioning was usually directed at the denomination, not at the ministers themselves. For example, a Protestant pastor related an incident in a recent adult Bible study class in which one of that denomination's fundamental beliefs was challenged not only by some of his church members in the class but also by the teacher, a lawyer who was also a member of that church. His response:

> They have their views and just because the

> church manual or our denominational literature
> says one thing, it doesn't mean that they auto-
> matically accept it. These people are sharp. I
> mean there are a good number of people here
> who are not theological dummies, nor are they
> Biblically illiterate. They know their stuff. I've
> got a lawyer here who really knows his stuff. I
> mean, he is very anti-[named one of his denomi-
> nation's doctrines], but he knows his stuff.

In this case the educational authority of the lay teacher, based on his personal study of the Bible, took precedence over institutional authority and the denomination's official interpretation. What was more common, however, was the predominance of the pastor's educational authority or the church universal's institutional authority over the denomination's institutional authority.

Besides educational and institutional authority, the pastor as an information provider enjoys two other kinds of authority that are not typically associated with information professionals: personal and divine authority. If the first two are based on technical competence, the last two are more issues of trust.

Personal Authority

Wilson's (1983, p. 25) statement that "authority can be acquired and defended on the basis simply of personal trust, belief in a person" is especially true in the profession of the pastorate, particularly in the private role of counseling and the public role of preaching. In one of the standard texts on American preaching, for example, Bosley (in Holland, 1969, pp. 29-30) lists personal power as second only to the divine in the history of preaching in this country.

Since the founding of rhetoric by Aristotle in Greece and Quintilian in Rome, two of the three legs upon which public oratory has stood are *ethos* (the speaker's personal character) and *pathos* (the personal bond between speaker and audience), the third being *logos* (a reference to the technical competence of the rhetorician). In the role of counselor, the image of the "wounded healer" underscores the significance of personal experience in ministry.

One of the first to emphasize the importance of the person as a basis for authority was Weber (1964) in his discussion of charismatic authority. Many of the examples he drew on were those of religious leaders: Old Testament prophets, shamans, cultic leaders, and other such figures. Weber went so far as to say at one point that "[c]harismatic authority is thus specifically outside the realm of everyday routine and the profane sphere" (p. 361), the opposite to profane, of course, being the sacred.

In discussing Weber, it is important to point out what is not meant here by the term "charismatic." Among ministers, the term carries a connotation of supernatural authority or "gifts," based on several New Testament texts that talk about such manifestations of "charisma" as speaking in tongues or performing miracles. That is not what is meant here. Nor is this term used here in the popularized interpretation of the Weberian concept, in the sense that Hitler or Roosevelt or Martin Luther were charismatic leaders. None of the pastors in this study could be appropriately described as charismatic in the popular sense.

For example, though two of the ministers in this study had weekly televised programs, they were certainly of a different nature than the highly publicized televangelists [local cable versus national networks]. None of the pastors interviewed gave any evidence of "cultic" authority. There were no Jim Joneses on the negative side, nor Martin Luther Kings on the positive.

To be sure, several ministers in this study had built up rather sizeable congregations of a thousand or more members, but none of the interviews or case studies involving these individuals uncovered any undue degree of this form of charismatic authority. No evidence of "Lone Ranger" leadership of this type was found. All were responsible to either local leaders or denominational judicatories or both. Yet, in a modified Weberian sense many of these ministers did give evidence of the power of the pastor's person as a basis for authority.[20]

The issue of the pastor's personal authority in "less charismatic" ways was evidenced in several instances in this study. In a tour of one church building, for example, owned by a congregation that had experienced several splits in its history, the pastor pointed out a long line of portraits of former pastors, some of whom had had very short tenures. His comment was, "this church has always split over pastors and personality, not theology." Another pastor, who was in the process of "relocating," handed me a list at one point that contained twelve complaints from the congregation's leaders. Most of the twelve points addressed issues of personal authority and personality conflict, which are not elaborated because of confidentiality.

Another example of the emphasis that some pastors in this study placed upon the person as a basis for authority concerns the pastoral task of preaching. A preacher at one large church observed that attendance dropped somewhat in the summer months when he was out of the pulpit for extended periods. His explanation was that:

> I [named his name] am the teaching arm of this church in the pulpit. I am the number-one teaching arm. I don't want it to be an ego kind of thing, because I do not view myself as God's gift to preaching. I've got people in this church who can think and write better than I can, who

> are superb illustrators. But if they were up there
> in the pulpit week after week, the church would
> diminish.... Part of that is true by virtue of the
> fact that they are used to [named his name]. It
> wouldn't matter if the other person's sermons
> were brilliant. They simply expect to hear me.

Several pastors of large churches reflected this attitude
relative to their preaching. They rarely "gave up" their pulpit on
Sunday morning because of the personal attachment (*pathos*) between parish and preacher. The authority these congregations
granted was based partly on the "known-ness" of these pastors
as persons. These pastors of large churches had all had long
ministries with these congregations, and their personal authority
had been established over a period of time. The sole exception
said emotionally at one point that it was "very lonely being the
senior minister of a large church" because his personal authority
had not yet been established. There was little *pathos* present.[21]

For some ministers the sermon was the major means of
establishing personal authority. One pastor commented that she
only became respected in the community after she delivered the
funeral sermon for a very prominent local leader, a sermon in
which she opened up and told them something about herself as
well. Another minister who had just earned his Doctor of
Ministry degree and had been asked by the regional headquarters
of his denomination to offer a college-credit course in preaching
offered this perspective on the power of the preacher as person:

> You know, I'm getting ready to offer this course
> on preaching, and I believe that it's more impor-
> tant to prepare the preacher than it is the
> message. You know, if I'm prepared spiritually
> as a man, then I'm just dumb enough to believe
> that God is going to be there somewhere along
> in the message.

This attitude towards the power of the person in preaching was reflected also in an interview with the pastor mentioned at the beginning of this section on authority, the one who stressed at some length the issue of trust in providing information. In explaining his approach to preparing and preaching sermons, he said with some feeling:

> When I prepare a sermon, I don't rely on some-one else's ideas. Now, I have to understand that there's no such thing as a completely original idea. But I want to puke when I hear guys, you know, preaching stuff that they've taken out of some book.... I put a high value on having something that's really out of my own heart.... Is this something that I am dealing with per-sonally? Do I know what I'm speaking about? ... The issue is, Can they trust me?

Again, the component of trust is a crucial one in the pastorate. When the personal authority of the pastor was eroded or the bond of trust broken, the consequences for these clergy were usually immediate and often catastrophic. Two of the ministers in this study were in the process of being dismissed for these very reasons, and a third's tenure was in jeopardy. In this same community five years earlier, six pastors had been dismissed in one year by six different churches because of ethical reasons, an issue which will be dealt with in more detail in Chapter 4 under the discussion of clergy malpractice.

Authority based on the person is an important part of the pastoral profession, not only because of its use by ministers but its misuse as well. Perhaps for this reason, the fourth and final basis for authority, the divine, was discussed much more openly by the pastors in this study.

Divine Authority

In complete contradistinction to all other providers of information, the religious leader not only looks to education, institution, and person as bases for professional authority, but also makes a divine claim for the authority he or she exercises. As noted earlier, divine authority is the most central theme that Holland (1969, p. 14) observed in his history of American preaching. While philosophical discussions of the supernatural are outside the scope of this study, the issue of divine authority is nonetheless a "social fact" that must be addressed here. As Durkheim himself explained, "a social fact is every way of acting, fixed or not, capable of exercising on the individual an external constraint..." (1964, p. 13).

The constraints evidenced by ministers in this study relative to the divine authority they claim were quite pronounced. Hardly a pastor did not make some reference, oblique or otherwise, to God in the research-gathering stage of this project. Three even prayed that, in effect, "God would bless my research." One inquired as to my personal relationship with Christ. There was no sense of overt evangelism in these incidents; they were perceived more as expressions of professional preoccupation with deity.

The highly educated pastor mentioned earlier--who also exercised institutional and personal authority--was both serious and representative when he noted that no diplomas hung in his office because his only authority came from his ordination. "I feel called of God to do what I am doing, and my authority is through the ordination and through the Bible that I was given authority to preach."

This pastor's comments highlight the dual nature of divine authority for the clergy in this study: the God Who is the Living Word and the Bible which is His Written Word. The difference was often indistinguishable among these ministers. One pastor commented on how frustrated he was with colleagues who relied too much on personal and even educational authority, especially in the pulpit:

> I believe if that is what we are going to do, we lose our authority. I'm not standing up there to give them my own thoughts [reference to personal authority]. I'm not standing up there to even give them my refined thoughts [reference to educational authority], you know. But there is always that authority that has to come from the Word of God. And that's why we have to refer to the Bible [in our preaching]. The Bible is our first source, and the Holy Spirit as He directs us.

For others the Bible was the means by which they manifested their divine authority, particularly in the pulpit and especially among the more theologically conservative ministers. This was made clear in the following exchange with a fundamentalist preacher whom I had heard preach four times:

> Interviewer: You seem to use the Bible quite a bit in your preaching, even your illustrations are almost all Biblically based.
>
> Pastor: Do you understand why, from our point, why we do that?
>
> Interviewer: I think I do. Maybe I'd better hear you explain.
>
> Pastor: It's that I feel that the Bible is God's Word, and the power of God's Word.... The problem that I think we've come into in 20th

century Christianity and soon in the 21st is that
the pulpit has become a lot of philosophy, where
psychologically pastors are not preachers
anymore. They're almost a psychologist or
psychoanalyst. They come in and give you their
thoughts, and there's the newspapers and the
books they have read. Now, all that's important, and I do that too, but when it comes down
to meeting the needs of the people, it's not....
I preach.... It's not important what Joe Blow
may say, what I say, because we can be wrong.
But if we believe the Word of God is true, that
it's infallible and God's message to us, then we
had better see what God has to say. So there is
always an illustration that He uses of people in
Scripture. There is something there to meet our
needs. So there is our basis, our foundation, the
absolute. Now other pastors may not do that
because they may not believe in the absoluteness
of the Scripture.... I don't ever speak on a
subject without having Scripture to back me up
if I'm in the pulpit. I believe that a message
needs to be peppered with the Scripture because
the power is in the Word of God.

Interviewer: Is that why I noticed so many
people leafing through their Bibles during the
sermon? Do you encourage them to do that?

Pastor: Yes. The idea is that what I say is of
little or no importance. What does God's Word
say? So we encourage them to look it up, to be
familiar with where the passages of Scripture
are. They can practice that right here when they
are in church.

The Bible was not the only tangible locus of divine authority for this group of clergy. For some this sense of the divine was manifested in the artifacts associated with the ministry. "When I place on my shoulders the stole," said one pastor, "that is the yoke of the proclamation of the Word of God, and I recognize that that is a heavy responsibility." When asked about his lack of use of a "stately wooden pulpit" in favor of a small lucite lectern and whether that somehow diminished his authority in preaching, another pastor quickly responded, "No, because you see the authority is here," reaching down and picking up a Bible on the coffee table in front of him. Even the Bible, on occasion, was treated artifactually. For example, in one church service I observed, a bejeweled, gilded Bible was carried down the aisle over the person's head, as if the object itself were on display, and when Scripture was read during the service, it was always from this book, which was always kissed before being opened (cf. Cressy, 1986).

For one preacher, the sense of the sacred was more visual than physical. After recounting a long story about how terrible his first effort at preaching had been because he had relied too much on his own expertise and not enough on God to the point that neither the "sisters of the church, not even the mothers," were responding, he concluded:

> You see, it was self, not the Lord. And nobody shouted. They all knew what was going on. So I don't do things myself anymore, you know. I try to work when the Spirit speaks, you know. Talk to God, and tell Him don't wait until the last minute. And every once in a while, He motions like that and there are the passages like that, you know.... It is almost like a television screen comes down to you, and you see the whole picture. You see everything, just like Ezekiel and the dry bones. It was a vision.

Well, the Lord showed him, you know. Well,
to me it is like a screen come down, like a
movie screen. Everything is laid out on the
screen. The whole thing is laid out on the
screen that you can see, and He explains it to
you, the essence, the meat of the sermon.

Another pastor stated his philosophy of preaching this
way, "You is to bring them what God has dictated to you."
When asked if he had a scheduled routine for his sermon preparation, he replied:

Usually when the Spirit directs me. It could be
at any time. I try my best to work according to
the Spirit who calls. Did you know that the
Bible says that the Spirit will not dwell with man
at all times? So there are times when the Spirit
will direct you in certain ways and if you don't
work right then, it slips away. So you have to
write down or note down certain things that the
Spirit directs you.

This particular view of divine authority is not necessarily
antithetical to more human modes of information gathering, even
for sermon preparation. This same preacher was also an avid
reader, as he revealed in these comments:

Yeah, I found out that reading is one of the
greatest assets that a preacher has. It gives him
a lot of information, and it also inspires him and
keeps his mind alert. If you close your mind to
knowledge, then you are closing out the Holy
Spirit being able to work with you. I have two
associate ministers here with me now, and one
is supposed to preach his first sermon in [a few
months]. I am trying to teach him now that the

one effect of preaching is reading. Read as
much and as often and as many books as you
possibly can. And I don't put no stipulation on
the books that he's got to read. All books is
good to read, even sometimes I find myself
wandering off into something that is not
spiritual, you know, because of the fact that if
you don't know wrong, you won't know wrong
when you see it.

The emphasis on divine authority among ministerial
information providers was also evidenced in other ways,
sometimes internally. A pastor who had received excellent
comments on her dramatic portrayal of a Biblical character in the
Sunday service prior to my interview expressed her discomfort
over such praise this way:

I feel awkward when someone tells me that they
"liked" my sermon. I remember one preacher
way back who used to respond to that comment,
"Yes, Satan already told me that as I was leav-
ing the pulpit." I guess I always feel--and the
prayer I always pray silently before I give a
sermon is, "You, not me, God."

When asked her approach to sermon preparation, another
pastor responded, "Well, first I pray, then I read the text, then
I pray, then I look at commentaries, then I pray--you get the
idea." As another said in answer to the same question, "Well,
I look at the text and then I say, 'Okay, Lord, what is this all
about?'" Two mentioned that they usually "got [their] texts in
prayer." As one charismatic clergyman said about choosing his
sermon texts, "You sit before the Lord and ask, 'What do You
want me to do?', and then you browse through the Scriptures."
He went on to relate his dissatisfaction with ministerial magazines and other pulpit helps "because I don't want some other

man telling me how to minister; I want to hear it from God."

Sometimes "divine inspiration" comes rather late in the sermon preparation process. "There have been occasions when I've prepared one message," confided one pastor, "and I've gotten to the pulpit and the Lord has given me another."

On a more rational note, some pastors wrestle intellectually with the role of divine authority. Not that they deny it, quite the opposite. The following example of cautious "thinking out loud" by one pastor about the various bases for authority in the ministry summarizes some of the tension that pastors feel:

> Interviewer: Do you often refer individuals whose problems you feel are beyond your expertise?
>
> Pastor: Oh, always.
>
> Interviewer: To whom?
>
> Pastor: To other individuals here in the community that I have confidence in.
>
> Interviewer: To [named a local counseling agency]?
>
> Pastor: No. Individuals here in the community. Fortunately, two of them are now in our church, so that's encouraging. But for a long time there was just no one here in the community that I felt confident in referring people to.
>
> Interviewer: You don't feel confident in the agency I just named?

Pastor: I would not refer anyone to their services here. I would not do that. [He chose his words very carefully here.] I'm sure there would be some that would.

Interviewer: I'm just curious. Is that because of their lack of emphasis on Scripture or...?

Pastor: Uh...

Interviewer: If you care to say...

Pastor: I would say... I have some question whether those people over there are actually born again. I have some question whether they are Christians in a Biblical sense. That's part of it. And then secondly, my philosophy is, my concern... The tension in Christian counseling, as far as I'm concerned, is that there is a real tension for people who are in the counseling ministry for the Scriptures to maintain functional authority over the humanities. And I'm convinced that they have to do that for it to truly be Christian counseling. And I guess I'm concerned if someone has had anywhere from four to ten years of advanced training in counseling, in the disciplines of psychology and counseling, okay? I won't call it a philosophy yet. I think it's too new to be a philosophy. But in the disciplines of psychology and counseling, if a person has had four to ten years of study and training and internship and something like that and has not had at least an equal amount of training in theology and in the Scriptures, I have a hard time believing that that person can maintain functional authority of the Scriptures in their counseling.

> So if there's a question on my part of whether
> this person is a Christian in a Biblical sense,
> and, secondly, if there's a question on my part
> whether the Scriptures can really maintain
> functional authority over the humanities, then
> I'm going to be very hesitant to refer someone
> to them--whether it's [that agency] or whether
> it's someone else in the community who hangs
> a shingle with a fish on it and says, "I'm a
> Christian."

This pastor's comments encapsulate some of the thinking that several pastors mentioned in their discussions of authority and the various bases for it. To him, as was the case for many pastors in this study, the two key bases for authority were personal ("Is this person a Christian?") and divine (expressed as the "functional authority of the Scriptures"), with some deference as well to the educational aspects ("training in theology and the Scriptures").

This pastor's comments also point out the significance of professional knowledge that is crucial to the role that pastors occupy as information professionals. What must they know to be pastors? How do they acquire that knowledge? What are the limits to their knowledge? When must they admit that they don't know, and will, therefore, refer? What is the pastor's professional knowledge?

The Professional Knowledge of the Pastor

As pointed out at the beginning of this chapter, a professional is one who has control over a certain range of knowledge. If pastors may be considered to be information professionals in the sense that a significant portion of the public grants them the authority to provide certain kinds of information, what is the range of knowledge over which they as professionals have control? In Abbott's (1988) terms, what is their jurisdiction? What are the kinds of questions for which they are asked to provide information? What is the nature of the pastor's professional knowledge that permits him or her to serve as an information provider?

Spiritual Knowledge

The traditional answer to these questions may be found in the five-part classification of knowledge devised by Machlup (1982, pp. 8-9). Of the five kinds of knowledge he posited-- practical, intellectual, pastime, spiritual, and unwanted--ministers obviously stake their professional knowledge claim in the fourth area, spiritual knowledge. On one level, pastors function as information professionals because they have spiritual knowledge, and people come to them because their information needs are of a spiritual nature.

Still, on a more complex level, the findings from this study suggest that the types of information people expect from pastors is not limited to the traditionally spiritual. To be sure, pastors in this study were often asked about their church's view on a given topic, or what the Bible said about some issue, or if they could help solve some spiritual problem.

Yet, ministers in this community were also asked such questions as these: How can I get help in paying my light bill? Should I put my mother in a nursing home? Can I get AIDS by hugging someone? Will you help us put our marriage back together? Should we sell bonds to raise money for our new building? Should I leave my abusive husband? Will you speak to city hall against this new ordinance legalizing gambling here?

For pastors to answer these questions appropriately required a range of knowledge that is not traditionally viewed as spiritual, but rather economic, social, legal, medical, and political knowledge as well.

This does not mean that the pastors in this study believed themselves to have professional knowledge in every one of these subject areas. Quite the contrary, most of the pastors were very quick to refer. But their very readiness to refer indicates that these pastors, like traditional information professionals, felt that part of their domain of professional knowledge was in knowing how to refer others to the "best" information. The sources they used in these situations will be discussed in detail in Chapter 3.

However, unlike traditional information professionals, such referring was almost always done by these pastors from a spiritual perspective and with spiritual motivation. Referrals were often accompanied by prayer, for example. A medically oriented question about AIDS might lead a pastor to suggest a local hospital for answers, but it would also occasion a theological discussion about homosexuality. Psychological help involving complex marital difficulties almost always led pastors to refer, but almost always to trained "pastoral" counselors, not to "secular" psychiatrists.

Three Kinds of Knowledge

In light of the complex nature of the questions the pastors in this study were asked, perhaps a better way of looking at the pastors' professional knowledge is to use categories other than the traditional subject labels, e.g. spiritual knowledge or medical knowledge or legal knowledge. The three categories that have been most useful in analyzing the findings from this study are these: 1) factual knowledge, 2) relational knowledge, and 3) limited knowledge.

FACTUAL KNOWLEDGE

The first type of knowledge in this schema is factual. Factual knowledge enables the professional to provide what Wilson described as "answers to closed questions" (1983, p. 18). Many of the questions that ministers in this study said that they were asked required this kind of professional knowledge. They cited such questions as "What do the Mennonites believe?" or "What is heaven like?" or "How do I join your church?" The information being asked for here was of a factual nature. "Factual" in this context means that the data being provided were typically limited in scope and bounded in nature. For example, "Mennonites believe these things...," which the pastor would then enumerate. Or "Heaven is like this...," and the pastor would refer the asker to the description provided in the Biblical book of Revelation. "You can join our church by doing these things," which the pastor then listed. The knowledge needed in these contexts was closed-ended and usually verifiable in some way, e.g. by reading Scripture. A few "facts," usually from the Bible or denominational publications, often encapsulated the information needed.

However, these kinds of closed questions were not mentioned very often by these pastors. Conspicuous by its rarity was one pastor's statement that "people just want Biblical information." The pastors in this study, when asked what kinds of questions were being asked of them, were much more likely to bring up open-ended questions that required more of a relational knowledge.

RELATIONAL KNOWLEDGE

The second type of knowledge exhibited by the pastors in this study may be described as "relational knowledge," a concept often used by these pastors in two senses. The examples of relational knowledge that they either noted or I observed took one of these two forms among these pastors, both usually in response to open-ended questions.

On one hand, relational knowledge refers to the trust relationship between pastor and parishioner. Pastors in this study displayed in their information provision role a type of knowledge that was dependent upon a relationship of some sort between asker and answerer. People often asked their pastors open-ended questions for which there were no factually correct answers. Pastors gave answers which were only opinions, but they were accepted because the pastor was accepted, because he or she had a relational knowledge of the person asking the question. The defining characteristic of this type of knowledge was trust, not competency.

For example, a student member of one campus ministry asked her campus minister, "Should I marry this man I'm dating?" That was an open-ended question to the pastor whose answer only had validity because of the relational knowledge that this pastor had of her parishioner. As one pastor commented, "People don't care how much you know until they know how much you care." This type of relational knowledge was very pronounced in this study.

In an interview representative of many ministers in this study, I asked a pastor to give me an answer to this hypothetical question: "How should I deal with my brother who has AIDS?" Instead of answering my question, he began asking me a series of relationally oriented questions: "Are you a member of my church?" "Have I known you long?" "Do I know your brother?" "Is he a Christian?" His questions indicated that he considered this type of relational knowledge that required some personal involvement between the pastor and the person asking the question to be vital in his role as an information provider.

One pastor bluntly admitted that he did not answer questions from people he did not know.

On the other hand, relational knowledge in this study frequently referred to the pastor's knowledge about relationships. To some extent, this is an example of a discipline-based knowledge, with the discipline being mostly that of counseling. This issue will be pursued more fully in Chapter 4 under the pastor as healer (counselor), but it is mentioned here because the great majority of the questions that pastors in this study were being asked were of a relational nature and required this second kind of relational knowledge.

Over and over again, the pastors said they were being asked such questions as: How do I get along with my husband? Why don't my kids listen? Should I be dating this girl? How do I heal the broken bond with my parents? Said one pastor, "Folks aren't interested in the spiritual; they want answers to relational problems." This pastor did speak from a spiritual perspective on these relational issues, but from the people's viewpoint the issues were primarily relational not spiritual. They wanted not spiritual knowledge, but relational knowledge. Complained another as he held up an issue of a professional journal in Biblical archeology, "You see the title to this article, 'Did Sarah have a seminal emission?' Who cares? I've got people wanting to know how to put their lives back together, and they expect me to read this?"

There is another reason to discuss here this type of relational knowledge. For some pastors the issue is not just a discipline-based knowledge of counseling that enables them to answer relational questions. The larger issue is a kind of "sense-making" knowledge that not only helps people deal with broken relationships, but also helps people make sense of their lives (cf. Dervin and Nilan, 1986, on this point).

The most elaborate discussion of this aspect of relational knowledge was provided by a pastor who discussed at some length the difference between relational and factual knowledge and how important that was in the ministry. When we first talked he said he was rather busy and, therefore, limited in his time. After an abbreviated interview, he inquired about my doctoral studies. When I mentioned to him my interest in how professionals use information, he responded, "You know, in your research among ministers you have really got two different issues going on?" When I asked him to amplify this comment, he explained in terms reminiscent of Price (1961):

> We are using this Bible study program [named the name] out of Pittsburgh that has a thirty-year history. They talk about a knowledge explosion. In one of their things they cite that if you took all the knowledge in the world up to 1700, there was just a given amount of knowledge. Then, that knowledge doubled between 1700 and 1900. Then, if I have the statistics right, it doubled again between 1900 and 1950, then again between 1950 and 1955 and again between 1955 and 1960, and somewhere between 1960 and 1965 it started doubling every twenty months.... So this knowledge stuff is going crazy, when you look at who's in charge of passing out this knowledge and how it's helped people, like in computers and stuff.
>
> But what we deal with in the church is a different kind of knowledge. And they [this Bible study program] have a chart. Here, let me draw it for you. [He then drew the figure below.]

[Figure 1]
[Two Kinds of Knowledge]

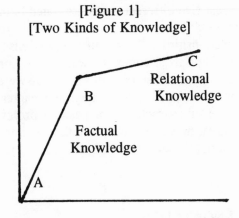

Now, they call this in their literature [pointing to the first half of the line in Figure 1] A-B knowledge. And they call this [pointing to the second half of the line in Figure 1] B-C knowledge. The A-B knowledge is factual. It's the data, the empirical, the stuff that's scientific knowledge. And the B-C knowledge is the relational. Now relational knowledge is not doubling at that rate like the factual knowledge. And when you are talking about what ministers are dealing with, they are dealing primarily in relational knowledge, in helping people interpret what's going on in their lives... what people are needing, co-dependency stuff, social issues, about dealing with AIDS and alcohol and other things like that in their lives.

He went on to explain that his task as a pastor, particularly in his preaching ministry, was to help people make sense of their lives, to deal with the relational issues. The key for ministry, he said, was not factual knowledge, but relational knowledge on inter- and intra-personal levels, especially as it applied to "helping people make sense of their lives."

At least five different ministers stated bluntly during the interview process: "The number one problem in this community is broken relationships. 'How can I make sense of this situation?' is the single most common kind of question that I get as a pastor." How the ministers in this study answered those kinds of questions is discussed more fully in Chapter 4 under the pastor as healer or counselor. The pastor's professional knowledge in this area, however, does raise the last important issue in this discussion, namely that of the limits to professional knowledge.

LIMITED KNOWLEDGE

The third type of professional knowledge, in addition to factual and relational, is what Wilson (1983) called "limited knowledge." If the first type deals with closed questions and the second with open-ended questions, the third type of knowledge is based on knowing what questions not to answer.

One of the elements in Wilson's definition of authority concerns the specific spheres in which an individual may be considered to be an authority. The knowledge domain over which one has control is an essential element in the granting of authority. Because one is an authority in medicine does not mean that he or she will be granted authority in the political arena. Likewise a pastor's knowledge is limited, and this fact was readily acknowledged by most all of the pastors in this community that I interviewed.

Ministers were quite quick to draw boundaries around their professional knowledge, especially in their role as counselor. Even an elderly Pentecostal pastor, who rarely read any "secular" magazines because of their "distortion of the truth," openly admitted his limitations, even over Scripture's role in counseling:

> It's been strange for us because I came into this
> area of ministry with the idea that, well, so who
> needs a psychologist? The Word of God will set
> you free. And all I have to do is tell them the
> Word of God says this and just have faith and
> believe and trust the Word of God and every-
> thing will be fine. Well, that's not true. I
> mean, it's true, but it is more complex than that.
> You are dealing with people's emotions and
> stress and anguish and bitterness and resentment
> and all those things that have got to be straight-
> ened out before the Word of God can ever take
> effect.... There have been times lately when we
> have told people..."You need to seek profession-
> al counseling."

For a Pentecostal preacher to admit this kind of limitation in
professional knowledge seemed unusual, given this group's
history. Among other denominations, this attitude was even
more prevalent. This interchange with a pastor of a mainline
denominational church was typical:

> Interviewer: Are there any particular kinds of
> questions you get in your counseling ministry
> that you try not to answer?

> Pastor: Oh, I think, for instance, if a person is
> in deep depression and wants help, then I feel
> that that is out of my territory, especially if it is
> near suicidal.

> Interviewer: How do you know when to draw
> the line? When to say you don't feel adequate
> to help them?

> Pastor: I think if it is going to be an on-going

situation, where someone really needs to be in
therapy, if it is going to be over several months,
then I think that is going beyond my training. I
can listen to them, and I can help them sort out
some things and make suggestions where I think
I can help, but after that I know my limitations.

As another minister noted about her willingness to refer
in situations similar to those just described, "I know enough to
be scared." Only four of the sixty-two pastors who were interviewed gave any indication that they did not put limits on their
professional knowledge. All four were young pastors in first-
time ministries, and one of them was facing dismissal partly
because of not referring one particular counseling case.

One older pastor acknowledged that in his first years in
ministry he "really couldn't do anything [in many counseling
situations] because [he] didn't have knowledge about it." The
problem, he continued, is that a stereotype exists that all pastors
have this kind of relational knowledge. According to one professional counselor in the area, however, most pastors in this
community knew their limits and knew when to refer.

As Wilson (1983) accurately observed, "Learning to be
a professional requires learning what questions not to try to
answer; it is learning to stay within limits. The professional is
well practiced in deference--deference to members of other professions" (p. 131). As one pastor commented, "Though I've had
some training in those areas, some questions are better left to the
experts." Like the traditional information professional, the
pastor does not always try to meet personally every person's
information need. The professional practice of deferring to the
experts (cf. Lancaster's 1990 similar call for librarians to do the
same) and referring to other information providers was found
frequently among the clergy in this community.

Summary

I have suggested in this chapter that an accurate understanding of the pastor as an information professional is a helpful framework for analyzing how pastors gather and disseminate information. Understanding how pastors are similar to and different from traditional information professionals, such as librarians, is important in looking at how pastors acquire and use information, the two foci of Chapters 3 and 4. A concluding summary of the concept of the pastor as information professional is presented in Chapter 5.

3. THE PASTOR AS INFORMATION GATHERER

"My periscope is always up" is how one pastor described the need he felt to be continually gathering information for the practice of his profession. Contrast that approach with this pastor's sentiment: "People don't need more information; we got information out the kazoo. That's not helping people." Somewhere between these two extremes is found the information-gathering behaviors of most of the ministers in this community.

This chapter will examine both the underlying information needs and the sources used by the pastors in this study to meet those needs. The information needs of these pastors will be discussed briefly from four perspectives: origin of needs, utilitarian needs, current awareness needs, and the problem of information overload. The discussion on sources will focus on the formal and informal channels used by these pastors to meet their information needs.

Ministerial Needs for Information

As Wilson and Streatfield (1981, p. 174) have observed, "the direct, objective perception of [a] subject's information need by another party...is not possible." Instead, information needs must be imputed to an individual on the basis of such phenomena as records of past information-seeking behavior, interviews about current information "needs" and how they are met, self-reporting of information-seeking behavior, and observations of individuals in their normal settings.

These methods were also employed in this study as a means of discerning the information needs of pastors. The predominant method, however, that was utilized in this study was the personal interview, supplemented by a written questionnaire. The questionnaire focused more on information channels, however, and will be discussed, therefore, in that section of this chapter.

Origin of Needs

An earlier study of how ministers use information (Tanner, 1991) noted that much of the information-gathering behavior of ministers is not generated by the pastor's own information needs. Rather, some information seeking is due to needs that others have and bring to the pastor so that he or she can seek information on their behalf. Thus, ministerial information needs may be categorized according to two points of origin: self-generated needs and needs generated by others.

Self-generated information needs come from pastors themselves. They are often related to some specific professional task that the pastor must perform. For example, the minister who said, "My periscope is always up," went on to add: "It has to be because I know that next Sunday morning at 9:00 I have to be brilliant." His expressed information need was related to his preaching. He gathered information based on his own very specific information need, research for sermon preparation. Among the ministers in this community, such self-generated information needs were frequently cited. These needs usually had an instrumental or utilitarian focus and will be discussed in that section below.

Information needs that were generated by others and brought to the pastor were also cited frequently in this study. However, unlike the earlier study (Tanner, 1991) among ministers in a smaller town where non-self-generated needs were uniformly present, the pastors in this larger community expressed considerably more variety in talking about this kind of information need. In fact, one of the most mixed areas of response during the interviews with these pastors was their answer to this query: What questions or kinds of questions are you being asked as a pastor? The responses tended to be of three types.

First, there were those pastors who simply said, "People don't ask me questions." Their information-gathering efforts were directed toward self-generated information needs. When probed for reasons, one pastor responded, "I think people are less open to asking pastors nowadays questions about anything deep. This community is mostly yuppie, and they are inclined to handle their own problems." Another pastor explained that his congregation of older people "just don't ask questions; they were not raised to do that." It could be that generational characteristics were the underlying causes. It could also be that the reasons were to be found in the pastors themselves. If there were any common features among these pastors, it was that they were either new to their congregation or they seemed to downplay the relational aspects of their ministry.

The results in both cases were that their parishioners did not feel comfortable in asking them questions. However, these are speculations, and more data are needed to determine actual underlying causes. It could simply be that the pastors did not remember accurately or were not responding fully to the query.

Second, there were those pastors who at first said they were not being asked any questions, but further inquiry revealed that what they actually meant was that they were not being asked "important" questions. Invariably these pastors meant by that term that the information needs being brought to them by others were not of a religious or theological nature. One veteran campus minister talked at some length about his frustration over the paucity of these kinds of information needs among the students in his parish.

> I don't find many students today asking religious questions, which, of course, I find exceptionally frustrating. I tell parish pastors, if they ask, that this is the most Biblically and theologically illiterate generation of students I have ever known. They know nothing. They ask nothing. And we're talking here about church kids, not non-Christians. This fall during one of our Wednesday evening communion services, I used it as a time to talk to the students about the different questions they had, particularly about the Bible. They didn't have any. One of the students said she thought it was probably wrong to study the Bible in her opinion, that one didn't need to do that, shouldn't do that. Many of them come into our fellowship group and talk about Jesus and how important God is to them, but theologically significant questions? Forget it.

Other campus ministers also echoed the dearth of these types of information needs among their parishioners, but it was not limited to the university setting. Several pastors of smaller, theologically conservative churches expressed the same sentiments. It wasn't that these ministers were not being asked questions. It was that they were not being asked the usual, traditional questions that they as pastors expected and even desired. Part of the explanation for this situation was offered by this pastor of a theologically conservative congregation.

> I think that the trend in the church world today is away from doctrinal issues and questions like

that [spoken in tones of disappointment]. It is
more towards people looking to have their needs
met. They need fellowship, something to belong
to, a friend, those kinds of questions. I am
disappointed to say that even among the [named
his denomination] they are not looking for a
doctrinally sound church. They want their
personal needs met. They want a church that is
more contemporary that way.

One pastor, who had served a church for ten years,
offered that he had, in essence, taught his parishioners to ask
more questions, especially about religious issues. He, too,
pastored a theologically conservative congregation and felt that
people had not been asking such questions because they had been
discouraged from doing so by the denomination.

I think I am definitely getting different kinds of
questions than when I began here. I think this
church has gone from being a really closed-
minded kind of people to one that is more open.
It is okay now for them to ask questions. I
guess I have tried to instill in them Luther's first
law of prayer: Be honest with God. I generally
believe that many of our churches have not
allowed their people to ask these kinds of
religious or doctrinal questions. I've tried to
focus that and help them ask those kinds of
questions.

This pastor's comments are indicative of the power of
the pastor to create an environment conducive to certain kinds of
questions. For example, the pastor's choice of sermon topics
and his or her expressed openness to certain kinds of issues are
examples of how pastors can help focus the questions they are or
are not asked.

There were, to be sure, several pastors who did not express a lack of religious questions. One pastor, for example, "guessed" that forty percent of the questions he was asked were of a religious nature. The most vivid example of religiously oriented information needs that were generated by others but which required the pastor to gather the information was found during an interview with a Catholic priest. When asked what kinds of questions he was asked as a priest, he answered by giving me a book that he had written.

The book was a 639-page compilation of the hundreds of questions he had been asked in his 38 years as a priest, particularly in his role as a syndicated columnist for a Catholic news service where he wrote a regular question-and-answer column. Reviewers of the book, such as *Booklist*, recommended it because the author did "his research well" and because he "provide[d] information for Catholics." Almost all of the questions were religious in nature: Why do Catholics have a different version of the Bible? Can priests now marry? Is it a mortal sin to use God's name in anger? Did the Church once approve of abortions? Is living together before marriage acceptable? Almost all of the sources he cited were either Roman Catholic publications or the Bible.

Still, there were at least eight pastors of the sixty-two interviewed who expressed some measure of dissatisfaction regarding information needs generated by others. Their dissatisfaction was that these needs that others were bringing to them were not of a religious nature.

Third, there were the majority of pastors who stated that they were being asked all kinds of questions for which they were expected to provide relevant information. These non-self-generated information needs ran the gamut from the routine to the religious, from the economic to the ecclesiastical. Sometimes the questions were very routine. "When is the next board

meeting?" "Do you rent out your building for weddings?" "Can
I get the mailing list for single mothers?"

The predominance of these kinds of questions led at least
five larger churches in this community to hire administrators,
one of whose tasks was to provide this kind of routine information so that the pastors could deal with more professionally
related information needs, whether overtly religious in nature or
not. One pastor who had not yet moved to such an arrangement
offered this perspective on these routine information needs in the
ministry:

> When you mentioned in your letter [of intro-
> duction] that you wanted to talk about what
> kinds of questions I was being asked, I thought
> that that was going to be very difficult to
> answer. Then it hit me. The most frequently
> asked questions that I receive are administrative
> ones. And I think that this is one of the critical
> problems for pastors, at least it is for me in my
> ministry and I think it is in our whole religious
> tradition. Let me use the paradigm of a legal
> practice or an architectural firm or a medical
> practice. They have office managers to manage
> the practice so that the physicians, the architects,
> the lawyers, can actually practice their pro-
> fession. We don't have that yet in our field in
> the ministry. An inordinate amount of my time
> is spent in answering questions that I shouldn't
> be answering. I should be dealing with pastoral
> questions, not managerial ones.

At other times the questions that the pastors in this
community received were all over the map. If there were any
two common themes, they were that the information needs
behind these questions were not generated by the pastor and that

the type of information need usually revolved around some emotional issue involving broken relationships, typically expressed in the context of dysfunctional families. These types of questions, requiring the relational knowledge discussed in Chapter 2, were the most commonly asked questions cited by the pastors in this study. Examples of these types of need will be discussed in Chapter 4 in the section on the pastor as healer.

The dual nature of ministerial information needs in terms of their point of origin--those generated by the pastor and those generated by second parties for the pastor--is not the only way of looking at the role of the pastor as information gatherer. Three other aspects of information need that were observed among the pastors in this community are utilitarian needs, current awareness needs, and the problem of overload in dealing with information needs.

Utilitarian Needs

One of Machlup's (1962) five types of information is what he called practical knowledge which is "useful" in the knower's work. It is information which has a specific utilitarian or instrumental purpose relative to a particular professional task, as opposed to intellectual, entertainment, or even unwanted knowledge. This focus on the intent, rather than the content, of information, i.e. the "usefulness" of information, was an important issue for many of the pastors interviewed in this study (cf. the discussion of information in the Appendix). When asked indirect questions about information needs in the ministry-- whether self-generated or generated by others, many pastors replied in ways that stressed this "point of need" focus to their information-seeking behavior.

For example, after more than one hour of discussing various facets of ministerial information needs, without using the

word "information," one pastor responded somewhat surprisingly, when she saw the term on the written questionnaire, "I was
wondering when you were going to ask me about my use of information." When I explained that I thought we had been
talking about it in light of our conversations about such basic
things as the kinds of books and magazines that she read, she
replied:

> Pastor: Well, I don't think about information
> that way.
>
> Interviewer: How do you think about it?
>
> Pastor: I mean I just do stuff. I research things
> as I need them. I mean I kind of find stuff as I
> need it.
>
> Interviewer: What do you mean?
>
> Pastor: Well, for one I like workshops and
> seminars because they're intensive. I learn
> much more by going to those than I do by read-
> ing a book. A book is fine when I'm reading it,
> but then after it's over, I can't remember what
> it said. Unless I do a paper on it or something
> like that, you forget.
>
> Interviewer: Do you ever mark in your books
> while you're reading...to help you remember?
>
> Pastor: Oh, yes, but then I still don't retain it.
> Well, because if you're not working on a
> sermon or something where you will use that
> information right away, you lose it. I mean, I
> read a ton of books for my D.Min. [Doctor of
> Ministry program], but the only ones I can

really remember are the ones I had to do papers on or something in order to get the information assimilated.... There's a lot of stuff you lose if you're not going to use it.

Interviewer: Is most of the stuff you read, then, related to a particular use, like a Bible study or something?

Pastor: Yes. Yes. I'm very practical in my attitudes there. I'll read a [particular] book because that's what I'm doing right now so it's of interest. But to just pick up some of the theology stuff and I'm not working on that, then no. If I'm doing a sermon, then I'll read those things that have to do with that particular subject. And I'll get into them even though I'm not going to use half the stuff in the sermon. I mean, that gets the juices flowing. But there has to be some kind of motivating factor for me to read something.

The "motivating factor" for this pastor, as for many in this study, was a utilitarian one: "I research things as I need them." Like the American historians interviewed by Case (1991), the "problem-oriented model" both motivated and controlled the information-seeking behavior of many of the pastors in this community. Several pastors mentioned that they kept a file folder for their next sermon in their briefcases and kept it with them at all times so that as they "bumped into things during the week," as one said, they could collect that information for that particular information need.

The utilitarian nature of ministerial information needs was also evident in the composition of pastors' personal libraries. Though this issue will be discussed in more detail under the section on formal channels, it is worth observing here that many pastoral libraries had a very instrumental focus, an observation also made by Porcella (1973).

"I have a very functional library," was more than just one pastor's statement. Many pastors during the course of the interview referred to their "counseling shelf" or showed me their "row of commentaries" on books of the Bible. The point was not just an organizational one; it was that these were the sources needed to meet their very focused utilitarian needs. One pastor's "ready reference" shelf consisted of a King James Bible, a Biblical concordance (Strong's), a dictionary, and the phone book. That was it. His major emphasis upon "Bible-based" preaching explained the first two. When I asked him about the phone book, he showed me the well-worn yellow pages section and explained, "If someone asks me a question I can't answer, I just refer to my yellow pages and I can usually find the information they need."

Another pastor kept a notebook full of brochures from a number of social agencies in town. "I decided to do that because I was getting so many questions from people about those kinds of issues, like bulimia and alcoholism. Now I can find the information I need to answer those kinds of questions or at least refer them to the right place." One pastor's book-buying philosophy provided another example of this utilitarian approach to information needs: "Usually I'll buy books when I run into some counseling problem that I don't know much about. Then I'll order three or four books on that topic, read them, and then sit down and try to help them with their problem."

The instrumental focus in ministerial information needs was sometimes of a more personal nature. One pastor in the process of relocating, when asked what ministerial magazines he read, commented that he didn't usually read any from his own denomination. "Except last fall," he said, "when there was this series of articles on ministry burnout that they had. That was a high stress period for me so I devoured everything they wrote." Another pastor, who was about to "go on sabbatical" for three months to another country (in an exchange program with another minister), responded to my question about his current reading interests this way: "I'm mostly reading about [named the country] because that's where I'm going."

These very focused, task-oriented, utilitarian-based information needs were not the only kinds of information needs observed among the pastors in this community. Some needs were nearly opposite in nature, and they will be discussed next.

Current Awareness Needs

While some pastors' information needs were dependent upon a specific "point of need" situation that had a particular utilitarian purpose, other pastors in this study expressed information needs that may be described in much less focused terms. These needs appeared to be reflections of some pastors' desire to collect information just to stay current in their profession.

To be sure, such "current awareness needs" still displayed some instrumental or utilitarian aspects (i.e. the information was generally used eventually for some professionally related need), but utility was not the focus of the need. Rather, the focus was upon the act of information gathering, not upon any immediate or direct attempt to satisfy some particular information need. For lack of a better term, this kind of information need may be described as a current awareness need, a term used by the pastors in this study.

One example of this perspective on pastoral information needs was noted by a pastor who related the following interchange between him and his wife.

> I get up at 6:00 to read my Bible for a couple of hours. My wife will say, "Well, what have you done so far? It's 9:30 in the morning." I tell her that I've already started working. I say, "Man, I was up at 6:00 and have been on duty ever since." I've been on duty and that's part of my job. You know, people will look at pastors' lives and say, "What does he do? Studies a little book."

> I need to do my own personal time of reading, and not just the Bible. So I sit and read for two hours, and my wife thinks I've done nothing. You know, because she's so active. She hits the floor running. But I'm reading this book, any book, and she'll say, "This guy's not doing anything today. He's sitting around reading." She doesn't realize that when I'm watching the TV or reading a magazine, that that's part of my job. I'll say, "I'm on duty. I've got to keep abreast of things because that's part of being a pastor."

This pastor's information-gathering behavior was not focused upon a specific purpose. To him, reading was pastoring. His information need was amorphous. While there was some sense of purpose to his "watching the TV or reading a magazine," the purpose was not to satisfy any specific need other than to "keep abreast of things." A similar "storehouse" approach to information gathering was also quite pronounced in an interview with a minister who over the ten years of his ministry had altered his view on the use of information.

> I try to stay alert to what's going on. Try to be

alert to stuff that's out there. I often tell people that my brain works more like yeast than gunpowder. It takes time for the leaven to rise to the top. I read rather widely and generally. Sometimes things come along that I think, "I could use that someday." So I'll tuck that away. There was a time that as soon as I read something, I used it like in a sermon or lesson. It was kind of like money, you know. Spend it now. I don't do that anymore.

In such cases, the pastor functions as a theologically value-added processor of information. This same pastor, who was theologically and socially quite conservative and yet also an avid reader of the *Atlantic* magazine, said he read it because "I think it gives me a window on a political and social spectrum that I'm not necessarily part of.... It is alert to social currents that are at work in our world. It's simply an information source."

This example illustrates the current awareness motif that controlled his use of this particular information source. Even an extremely conservative pastor who refused to "read any secular magazines" because "their version of the truth is always distorted" later admitted, "I watch the world news on TV probably every day just to try to keep a grasp on what is happening, not for any particular reason, just an awareness type of thing."

The wide variety of books and magazines cited by the pastors in this study (see following section) attests to this broadly based, almost "shot gun" approach to information gathering that stemmed from current awareness needs. The desire of many pastors to stay current in everything from preaching to counseling to world events also contributed to what some pastors in this study referred to as "information overload."

Information Overload

The pastor's comment at the beginning of this chapter, "We got information out the kazoo," is representative of several ministers in this community who were wrestling with what they perceived to be an information overload. It should be noted that most pastors did not express any strong sense of being overloaded with information. They either did not perceive a problem in this area or they had found methods of coping that were so satisfactory that it was no longer an issue for them.

This section will look only at those ten or twelve pastors who did talk about this issue in terms that suggest they were still wrestling with problems of information overload. One such pastor was the one whose comments begin this section. Though he felt that information was overvalued in the ministry, he did not mean by his statement that he did not gather information. Quite the contrary, as he went on to explain:

> It seems like I'm constantly getting information.
> I got a problem with information. I mean, I'll
> be in the bathroom, and I'll have the radio on so
> I can hear the news and I'll be reading a maga-
> zine at the same time. I've got so much stuff
> coming in to me. I like to watch the news. I
> read a lot. I listen to tapes at least two hours a
> day. I'm addicted to information.

Another pastor, a self-described "information junkie," after giving me his typed list of 101 magazines that he subscribed to, said, "You know, one of the best things that I've come across lately is *Current Thoughts & Trends*. That is an exceptional resource." The publication he named is an abstracting service from a religious publishing firm in Colorado that publishes a monthly summary of significant articles from over fifty magazines and journals, ranging from *Time* to *Christianity*

Today. The summaries are all classified according to seven major topics: the Church, the Christian, the pastor, the family, the denominations, the nation, and the world.

His reference to this abstracting service, mentioned by at least seven other pastors, indicated that one means these pastors had chosen to address the problem of information overload was to use an abstracting service. This particular kind of information source will be discussed more later, but its growing use among these ministers represents a new approach in the pastorate to dealing with overload.

Another example of how pastors dealt with information overload surfaced in a question about what books these ministers were reading. One of the most frequently mentioned authors was George Barna, who directs a religious research group in Glendale, California. Barna has published a number of books that summarize a variety of social science research data in terms of their implications for ministry, including a 100-page bibliographic and information guide, entitled *Sources of Information for Ministry and Business* (1990). His newest product is a periodical, *Ministry Currents.* The promotional piece for this publication that several of the pastors in this community received alluded to the growing perception of an information overload problem in the pastorate:

> *Ministry Currents* is a newsletter...designed to serve as a research assistant for your ministry. You may be familiar with the books and reports we produce concerning ministry. In fact, Barna Research conducts more research on Christians and Christianity in America than any other organization.... In the course of our research, we uncovered an unmet need among Christian leaders. With time at a premium, they said they need a ministry-oriented, information-based, to-

the-point publication.... Our intent is to provide
you with an in-house research assistant--one who
won't call in sick or demand pension benefits,
but will supply answers to your questions based
on credible, current information, in an easy-to-
digest format.

The sample issue of *Ministry Currents* sent to some of
these ministers included an article on "Intimacy with the
Community: Developing In-House Research Capabilities," in
which ten different local sources of information were cited,
including the public library. One pastor, after listing several
Barna books among the titles he was currently reading, said, "I
read those things because I really feel that he's on the cutting
edge of giving us the research we need in the form we need to
keep up with our culture and the people in our pews." The
popularity of Barna's digest-oriented publications was further
evidence of these pastors' struggle with information overload.

The frequent mention of *USA Today* was another indication of this problem, in that brevity was the reason usually given
for why these pastors read it. As the pastor of one very large
church with a staff of five explained: "The paper that I like is
USA Today. I'm not interested in long, laborious kinds of
articles. I'm the one-minute manager kind of person. Give me
the issue in four or five paragraphs." He immediately went on
to add that he was currently reading "Barna's new book on *What
Americans Believe*." Since the most-cited reason for not reading
more was the issue of "not enough time," it seems apparent that
more efficient means of providing information to pastors was
viewed by these ministers as helpful.

No attempt was made in this study to determine whether
the problem of information overload was "real" or only "perceived" by the pastors in this community. However, since the
interview method by design focuses on perception, the actual

state of affairs is not the issue. The perception was real, and that is what this study is about. How pastors dealt with the problem of gathering the information needed is discussed next.

Ministerial Channels of Information

Information-seeking behavior may be classified into two major categories: formal channels and informal channels. The former consists primarily, but not exclusively, of such traditional print-oriented sources as books and periodicals. The latter includes more personal sources, such as colleagues and conferences. This dichotomy is not only a standard scheme in the field of library and information science (Lancaster and Smith, 1978), but it is also reflected in the vocabulary of the pastors here.

For example, when asked what sources he used to bridge the gap between the first-century world of the Bible and the twentieth-century world of his audience, one preacher made this comment: "One of the ways I try to bridge that gap is to stay updated in my *reading*; the second is to be a good *listener*" [emphasis mine]. This distinction between reading and listening is a fair, though overly simplistic, summary of the differences between formal and informal channels.

Even more pointed was the following pastor's observations about the two different emphases in ministerial information sources. When asked what he was currently reading, he replied:

> I've given up a lot of my reading. Part of it is time, but... Let me put it this way. In the ministry you can either be with people or with paper. Now, I go in cycles but during the last few years I have chosen to be with people rather than with paper.

Most of the pastors that were interviewed likewise, in one form or another, expressed this preference for people over paper, for informal over formal channels of information. It is not surprising, therefore, that on the written questionnaire used in this study to supplement the interview data, informal channels were rated more highly by the pastors in this community than formal ones. Table 2 below summarizes these data from the written questionnaire. Ministers were asked to rate on a scale of 1 to 5 (where 5 = very important) the following twenty-five items as to the importance of each in providing them with the information needed to perform their ministries effectively.

Table 2
Importance of Information Sources for Ministry

Printed Sources of Information:	Rank of 25	Mean Score	Std. Dev.
1. Articles in general magazines	14.5	3.04	1.023
2. Articles in ministerial magazines	7	3.70	0.989
3. Books by religious publishers	4	4.31	0.696
4. Books published by other publishers	10	3.32	1.012
5. Biblical reference works	3	4.34	0.911
6. New Testament Greek-language tools	13	3.06	1.539
7. Old Testament Hebrew-language tools	18	2.65	1.471
8. Denominational literature	9	3.36	1.195
Audiovisual Sources of Information:			
9. Religious radio programs	22	1.86	0.903
10. Other kinds of radio programs	25	1.12	1.128
11. Religious television programs	23	1.73	0.964
12. Other kinds of television programs	19	2.50	1.081
13. Audiocassettes on religious topics	14.5	3.04	1.244
14. Audiocassettes on other topics	21	2.11	1.112
15. Videocassettes on religious topics	17	2.70	1.216
16. Videocassettes on other topics	20	2.18	1.113

Table 2 (continued)

Personal Sources of Information:

17. People in my own congregation	2	4.41	0.739
18. Other ministers in town	11	3.26	0.988
19. Ministers on staff at this church*	5	4.29	0.783
20. Ministers from my own denomination	8	3.62	1.065
21. Meetings that I attend at my church	6	3.74	1.060
22. Denominational meetings I attend	12	3.20	1.225

Other Sources of Information:

23. Items in my own personal library	1	4.63	0.517
24. Items in other libraries in town	16	3.03	1.197
25. Social agencies in town	24	1.21	1.211

* N = 32 (30 of the 62 pastors had no other ministers on staff)

The data from Table 2 indicate that of the twenty-five different sources listed on the questionnaire, the six informal, personal channels were all scored above the 3.0 median (on the 1 to 5 scale), with a composite mean score of 3.75. The sixteen formal channels of printed and audiovisual sources garnered only a 2.83 composite mean score, though there was a statistically significant difference between print sources, which were given a composite mean score of 3.47, and audiovisual sources, which were rated at a composite mean of only 2.16.

Two of the three "other sources" listed in Table 2 above were rated above the mean, with the pastor's own library rated higher than any other single channel of information. The interview data tended to confirm these numerical ratings and will be discussed below from two perspectives: the formal channels that these pastors used to gather information and the informal channels that they used to gather information.

Formal Channels

The formal channels used to gather information by the
pastors in this community included books, particularly the Bible,
periodicals, audiovisuals, computer databases, and libraries (both
personal and institutional). These five types of formal channels
will be discussed in turn.

BOOKS: THE BIBLE

When examining the variety of books that pastors use to
gather information to help them in their ministry, it must be emphasized at the outset that, unlike other professions, the clergy
are "a people of *the* Book." This was made clear in how the
pastors in this study completed the written questionnaire. There
was no category for the Bible listed, since its use was just
assumed, but at least a dozen pastors either wrote in or made
comments such as "Well, the Bible" under the question, "Are
there any other sources that you rely upon for your information
needs?"

Without peer among the books cited by these pastors
throughout the interview process was the Bible. This is another
aspect of the information-gathering behavior of pastors that has
no parallel among traditional information professionals. There
is no comparable "book" in the library and information science
field that carries the same kind of influence or authority that the
Bible does for clergy. This position of supremacy accorded the
Bible by the pastors in this study is reflected in the following
comments by a pastor who was asked how he had tried to help
a single parent who needed information about raising his
daughter. His response:

> Well, my first source for answering questions is
> always the Bible. I tried to share principles of

Scripture with him because, after all, I feel that
as a minister that is my responsibility, to apply
the Scriptures to people's questions and to their
lives. That's what being a pastor is all about.
You've got to know the psychological and many
other disciplines, but basically it is taking the
Word of God and applying it or helping them
apply it.

Another pastor, in reflecting upon a sermon he had
recently preached about Jesus' use of Scripture to thwart
temptation, said:

So my point of the sermon was: What is the ultimate weapon we have to fight temptation? Jesus
didn't use His almighty power. He used God's
Word, which is also our ultimate weapon. In
my preaching I always start out with the text. I
don't usually use many or sometimes any outside
sources. I just look at the text.

This concentration on "the text" was frequently echoed
by theologically conservative pastors. Said one, "I only use
commentaries to check my own exegesis of the Scriptures; otherwise I rely on the Word." Said another, "I don't ever speak
publicly on any subject without having Scripture to back me up."

Close to two thirds of the pastors described their preaching style as "expository." By that they meant that they used
extensive portions of the Bible, usually an extended pericope, as
the basis and core of their sermon. As this preacher explained,
"I always use Scripture to support and undergird my sermon so
I'm not just saying what I think. There has to be a 'Thus says
the Lord.'" He even wrote his sermon notes with a red pen for
those sections that were Scriptural quotations, as did several
other pastors in this community.

However, this concentration on the Bible was not limited to conservatives. The pastor of one of the most theologically liberal congregations in this community, where "only 10 to 15% of the members could be described as Christian," also acknowledged the influence the Bible had upon his information-seeking behavior.

> I probably use the Bible quite a lot. Now some ministers in my denomination don't use it as much as I would. I think the [denominational] view of the Bible is that it is a source book of immense value and an expression of our developing understanding and faith. It also, in a sense, is a normative thing in our society and culture. It's something that a lot of people relate to. It provides symbols and events which people can relate to. We also reserve the right, which is a very old right going back to the Reformation, to interpret the Bible for ourselves. Of course, there's an awful lot of immense value in the Bible that is often locked up simply because people don't understand the symbolism or the setting. So, in a sense, it's part of my role to try to unlock some of that wisdom in the Bible for the people in my preaching.

The use of the Bible as an information source was not limited to such professional tasks as preaching. For many pastors, the Bible functioned also as a devotional book, which was not surprising given the spiritual, reflective nature of the ministerial profession. What was surprising was how infrequently this use was noted by these pastors. While no pastor denied using the Bible devotionally, only five pastors mentioned any significant use of the Bible for this purpose, and one of those did so in a self-accusatory manner for not doing more of it.

Though imprecise, the numbers from the written questionnaire also tend to support this perception that the Bible was not used by these pastors primarily as a devotional book. In "guesstimating" the number of hours they spent per week reading in each of four categories, the time spent on personal devotions garnered the lowest total, with a mean of only 3.06 hours per week and a median of only 2 hours per week. By contrast sermon preparation, in which the Bible was the predominant source, totalled twice as many hours, with a mean of 6.17 hours and a median of 5 hours per week.

These numbers, as well as the pastors' comments during the interviews, underscore the observation that the primary use of the Bible by the clergy in this community was for preaching. Nearly every example cited by these ministers regarding their use of Scripture was in the context of sermon preparation. Even when the Bible was being used as a textbook, as was the case for one pastor taking Biblical correspondence courses, it was in the context of preaching. As this pastor/student explained:

> I am going through an Old Testament course and right now I am studying through Samuel. I've incorporated some of the courses into my preaching. So I am studying now about David in the Old Testament and also preaching about David. I just felt God would be pleased with me doing that, and I felt good about it.

The importance of the Bible for preaching is also underscored by something unique to the ministerial profession, the lectionary. The lectionary is a "book of Scripture readings for worship services" (*Interpreter's Dictionary of the Bible*, 1962, s.v.). Dating from the Old Testament synagogue, the lectionary is a system of selected readings from Scripture for liturgical use according to the church year (see *The New Westminster Dictionary of Liturgy and Worship*, 1986, s.v.).

In fact, the predominant use of the lectionary in most American denominations has spawned almost an entire cottage industry supplying Bible-based aids for preaching. Only among some of the theologically conservative pastors in this community were the lectionary and its accompanying aids not used regularly.

In its simplest and most common form the lectionary is a three-year cycle of Sunday-morning Biblical readings that are used by pastors to provide both a theme for the worship service and a text and topic for the sermon. In its most complex form, the lectionary and its accompanying aids provide a completely scripted service and sermon, complete with hymn selections and homiletical illustrations. Some publishing houses even provide a typed outline of the sermon that the preacher can take to the pulpit, in addition to a complete manuscript of the homily.

Most of the pastors in this study were quite enthusiastic in their support for and use of the lectionary, though most did not use all of the accompanying aids. For many, the primary benefit was simply the regular cycle of Biblical readings from a variety of Biblical books. As one pastor admitted, "It's helpful in that I'm able to expose myself to Scripture that I wouldn't normally be open to. If it was up to me, I'd preach from Romans every Sunday." Another pastor gave this example:

> I like the lectionary because for one thing it forces me to wrestle with texts that I might just as soon avoid. When one of the texts on divorce, for example, came up in the readings, I could just as easily have said, "I don't think so. No, we're not going to wrestle with that." You see, our church was going through two nasty divorces at the time. That was probably one of my hardest sermons, but I felt it was necessary and helpful. It gave me a chance to talk about Christ's compassion and not confusing

the issue with our own cultural norms and about not being superjudgmental.

This sentiment was echoed by a downtown pastor who talked about how the lectionary "forces you to deal with Scriptures that you may never deal with." In one particular case, this pastor of a very traditional, wealthy, downtown congregation, had preached a sermon on the lectionary reading from Hebrews 12:29, "For our God is a consuming fire." It was a sermon that was otherwise out of character for this pastor and this church, and he had been told so, despite his ministry there of more than twenty years. Still, the lectionary provided him an occasion to talk about his wrestling with using the Bible and its implications for preaching that he might not otherwise have had.

A rather lengthy portion of his sermon, which I both observed and obtained a complete manuscript for, is cited here as a means of illustrating to what extent the lectionary readings can stimulate an otherwise staid pastor to preach on an extremely unusual topic in extremely uncharacteristic terms.

Today's text is from Hebrews. My guess is that some of you have never heard it before. It isn't the usual good and kind and Jesus sort of thing. It's big, dark, threatening. This isn't kids' stuff, Pablum to be fed to a comfortable, toothless congregation. This isn't a common worship experience of most people. Today, we build our churches like great carpeted living rooms, where every hard edge is cushioned, and most of the time we preach comfort and contentment lest someone be even mildly moved. Our pastors are usually relegated to the "helping professions," chaplains to the afflicted affluent and preservers of the status quo, affirmers of things as they are....

TV preachers promise to "make Jesus work for you." If the Bible's world clashes with my experience or my needs (as I define my needs), then so much the worse for the Bible.... When I was in seminary, taking preaching classes, they told us repeatedly, "The task of the preacher is to close the gap between the Bible and the modern world." The preacher is the one who stands in the pulpit and holds the Bible in one hand and today's newspaper in the other. In twenty-some odd minutes I am supposed to close the gap between the old, outmoded world of the Bible and the new, fresh, modern world where you live. I am trying to stand with one foot in the old Bible and the other foot planted in the modern world. And what I get is a hernia. No! I refuse to do that anymore!...

I've decided from now on to make the modern world credible to the Bible. The modern world that not only gave us the telephone and the TV and the computer, but also Selma, Alabama; Hiroshima; Auschwitz; and the murder of millions of native Americans. This is what I'm supposed to make the Bible credible to? No! I've decided to open up the gap between you and God, rather than close it because it is in the gaps that you are free to roam, envision, dream dreams, hear a new word, see a new world, and long for the one true God....

While there were undoubtedly other dynamics at work in this sermon (e.g. the church's recent decision to expand staff and facilities, the pastor's own personal and professional struggles), the use of the lectionary and this pastor's own wrestling with difficult texts were also major contributing factors.

For other pastors, the lectionary was valued as an information source in preaching primarily because of its pre-programmed approach to Scripture. "It helps me focus on how to preach the text," explained one pastor, "not on what am I going to preach." This focus on "how" was another reason given for using the lectionary, particularly with all of its accompanying aids. Even for a self-described "information junkie" who had an extensive library of his own, this benefit was a major reason for his use of the lectionary:

> One of the neat things about the lectionary is that there is so much resource material that goes with it nowadays. You can subscribe to services that provide you with sermon illustrations. You can subscribe to groups that do a lot of the exegetical work already for you. So I read a lot of that stuff, and there is always one or two stories in there.

Another pastor, when asked about how she went about preparing the last sermon she preached, responded by talking about several lectionary aids that she had read and how they "gave me statistics and stories on that issue that I had no idea existed." For her and for many, in fact, the lectionary aids served as a *de facto* abstracting service, summarizing the results of some other person's or persons' information gathering on a particular homiletical issue. One pastor subscribed to so many lectionary-based services that he rarely wrote his own sermon since "they do a much better job than I could ever do."

This intermediary role that the lectionary performs was also the very reason given by some pastors for not using it. Said one fundamentalist pastor, "I don't want someone else telling me what to preach. I want to hear it from God." What was perhaps not so obvious to this pastor was the intermediary role that he and all pastors play in the overall information-transfer process, as they stand "professionally" between deity and humanity (cf. Berger's [1969] description of the "sacred canopy" that clergy maintain, and the earlier discussion of the pastor as interpreter in Chapter 2).

The issue of "inspiration" was raised by even theologically liberal pastors. When asked why he did not use the lectionary even though almost everyone of his denominational colleagues did, one pastor candidly admitted: "I was part of the committee that helped create the new lectionary, and I guess I'm less inclined to think that the Spirit did the whole thing." One pastor had cancelled a number of lectionary services that the former pastor had had the church subscribe to because "I don't like canned sermons." The pastor working on a Doctor of Ministry thesis on Gadamer's interpretive method was particularly unappreciative of this aspect of the lectionary. "Most of the material that they put out for help with the lectionary is poor because it shuts down creativity," he said. "They don't open up the text, they close it." Explained another pastor, "The lectionary is a good framework for dealing with Scripture, but many times when I look at their material, I just say, 'What am I going to do with this?'"

For many of the more conservative pastors in this community who did not rely on the lectionary, the sources of choice were either commentaries on different books of the Bible or Greek- and Hebrew-based exegetical aids. Actually, the use of such Biblical reference tools as commentaries was ranked higher than any other single printed source on the written questionnaire, with a mean score of 4.34, where 5 signified "most important." Of all twenty-five sources on that form, only the pastor's own library and people in the congregation were rated higher.

The use of Greek-language tools (*Koine* Greek being the original language of the New Testament) was also rated relatively high at a mean score of 3.06 (see Table 2 above). The importance of Old Testament Hebrew-based sources, on the other hand, was rated the lowest of all print sources with a mean of only 2.65, though fully a third (35%) of the sixty-two pastors gave it either a 4 or 5 rating. Tools based on these languages also had the two highest standard deviation values (1.539 for Greek and 1.471 for Hebrew), indicating that there was considerable difference of opinion among the pastors in this community over the value of these Biblical languages.

Statistical tests for significance found no quantitative explanation for this difference in terms of such numeric variables as age, years of education, or length of ministry. However, it was my observation that those pastors who talked about the value of Greek and/or Hebrew in interpreting the Bible were almost all theologically conservative. It was not true, however, that all theologically conservative pastors upheld the benefits of knowing Greek. Sometimes the value of knowing the Biblical languages was expressed in almost nostalgic terms, as the following middle-aged minister stated when asked why he continued to use these languages:

> Well, I made an agreement with myself in the seminary that if I spent five years with Greek and four with Hebrew, then I really didn't want to make that wasted time. So I've kept up with it. One thing I respect about [the conservative branch of my denomination]--though they are in a lot of ways reactionary--is their 80-year-old pastors who maintained and got up every morning and read Hebrew and Greek. In some of the old system you could get one of these pastors and a Jesuit from Europe together, and they could both speak the same language. It was a very classical education. They had Latin in junior high and Greek in high school. Then

they'd have their Hebrew in college. So they
were doing that sort of exegetical work their
very first year in seminary. I get upset by those
who have been trained in them, but don't use
them. But then I enjoy languages.

At least six pastors had their Greek text or Greek lexica
lying on the desk during the time of the interviews, another
indication that the use of these types of Biblical aids was not
merely an espoused one. One pastor had even organized a small
class on the Greek language for his parishioners, and had also
helped design a Greek font for a computer program that was
being sold to ministers in his denomination. Several pastors also
showed me their sermon notes, where they had special markings
for explanations of Greek terms that they wished to provide the
congregation, a practice which appears to underscore the importance these pastors attached to this kind of source.

Yet the use of these "scholarly" tools was not highlighted
publicly. As one said, "My Greek stays in the study." During
the ten months of participant observation at Sunday morning
worship services, for example, I observed only two occasions
when the pastor used an expression like, "the Greek word here
means...." It was common practice to explain the meaning of a
Biblical word without mentioning the word "Greek" or "Hebrew." This practice appears to be one instilled in pastors in
seminary, where some homiletical texts suggest that such
citations may seem "academically arrogant" (see, for example,
Robinson, 1980, and the discussion on this issue in Chapter 4).

Whether a pastor utilized Biblical languages in interpreting and preaching the Bible, however, was often a matter of
time. A number mentioned that they just didn't have the time to
keep up their proficiency. Others just doubted the value or need
to know the original languages when "there are so many good
commentaries out there now that will do that for you." One

even mentioned at the close of the interview that her seminary had done a survey of all their alumni who were now preaching and found that 95% listed Greek as the least effective course that they had had in seminary in terms of its value for ministry.

These comments only serve to underscore the variety of approaches that the ministers in this community take to understanding the Bible. This variety was even more pronounced when books other than the Bible were considered.

BOOKS: NON-BIBLICAL

"Well, books, books, books," is how one pastor responded when asked what sources of information he relied upon in his ministry. Another pastor, who had had no seminary education and yet was now in his fifteenth year of ministry, offered that he had made up for his lack of formal training by "doing a lot of reading."

The emphasis upon books as sources of information that many of these pastors made during the interview process is another point of comparison between the ministry and librarianship. In fact, one of the two librarians-turned-ministers in this community suggested that this was probably the most significant parallel between the two professions: "A minister friend of mine, you know, was also a librarian. It's funny but there does seem to be a link. Ministers, like librarians, do tend to spend a lot of time with books."

The most vivid example of the pastor's passion for books was the minister in this community who had a personal library of over 10,000 volumes, accumulated over a 25-year ministry. [While precise data were not gathered during this study regarding the size of ministerial libraries since many ministers kept libraries at home as well as at their offices, a count based on linear shelf space in pastors' church offices suggests a mean of approximately 750 volumes.] The following interchange not only revealed his somewhat defensive justification for the books he bought, but his own "collection development" policy:

Interviewer: How many books do you have?

Pastor: Oh, we are probably talking over 10,000 books.

Interviewer: Really? You have some very fine works here. Some that any theological library would be proud to have. Obviously a life-time of building.

Pastor: Well, at least 25 years. You know, books are my hobby, and I love them. I am also very aware that I've got too many, but who's hurting. I mean, it's my love and my passion. If I've got the money and the time to do it... I get criticized a lot for it, which I resent, but that's their problem.

Interviewer: How do you acquire most of your books?

Pastor: Since I buy so many, I refuse to pay full price. Sometimes I find them at book sales at professional conferences. I don't buy books here. This town is a vast wasteland for books so I usually go to used bookstores in Chicago whenever I'm in the area. I mean I probably bought 250 books last year, and there's been some years that I've bought as many as 600.

Interviewer: How do you decide what to buy?

And how do you keep track of them all?

Pastor: I have them by topics in sections. And I basically have a good memory on the things that I have. I read extensively book reviews and the essential library booklist kinds of things. I correlate those with what I have and don't have. Then I look at what they suggest and if it looks pretty good, then I will write it on a shopping list that I always carry with me. And so I always have a want list. One of the best things I've come across lately is *Current Thoughts & Trends* [an abstracting service for ministers discussed in the next section of this chapter], which alerts me to key items for my library.

Interviewer: I think there's a computer version of that abstracting service. Do you use it?

Pastor: No, I'd rather have it in print. I use the computer for word processing, but I'd rather use a book than a computer. When it gets right down to it, it's reading that strengthens my ministry.

While it would have been helpful to pursue his use of books even further, he was pressed for time and the interview had to be abbreviated. Still, it seems clear that he represented a significant minority of ministers (seven of the sixty-two pastors in this study had libraries of several thousand volumes; see below under "Personal Libraries") who exhibited a pronounced appreciation for books as sources of information.

In his case, information was viewed not merely as disparate bits of data, but rather as a complex, interwoven fabric that covered his ministry in many ways. His use of the phrase "it's reading that strengthens my ministry" indicates this broader level of information. His information-gathering behavior was very much akin to the "current awareness"-based information needs mentioned earlier that were not situation specific, but much more amorphous in nature.

Even ministers with smaller libraries mentioned their "love of books" though they were either not able or interested in building large private collections. One pastor whose personal library was less than 500 volumes responded to a question about what books he was currently reading in this way: "I constantly read," another example of broadly based information needs and information gathering.

The clergy in this study listed several factors that led them to choose the particular books they read. Those in the Doctor of Ministry program uniformly stated that their current reading was mostly prescribed by their classes, even though some of those books "made Leviticus look exciting." Others cited personal relationships with the authors. For example, one pastor was reading a book on the Civil War because one of his parishioners, a history professor at a local university, had written it. Another was using a commentary on Jesus' parables because a former pastor of his was its author. Another cited a title, adding it had been written by a denominational colleague of his.

For still others, book selection was based upon recommendations made either by friends or professional colleagues or the denominational headquarters. Some pastors even had to submit an annual reading list to their judicatory.

For many ministers, the reasons they chose certain books to read were quite utilitarian, as was discussed earlier. They read to prepare a sermon or answer a question or counsel a parishioner. For some, the reasons were less instrumental with several pointedly stating that they did not read "for sermon illustrations" or "to get up a sermon." They were avid book readers, but they read because of only very general and vague information needs, not because of any particular information need. Several of these ministers were members of book clubs that offered them a variety of titles with only indirect application to their profession, e.g. two were members of history book clubs; one, a Jewish book club; another, a Western book club.

There were also at least three different "ministerial reading groups" that met regularly to review books that the members had chosen to read. The reading fare of these groups was typically of a religious nature. One such group, for example, billed itself as the "Guild of Soup and Salad Theologians" because it met over the lunch hour to discuss new theological books. The other two were composed of denominational colleagues in the area who met monthly to talk about different books relevant to ministry.

However, not all pastors in this community viewed books so highly. For a few, the stated reason for not reading books was their high cost. For most, the rationale was lack of time. Two pastors had even found a somewhat novel method of dealing with their inability to schedule reading time. They relied on their wives as surrogate readers. As one explained:

> I find it very difficult to read books because of
> the time pressure point. I usually don't. I use
> my wife. She reads more than I do anyway, and
> I rely on her to share with me what she's read
> that she thinks would be helpful to me.

This would be an area worth pursuing to determine the effectiveness of the surrogate reader model, a model of information delegation that other busy professionals also use. A similar model was found in these pastors' use of abstracting services (see below under "Periodicals and Newspapers").

   One of the interesting findings in this study was the considerable variety of books that clergy read. This variety may be classified according to religious and non-religious books. Though both types were cited frequently by these clergy, religious books predominated. For example, of the 297 different titles that these pastors cited when asked what books they were currently reading--and only five listed none, 181 (61%) of them were religious in nature. The results of the written questionnaire also support this conclusion, as indicated in Table 3 below.

Table 3
Importance of Books as Information Sources

Type of Book Rated	1/2* Score	Mean Score	Std. Dev.
1. Books by religious publishers	0	4.31	0.696
2. Books by other publishers	14	3.32	1.012

* Number of clergy (out of 62) rating this source at a "1" or "2" on the 1 to 5 scale, where 5 = very important.

   None of the sixty-two pastors ranked religious books below "3" on the 1 to 5 scale in terms of their importance as ministerial information sources, while fourteen did so for non-religious books. The mean score for the latter books was only 3.32 compared to 4.31 for the former. The standard deviation for the 4.31 rating of religious books was also only 0.696, the second smallest value (next to the 0.517 value for personal libraries) of all twenty-five information sources listed on the questionnaire, suggesting the uniformly high regard in which these pastors held religious books.

   The specific titles of the religious books read by these pastors were quite varied. Since pastors often could not remember complete titles or often mentioned only the book topic, it is most useful to analyze this variety in terms of categories of religious books. One such category was books that were denominationally focused. This was how a Baptist pastor described his book reading interests:

> You try to buy good books because there is a lot of stuff out today that you don't want to bother with. You've got to try to get good books. If you're Baptist like me, you try to read books on the Baptist faith and belief, on their doctrine. You try to buy all those kinds of good books you can because there's some stuff that ain't worth buying.

To him, "good" books were "Baptist" books. This denominational focus to how some pastors chose religious books was not always self-evident. One minister stated that he did not limit himself in the types of religious books he bought or in the sources he used, but nearly every book title he listed was published by his own denomination, as were the majority of books in his personal library. Another pastor said he preferred to read "spiritual books," then mentioned four titles he was currently reading, all from his own religious fellowship.

Another category was religious books that dealt with a specialized aspect of ministry, an area that Porcella (1973) also noted as significant. The three most frequently mentioned professional specializations that the pastors in this community cited in terms of their religious book reading interests were church growth, counseling, and preaching--in that order.

The emphasis upon preaching was not surprising, given that not only was that area cited more than any other as taking the most amount of time in the ministry, but also was listed by almost half of the respondents (30 of 62) as the area in which they read the most (see Chapter 4). There was a strong sense among these pastors, almost all of whom preached at least once a week and some as many as thrice weekly, that sermon preparation was the area in which they did most of their reading. However, most of these pastors' reading in preaching was not in homiletical theory (though Craddock was often mentioned) or even in sermon books, but rather in reading a variety of books (many of which were sermon illustration books) that provided them with information for some sermon they were researching.

In addition to preaching as one of the three professional areas of reading interest most often cited, the subject of counseling was the second-most frequently mentioned when asked what books these pastors were currently reading. However, while counseling books were mentioned frequently, no particular titles or authors predominated. The one common theme was that these pastors were reading books that dealt with issues of recovery in the context of dysfunctional families. This also was not surprising given that the single biggest problem facing the ministers in this study, according to the ministers themselves, was the issue of broken relationships among their parishioners, usually within the context of individual families. This issue will be addressed in Chapter 4 under the pastor as healer.

In addition to books on preaching and counseling, however, books about church growth were by far the most widely read items among the pastors in this community. This interest may be explained partly because of the fact that this particular town had been targeted by a number of religious groups for "church plants" because of its rapid growth in population. In fact, 10 of the 58 different churches in this study had been begun just within the last decade. In addition, a total of 44 (76%) of all 58 churches were experiencing either moderate or significant growth at the time of this study.

This demographic dynamic no doubt influenced the type

of reading material that many of these pastors were choosing. Among the many books on church growth that these ministers listed, the most frequently cited authors were George Barna, whose works were discussed earlier, and Carl George, a professor of church growth at Fuller Theological Seminary in California.

One final category of religious books can only be described as "miscellaneous." There was so much variety that no single label can suffice. These religious books ranged from such authors as liberal German theologians (Hans Kung) to conservative American fundamentalists (Frank Perretti). Part of this variety was due undoubtedly to the inherent individuality of these pastors, as Strang (1942, p. 3) observed about all professionals.

Part of the book-reading variety may also be attributed to the three ministerial reading groups in the community which, in effect, encouraged ministers to read books on religious topics that they otherwise might not. Since nearly a third of the pastors interviewed were members of one of these groups that assigned different books to be read each month or two, this programmed variety undoubtedly contributed to the wide range of religious books that these pastors read.

Religious books were certainly not the only kind of books being read by the pastors in this study. As one pastor, who listed "more than 40" as the number of hours per week he spent in reading (the mean number for all pastors in this study was 16), succinctly put it: "All books is good to read. Even sometimes I find myself wandering off and reading something that is not spiritual." The non-religious titles cited by the pastors in the study ranged from *Zen and the Art of Motorcycle Maintenance* to *Victorian Reminiscences of Christmas*, from *The Day America Told the Truth* to *Riders on the Range*. One minister read children's books because:

I'm a strong believer in children's books. I read
a lot of children's stories. My funeral sermons
always contain a children's story about death because I think that's as basic as you can get, and
that's what people need right then.

Another was fond of the literary classics, especially
Melville. "I use a lot of Melville in my preaching," he noted.
"I took a course on him with a fanatical professor, and we knew
Billy Budd all the way through and *Moby Dick*. So there is quite
a bit of them in my sermons." This connection to prior interests
in college was mentioned by several pastors. One, a literature
major in college, liked nothing better than to "sit down in front
of the fire with E. E. Cummings for an evening."

Another pastor mentioned his recent readings in Wittgenstein, having been a philosophy major. In discussing his use of
a nearby university library, he explained his admittedly unusual
interest in this philosopher in terms that suggested multiple
motivations.

Just yesterday I was there, and I picked up a
book. I had read the reviews on it that not
many ministers would read. You see, I was a
philosophy major in college, and there's a new
biography out on Wittgenstein that I started last
night. I like to read biographies. I've never
been able to understand Wittgenstein's philosophy, so I thought, why not a biography? He
was very receptive to religious faith. I'm not
sure exactly what his commitment was, but for
a major modern philosopher to have that kind of
openness to religious faith is kind of significant.
I think I need to know more about him. I
thought maybe the biographical approach might
be better than trying to read his technical works.

The motivating factors here were several: a philosophy major in college, the catalyst of a recent review, and his own personal preference for biography. This interest in biographical books was also expressed by several other pastors, who cited such diverse subjects as Vince Lombardi and Chaim Potok.

Sometimes the reasons given for reading certain books were purely matters of personal interest, with no other apparent motivation at work, at least not any professional ones. This, too, is consistent with Strang's (1942, p. 2) observation: "Persons engaged in a particular profession, while devoting a great deal of time to their professional field, will vary their reading widely in other areas." This was clearly the case with the pastor who cited Pirsig's *Zen and the Art of Motorcycle Maintenance*. He admitted his fascination with this author in these terms:

> Have you ever heard of Robert Pirsig? [I nod-
> ded yes.] I've read *Zen* through three times. I
> just finished it again. My wife and I went on
> vacation, and we read it aloud to each other in
> the car. I'm reading one by him now called
> *Lila*. What an author!

Several of the pastors admitted a fondness for a particular author, reading everything by him or her that they could. One was, as he put it, "a Louis L'Amour fan" and read all of his westerns. A campus minister was reading a novel by Larry Wentworth because "he is one of the best American novelists, and also part of it takes place in [named a nearby town]." One pastor, an avid sports fan, was a devotee of a certain physical education writer: "I've read most of his books, and I'm just fascinated by a lot of things that he says about the whole person. He talks about the spiritual, as well as the physical."

Sometimes the purely personal motivation for reading

certain books overlapped into professional interests. This overlap is consistent with the variety of information needs that many pastors in this study expressed. On occasion, these pastors' information-gathering behavior originated as a personal interest and then found focus in a utilitarian need.

For example, a pastor who was an adult child of an alcoholic read almost everything she could on the topic, to the point where she decided to write her doctoral thesis on the issue. Several years later, she now admitted having slacked off because "they just keep repeating the same things." This pastor's utilitarian need was now being supplanted by a different personal interest that also exhibited features of professional information-seeking behavior. Her current interest was science fiction. Her explanation highlights this personal/professional overlap that many pastors indicated, suggesting that many pastors read non-religious books for very religious reasons:

> I read Star Trek books. I love that stuff. I'll even bring that into my sermons. I think there's a lot of stuff in there that's theological. However, that's not why I read it. I read it because I enjoy it. But they deal with a lot of issues that are real-life issues and in more creative ways than many religious books do. Dealing with religious questions in the 23rd century is different, and I enjoy reading how they approach that. I really enjoy that different perspective. I probably spend an hour a night reading that kind of stuff.

While on one hand, she read science fiction "because she enjoyed it," she also clearly saw the religious values inherent in this literature and used these books for professional purposes as well. There were, however, a number of pastors who talked about "recreational reading" for purely entertainment values.

The most often cited genre was murder mysteries. Said one, "I just don't have time to read books on the ministry. When I have a minute to relax, I do like to read but it has to be recreational reading, which for me is murder mysteries."

Some book reading by these ministers was even tied to the calendar. For example, during those interviews that took place in February several pastors mentioned that they were reading books on blacks because it was black history month. Another pastor was reading books on money and investments because his retirement was approaching.

One of the most surprising findings in this study was the number of ministers who, unbeknownst to each other, were all reading books on the men's movement. Ten of the sixty-two ministers interviewed cited such books as Robert Bly's *Iron John*, Robert Hick's *Uneasy Manhood*, and Sam Keen's *Fire in the Belly*. One pastor was even a member of a men's group which had started because they had seen a videotape version of a book entitled *The Gathering of Men*.

When asked for possible explanations for this widespread interest in the men's movement among the ministers in this community, one responded, "I don't think it's just a men's issue. I think it's a cultural issue that we as pastors are trying to deal with. It's related to the denial of our full expression as people." On a more extended note, one pastor offered this explanation:

> You know, this whole idea of the men's move-
> ment... I've just taken a man through this book
> on it, and I've found it to be a very cathartic
> kind of experience. Part of what I'm doing is
> getting ready for a sermon series on marriage
> and family, and I want to address the men on
> some of these issues. These books are raising
> some very exciting concepts in my opinion, con-

cerning the healing of past relationships and the finding of our own masculinity...keeping it all in a Biblical framework. In fact, I just counseled a couple recently where the husband did not have a good role model for being a father. And I'm sensing a real desire in men to find out exactly who they are. You even see it on television with shows like Tim Allen's *Home Improvement*. "Let's go to Sears." I like that.

Several motivations for reading were evident in his comments. It was not only of personal value ("very cathartic"), but reading books on the men's movement was also of professional value as a pastor ("I've just taken a man through this book"), as a preacher ("getting ready for a sermon series"), as a counselor ("I just counseled a couple where"), and as an observer of popular culture ("you even see it on television").

Books, however, were not the only formal channels of information used by the pastors in this study in their information gathering. The use of periodicals was also frequently mentioned.

PERIODICALS AND NEWSPAPERS

Not counting the pastor who gave me a list of the 101 periodicals to which he subscribed, the ministers in this study listed 91 different titles of periodicals and newspapers that they received and read regularly. Of these 91 titles, 57 (63%) were religious in nature, and 30 of those were published by denominational presses. These data suggest that the pastors in this study read mostly religious magazines, primarily those that were of their own denomination.

The responses to the two questions on the written questionnaire concerning magazine reading suggest a similar conclusion, with ministers rating ministerial magazines at 3.70 and other magazines at only 3.04. The results of the interviews tend, as well, to support this finding.

However, the interviews also indicated some diversity in this uniformity. For example, other than denominational publications, these pastors mentioned what appear to be a central corpus of fifteen serials. These fifteen most frequently cited periodicals and newspapers are listed in Table 4 below.

Table 4
The 15 Most-Cited Serials Read by Clergy
(N = 62)

Title of Serial	Number Citing	Percent of Total
1. The local newspaper	59	95%
2. Time	26	42%
3. Newsweek	17	27%
4. Leadership (for ministers)	15	24%
5. USA Today	13	21%
6. Christian Century	12	19%
7. Christianity Today	10	16%
8. Reader's Digest	8	13%
9. Moody Monthly	7	11%
10. Biblical Archaeology Review	6	10%
11. Homiletics	6	10%
12. Pulpit Digest	4	6%
13. The Clergy Journal	4	6%
14. Utne Reader	4	6%
15. Theology Today	3	5%

Though heavy in ministry and current events, this core list also suggests some of the variety evidenced in these pastors' book reading interests. When asked about the magazines he read, this pastor gave the following explanation for his varied interests:

I probably read about 20 magazines a month:
Vanity Fair, *Gentleman's Quarterly*, *Vogue*,
Esquire, *Time*, travel magazines, management
magazines, usually one computer magazine a
month, *Dance America* occasionally, *Better
Homes and Gardens*, plus many of the technical
journals in ministry. I'll even sometimes pick
up the women's magazines at the check-out
counter because what I understand magazine
reading to be is to pick up the pulse of a culture
that I'm part of. Your people in most churches
may pretend that they don't read those magazines, but the subscription lists would suggest
otherwise.

I want to know, for example, what does the
primary men's magazine, *GQ*, say about what's
in in clothing, in lifestyles, in health issues.
What are the addictive issues? Those magazines
are not trying to write for a religious group of
people. They're trying to write for where
people probably are, and they have a wonderful
ability to be able to market all that. I pick up
Sports Illustrated for the same reasons.

"To pick up the pulse of a culture" is how many pastors
would describe their motivation in non-ministerial magazine
reading. When asked why he subscribed to *People Weekly*, one
pastor responded: "I need to know what are the people of the
world looking at and thinking about. Sometimes I think in the
church that we lose touch, particularly ministers, with what's
going on in society, because we have a tendency to just spend
time reading Christian things." Another pastor of a mainline
Protestant congregation even admitted to reading the *National
Enquirer*. This was his rationale:

Well, it's not that I agree with the type of articles or in the way that they present these movie stars and things like that. Now these publications like the *Enquirer* and the *Star*, I don't read them every week. But I do look at them from time to time because a lot of people are reading these things, and I need to know what my people are reading. Sometimes I pick up things like that when I go to the hospital and am waiting to see a patient.

He offered a similar explanation for reading *USA Today*: "The articles are not only concise, but they tell you what you really need to know--what people are thinking." This "I'll grab anything" sentiment that another pastor expressed reflects the diversity of these pastors' periodical interests. This diversity will be discussed from two perspectives: religious magazines and other, general magazines and newspapers.

Religious periodicals were of three types: denominational, specialized, and ministerial. Denominational magazines were cited by almost all of the pastors in this study, even those who expressed dissatisfaction with their value. No doubt part of the reason for their popularity among these pastors was that they were free, but also perhaps because they were viewed as politically necessary from a professional standpoint.

The rare exception was one pastor's decision to cancel all denominational publications because his church was a result of two denominations' merging and he did not wish to favor either position. Even those who described their denominational publications in very unflattering terms continued to read them. Some pastors even extended their denominational reading interests to include church bulletins produced by ministerial colleagues in their denomination so they could read what their counterparts were doing.

Another type of religious periodical mentioned often by these pastors were those that specialized in a particular area of ministry. Four of the fifteen titles cited above were of this type: *Homiletics* and *Pulpit Digest* for preaching, *Biblical Archaeology Review* for Biblical teaching, and *Theology Today* for theological reflection. The mention of the last journal was only a little surprising since its primary audience is theological educators, but a number of pastors not only cited such journals but indicated they would subscribe to more except for their high cost.

The relative popularity of these kinds of religious journals suggests a certain level of theological sophistication among the pastors in this community, a sophistication that found some support during the interview process. For example, in explaining why he was beginning a small-group "healing service," the pastor of a very traditional, mainline denomination with more than two dozen physicians and surgeons as members offered a rationale that indicated he was theologically well read.

Interviewer: I'm not sure what you mean by "healing service." Is this part of the charismatic "signs and wonders" theology that has come out of some professors at Fuller Theological Seminary recently?

Pastor: No, no, no. I'm afraid that emphasis would not be theologically acceptable to [named his denomination]. No, what I mean by "healing service" is... Let me approach it this way. Most of the new research on the Psalms would indicate that what we used to think were the individual psalms of repentance probably came out of the cult and the family circle, or the family circle equivalent, the small group. This research indicates that family and friends would often come together when someone was ill to essentially help them pray, to help them come to acceptance of their illness, their impending death, or whatever.

So I think that a theologically correct understanding of the Psalms leads us essentially to the small therapeutic group. Most Biblical scholars are now beginning to say that that does make sense as an appropriate interpretation for the Psalms. That is the kind of experience we're hoping to be able to regenerate with our "healing service."

We worship better than anyone, but we're very individualistic in our piety. And what we're learning, as other churches here in town are learning, is that what we have missed is the family/small group/household setting of faith. We want to recapture what the Israelites had in their cultic faith, the small group coming together to read the Psalms, to pray, to quietly lay on hands and bless one another, to pray for individuals within the group.

The cases mentioned earlier of pastors wrestling with Gadamer and reading Wittgenstein give additional support to the conclusion that many of the pastors in this study exhibited a fair degree of theological acuity. This finding is actually not all that surprising given the emphasis placed upon the minister as "theologian in life and thought" in the massive study of pastors in *Ministry in America* (Schuller et al., 1980, p. 25). In this sociological survey, 1,200 general descriptions of ministry coalesced into "eleven major areas of ministry" that were considered crucial characteristics for pastors, one of which was this emphasis on the pastor as theologian. In their information-gathering roles many pastors also display this concentration on their professional core, particularly in their journal reading interests.

As information gatherers, the pastors in this study also cited other specialized journals in their profession besides theological periodicals that were important sources of information for them. The journals they cited as being helpful to a particular specialization were those in church growth and youth ministry, as well as campus ministry newsletters for the campus ministers in this study.

Preaching periodicals, however, were the most often cited. Usually the stated reason was to "get sermon ideas" and to "stay current in the contemporary practice of preaching," but a few admitted that their sermons sometimes came straight from these periodicals. At the beginning of one interview, a pastor discussed the last sermon he had preached, citing three points about Abraham's laughing at God that he, the pastor, had used in a very creative approach to a sermon on Abraham. Sometime later in the interview, when discussing journal reading, he said:

> I also get some preaching journals, like I subscribe to *Pulpit Digest* and I also get *Homiletics*. Occasionally I find good illustrations in them. And it so happens that last week actually there was a sermon based on Abraham in one of them. "Laughing at God" was the title. To be honest with you, I relied on that for last Sunday's sermon.

Many theologically conservative ministers cited a great number of preaching magazines, ranging from the fundamentalist *Sword of the Lord* to *Brian's Lines* (a regular compilation of sermons and sermon ideas produced by one pastor--Brian). One received *Proclaim*, a Southern Baptist preaching periodical, because he "knew the editor" and "liked it for sermon ideas."

The third type of ministerial magazines mentioned by these clergy, in addition to denominational and specialized, were those that dealt with the ministry in general. They were neither denominationally focused nor did they specialize in a particular area of ministry.

By far the most popular general ministry magazine was *Leadership*, a quarterly journal published by Christianity Today, Inc., the same publishing firm that produces *Christianity Today*. *Leadership* was listed for several reasons. It had "gifted writers" with such authors as Billy Graham, Charles Colson, and Carl Henry. It looked at "current issues" in ministry with articles ranging from sexual misconduct to ministerial salaries. It took a "creative" approach to the issues, including not only "helpful bibliographies," but also "great cartoons" that many pastors used in their preaching and teaching. And it had an "evangelical" orientation, which particularly appealed to those ministers who were mostly conservative in their theological perspective, but which did not prevent its use by theologically liberal pastors.

However, this tolerance for evangelicalism did not extend to this journal's sister serial, *Christianity Today*. Though it too was used widely by conservative pastors, it was not read by the other ministers in the community. As one explained, "I've backed off of it because it was just getting too conservative." (Ironically, some of the very conservative pastors in the community had done the same because it was "just too liberal.") For the more ecumenically minded ministers the publication of choice in this area was *The Christian Century*, one of whose editors is Martin Marty of the University of Chicago Divinity School.

Two ministers also mentioned that they received "free" and "appreciated" the general ministerial orientation of a magazine entitled *Ministry: The International Journal for Clergy*, though they did not know why they were getting it. Actually,

Ministry is published by the Seventh-Day Adventists and every other issue is sent gratis to ministers all over the country as part of that denomination's public relations efforts. Somewhat surprisingly, neither of the pastors who mentioned using this publication seemed to be aware of that fact. Other religious periodicals ranged from the charismatic *Charisma* to the social justice journal *Sojourners*.

The second kind of periodical cited by these pastors, besides ministerial magazines, were of a more general, non-ministerial nature. These ranged from *Time* to *British Heritage*. Sometimes the interests were hobby-related: photography, motorcycle, and computer magazines were examples of such.

One pastor read *Utne Reader* because he was "a child of the sixties." Several took *Reader's Digest* because there were "a lot of good sermon illustrations in it." It was not uncommon for the pastors in this study to use magazine material in their sermons, such as an article on the Chinese in *National Geographic* or one on decorating in *Architectural Digest*. One subscribed to the *Journal of Psychohistory* because of its helpfulness in his counseling. Another took several education journals because he taught adolescents. One even read *McCalls*, *Modern Romance*, and *Home and Away* because his wife worked in a medical clinic and brought them home for him to read. Another read *Redbook* because "my wife gets it so I scan it to see what families, what women are reading about current lifestyles."

Sometimes the stated rationale for reading a particular general-interest periodical was nothing more than a broadly based desire to "get a window on...social currents" or to understand a "variety of perspectives." It seems apparent from the interview data that many ministers read popular periodicals in order to understand and sometimes critique the values of society that were being reflected in these publications. In these situations, clergy exhibited something of a love/hate relationship with these popular periodicals and the values they espoused.

In some sense, their information-gathering habits relative to such publications demonstrated the tension noted by the theologian Niebuhr, who wrote a generation ago of the need for the Church to be "in the world but not of it" (Niebuhr, 1951). Clergy, too, in their information gathering from popular sources are at once citizen consumers and clerical critiquers of the information they acquire through such popular periodicals.

On a more superficial level, the desire to stay up on current events was the most frequently cited reason for reading news magazines and newspapers. *Time* was the most popular of the former, and the local newspaper of the latter. There were a few, however, who criticized *Time* and *Newsweek* because of their "lack of substance," preferring instead to get their news from the *MacNeil/Lehrer Report* or the *Christian Science Monitor* or the *Wall Street Journal*.

Most of the pastors read the local paper, but not all. One refused to since he had come from a large metropolitan area and "the move from that to [the local paper] was such a shock and I couldn't find any place to recycle it." Another pastor had a subscription, but made disparaging remarks about it ("my cat loves it"), even though a member of her church was a reporter and had written an article featuring her as a woman minister. Even some of those who read the local paper did so only when they "dropped off the kids at the public library" or when they "had breakfast at Hardee's" where it was available free.

Some who read the local newspaper also subscribed to such standard sources as the *New York Times* or the *Chicago Tribune*. More than a dozen (13) also read *USA Today*, because of its "conciseness." Besides keeping up with the news, other reasons mentioned for reading the newspaper were "so I can find out who's died to see if I'll be doing any funerals," in order to "find sermon illustrations," and as a catalyst for sermons ("some-times I'll be reading the paper and a sermon idea will hit me").

Only one pastor refused to read "secular magazines" because of this rationale:

> Number one, I don't trust what secular maga-zines say. If they are telling the truth, it is probably half the truth. It is not the whole truth and nothing but the truth. It is always distorted.

Yet even he later added that "you know, in my personal reading, if I have time, I will pick up a magazine for my own pulse of what is happening in the world."

One of the more common refrains sounded during the interviews was the problem with lack of time that pastors had in keeping up their periodical reading. More than a dozen of the clergy in this community dealt with this type of overload by subscribing to periodical abstracting services. Part of the underlying rationale for their use may be found in what Wilson (1983) said about professionals in general regarding their information-gathering habits.

> In theory the professional might seem to be faced with a huge and open-ended task of look-ing for relevant information, trying to evaluate the credibility of sources.... But in practice a professional can be as informationally passive as any routine worker.... The job of search[ing] the external environment for relevant information can be delegated to other specialists, such as editors of professional magazines.... (pp. 132-133)

For many of these ministers he might also have added "and abstracting services." This was a somewhat surprising finding in this study. While abstracting services have long been popular in many professions, including the library field, their use in the ministry has not been discussed in the literature to my knowledge. Their importance to a number of the clergy in this community, however, was unmistakable. The reason given for such "delegation" was usually that of time, coupled with the pastor's particular prerogative, guilt. Listen to this minister's musings about magazines:

> I try to read certain journals, but I am very selective. I try to read *Leadership,* for example, but I do a pitifully poor job of keeping up even with that. I have reduced my reading there to only those articles that are very current for me in the areas that I need help with. Otherwise, I just file them for later reference. I briefly index what's there for my 3" x 5" file so I'll have it later if I need it. Let's see what else. I don't read *Moody.* I don't read *Christianity Today.* I don't read *Newsweek* or *Time.* No, actually what I do is read another work that's put out called *Current Thoughts & Trends.* I read that. I used to subscribe to all those magazines, but it sent me on such a guilt trip because I couldn't keep up with them. I thought, this is foolish. I'd just sit down at my desk and look at the piles and think, boy, I need to do it, need to do it, need to do it. Can't get it, can't get it, can't get it. So now I rely on *Current Thoughts & Trends* to do my reading for me.

As mentioned earlier, *Current Thoughts & Trends* is a religiously oriented abstracting service that summarizes the contents of key articles from over fifty different magazines. Though most of these periodicals are of a religious nature, selective abstracts are also provided for *American Demographic,*

Time, U.S. News & World Report, World Monitor, and *Psychology Today.*

At least eight different ministers in this study mentioned their subscription to this service (which costs $36 annually in paper format), three of them in its more expensive, computerized form that is sent out monthly on floppy disks. The automated version, called "InfoSearch," allowed pastors to easily incorporate the data into their sermons or lessons on the computer. One minister even gave me a lengthy demonstration of the computerized version in his office. And the minister who subscribed to 101 different journals said that the print version was "one of the best things I've come across lately." One middle-aged pastor noted how much more efficient this publication had made him in terms of his information searching:

> Now I subscribe to a newsletter called *Current Thoughts & Trends.* It's a compilation of statements and quotes that are helpful for ministry. That's probably been a weakness in my life. Early on in the ministry when I was just out of seminary, I was into magazines like *U.S. News,* and I kept trying to keep contemporary in all the right sources. Maybe it was inexperience or something, but I just never did learn how to glean the information out of those that I needed to help me. Now I just use *Current Thoughts & Trends.*

While such tools obviously left ministers at the mercies of the abstractors, it was a tradeoff well worth it in their minds. This preference for relying upon others for information gathering was also evident in this pastor's comments:

> I read a lot of periodicals on research in adolescence and education. There are a lot of

nice pieces out there. Actually, what I usually do is read *Youth Worker Update*. That is a periodical that basically summarizes all the research out there, kind of cans it for you a little bit so that you can stay on top of it without having to see what the library has on it so often. I'm sure that doesn't make librarians very happy [a reference to my role]. But it refers you to the source if you want to look up the original research in the library. And I do look up stuff here at the university library if I see something that really catches my eye.

Three other pastors also subscribed to abstracting services, but they were specifically designed to provide sermon illustrations that could be used in preaching. One came preprinted on 3" x 5" cards so that they could be interfiled with the pastors' own illustration files. Sometimes the abstracts consisted of lectionary aids that even had pre-packaged sermons. It appears that the use of abstracts for pastors as information-gathering delegation devices warrants further study in the future.

The use of periodicals as sources of information was quite pronounced among the pastors in this study. Though these periodicals may be classified into two major groups, ministerial and general, both groups displayed a considerable degree of diversity, as was found with the book reading patterns of these clergy. The information needs that served as catalysts for using periodicals were both utilitarian and current awareness in nature. The perceived problem of "information overload" had also caused more than a dozen pastors to subscribe to periodical abstracting services. In addition to the print-based media of books and periodicals, audiovisual sources were cited as sources of information.

AUDIOVISUALS

Another source of information for the pastors in this study was their use of audiovisual sources, though these were not used nearly to the same extent that book and periodical sources were. For example, while the respondents to the written questionnaire rated the eight items about printed sources at a composite mean score of 3.47 (3.68 if Greek and Hebrew tools are excluded), the eight audiovisual items were given only an average mean score of 2.16 (see Table 5 below).

Table 5
Importance of Audiovisuals as Information Sources

The relative ranking (out of 25 sources) and rating (on a 1 to 5 scale, where 5 = very important) of audiovisual sources by the 62 pastors in this study are listed below.

Type of audiovisual source	Rel. Rank	Mean Rating	Std. Dev.
1. Religious radio programs	22	1.86	0.903
2. Other kinds of radio programs	25	1.12	1.128
3. Religious television programs	23	1.73	0.964
4. Other kinds of television programs	19	2.50	1.081
5. Audiocassettes on religious topics	14.5	3.04	1.244
6. Audiocassettes on other topics	21	2.11	1.112
7. Videocassettes on religious topics	17	2.70	1.216
8. Videocassettes on other topics	20	2.18	1.113

The mean scores for audiovisual sources ranged from a high of 3.04 for audiocassettes on religious topics to a low of 1.12 for non-religious radio programs (see table above). This section will look at both audio sources (audiocassettes and radio) and video sources (television, movies, and videocassettes). The growing popularity of these two types of information sources among many of the ministers in this study was reflected in this pastor's comment when asked about her use of books: "I don't use many. You know I've heard statistics that only 11% of people read. So I think if you're going to reach people, you need to focus on videos, tapes, other forms besides books."

In the highly oral culture (see Chapter 4) in which clergy live their professional lives, it is not surprising that audio-based resources constitute an important information source for pastors. Among the ministers in this community, the preferred audio source was audiocassettes. When asked, for example, if he read any books on preaching, one pastor responded negatively saying he preferred tapes because:

> Like Craddock says, preaching is an auditory thing. To read a sermon for me is like looking at music. It is meant to be heard. It is not meant to be read. Black notes on a staff don't turn me on. When people come up to me on Sunday and say they'd like to have a copy of my sermon, I say, "Fine, here's a tape of it."

In fact, tapes of other preachers' sermons were the most-cited kinds of audiocassettes mentioned. One pastor, who admitted "borrowing" his previous sermon from an audiotaped message he had recently heard, said he listened to a lot of tapes, adding "tapes are my single biggest source of information." The information, in this case, was something more than raw research data. It was information that was already packaged for public dissemination. Another subscribed to a monthly audiocassette service of sermons because they "helped me increase my knowledge."

Several pastors had extensive tape libraries, both of sermons and of lectures from professional conferences. One even showed me a catalog from a firm in Arizona that sells audiocassettes of lectures from more than a hundred different ministerial conferences held across the country. One minister said he spent "about two hours a day" listening to recorded lectures from ministerial conferences--on topics ranging from church growth demographics to miraculous healings.

Sometimes the content of the tapes was simply an audio version of a magazine format, such as *The Pastor's Update* produced by Fuller Theological Seminary. This particular audio magazine for clergy was mentioned by seven different pastors, but somewhat surprisingly a cassette series by Christianity Today, entitled *Preaching Today*, was not mentioned by any, even though it is probably one of the most popular products nationwide among pastors. Its absence among these pastors was inexplicable.

One final reason given for the popularity of audio-cassettes, at least religious ones, was that pastors could simply "pop them into the car stereo" and listen to them during the many hours they spent riding between hospital calls and attending out-of-town events. The only statistically significant variables associated with the high use of tapes by some pastors were the size of the ministerial staff and the size of the personal library. In other words, ministers with larger libraries working in multiple staff situations tended to use tapes more, but the strengths of the correlations were only .40 and .47 respectively. I was not able to uncover an explanation for these two correlations.

The use of the radio as an audio-based information source did not rate nearly so highly as did audiocassettes, despite the oral bias of both. The only radio programming mentioned to any degree at all were either call-in radio talk shows (the community had one of the country's oldest such shows and it was very popular) or news programs. Several of the sermons I heard made reference to such popular radio fare as Tom Bodett's Motel 6 commercial ("We'll leave the light on for you"), Paul Harvey's news and comments, and Garrison Keillor's public radio show. One minister did comment that he had been supernaturally "called to the ministry" while listening to Charles Swindoll, a well-known California minister, preach on the radio.

There was also one pastor who "enjoy[ed] listening to the 'Radio Reader' program" on the local university radio station. That was where he "heard a review of Umberto Eco's *Name of the Rose*" and decided to read it. He said he also had seen the movie starring Sean Connery, but it "didn't do justice to the book." So in one critical incident oral, print, and video sources all impacted on this pastor's information-gathering behavior. His preference for the oral and print over the video did not extend to every minister.

In addition to audio-based sources of information, some of the pastors also exhibited a propensity for video-based sources. Among the three most-cited examples--television, movies, and videocassettes--television was the dominant information channel. The average age (42) of the ministers in this study, indicating most had grown up in the "TV generation," no doubt played a role in this preference. The use of television as an information source was most pronounced in the pastor's role as preacher. The following comments were typical of the more experienced pastors in this community. When asked how he prepared his sermons, this pastor in his forties replied:

> I guess I tend to get a lot of my stuff where a lot of pastors do. I guess being someone who grew up in the sixties, I tend to reflect on television and old movies a lot. I mean, we had a young guest preacher in here last month, and it was so obvious that he was still in seminary. He was preaching and pulling from Socrates, he was

pulling from Spurgeon, and he was dying. And
I thought, you know, I'd be much more likely to
quote from the Bill Cosby show. The people
are going to be more interested if you use something that they are interested in. Who cares
about Socrates and Spurgeon? So I tend to use
television and movies.

The particular kinds of television that were most often
mentioned were news programs and talk shows. For example,
in responding to the item on the questionnaire about non-
religious television programs, one pastor penciled in "just Phil
and Oprah," referring to the network television talk shows hosted
by Phil Donahue and Oprah Winfrey. He went on to explain
how helpful it was to him in his counseling ministry to hear how
these two talk-show hosts dealt with personal issues and also
what issues were current.

Another pastor related in great detail how she had
stopped by a local bar to eat lunch with a friend and stayed to
watch a television talk show on child abuse because "I deal with
that stuff all the time." A third pastor told a story in one of his
sermons during the Winter Olympics about a member's relative
who was an Olympic athlete because "many of our members had
just seen him compete on TV the night before."

The relatively low rating given to religious television
programs (see Table 5 above) was not too surprising in light of
recent well-publicized scandals in this country involving televangelists. Two pastors, for example, whose sermons were
televised locally said that they rarely watched their more
publicized counterparts because they did not find such programs
appealing or useful, "except maybe Robert Schuller." When
asked about a negative reference in one of his sermons to a
religious television program, another pastor responded, "They
just offend me."

Except for the little use of religious programs, the television medium in general appeared to be used by a number of pastors in this community as a cultural common ground, much as the Bible was used as a spiritual common ground. This evocative nature of television as a type of shared experience, a contemporary form of the village storyteller, has been rarely discussed in the professional literature of the ministry. Most articles simply decry the morality of the medium, but there is at least one brief argument for the other view in an article by Wall (1988), entitled "Beyond Blandness in Preaching." To be sure, the "offensive" nature of some television programs was cited by several ministers in this study, but not very many. When one very conservative pastor of a "holiness" church was asked if he ever used television to help him in his ministry, particularly preaching, he responded:

> Well, in our church manual it discourages people from participating in too many such things as that, movies, modern dance, that kind of thing too. Now probably everybody in our church has a television, but we think we need to be very careful in what we select for viewing. We feel that many tend to tear down the natural inhibitions of modesty. Now, if everything was like "Leave It to Beaver," it would be a different story, but it's not.

For other pastors, the culture's fascination with television was the very reason they said they needed to watch it. "I force myself to watch at least an hour of MTV every week," said one minister, "because how can I ever know what's going on with our young people if I don't?" One pastor pithily noted that "the day of the MTV youth minister is here." One church even had a large-screen television set in its activity center so that the community youth could come in three nights per week to watch musical videos as part of a community outreach effort. The program was in its first year and had already grown to over 600 teenagers in attendance each week and had been favorably reviewed in the local newspaper.

The other major mode of visual information mentioned by the clergy in this community were movies. On one hand were those pastors whose sentiment was captured by this minister's comment: "I love the arts. There probably isn't a movie I haven't seen." On the other hand were those pastors who felt something of this preacher's feeling: "I rarely go. It's not that I'm against them, but I was raised where that was frowned upon."

Nationwide, there is some evidence that clergy actually see more movies than do their church members (Lindvall, 1986, p. 23). The old taboo among some very conservative churches against "theatres" is now breaking down partly because of the increase in videocassettes. As one pastor noted, "It's hard to distinguish movies from videos any more."

Though movies may be important sources of information, not many ministers when pressed could think of any ones they had seen lately. This silence may also be related to a desire for privacy or it may be that they did not feel comfortable talking about this type of source. This attraction/aversion tension is reminiscent of the love/hate relationship the pastors in this study displayed relative to their reading of popular periodicals as discussed earlier.

The only movies that were mentioned in the interviews were *Beauty and the Beast*, the only G-rated movie playing at the time; *The Black Robe*, a movie about Jesuit missionaries in 17th-century Canada that was also playing locally at the time of the interviews; *Boyz 'N the Hood*, an Academy-Award-winning portrayal of young men in an urban neighborhood which one pastor noted for its powerful portrait of "sin's unrelenting grasp on people"; *Backdraft*, a movie about firefighters; and *The Dead Poets Society*, which one pastor used in a sermon on grief because of

> the scene where the kid, the roommate of the kid who kills himself, goes out the morning after and the world is beautiful. It's snowing and everything looks the same. I mean, the world goes on. It looks like nothing has changed. Then he just goes nuts. He loses it. There is something about that contrast, about how difficult it is to talk about grief because the world goes on and everything looks the same. And the world expects you to act as if everything is the same. Except it's not, and inside, you're not.

Like the earlier pastor's reference to the Cosby television show, this pastor used movies as a type of shared experience to make a point about grief. The information in this source was similar to the information conveyed in storytelling. It is information about how people (via the arts) deal with problems, and how their experiences can be models for others.

The last type of video-based source cited in this study were videocassettes. Other than as alternative means of viewing movies, this form of media was rarely mentioned. The one exception was that many pastors used different series of counseling-oriented videotapes for their premarital counseling information needs. Typically, a pastor would have the couple planning a wedding view one to six hours of videotapes on various aspects of marriage, and then they would discuss as a small group the issues raised in the videos (see Chapter 4 for further discussion). Otherwise, videocassettes were little used by most of the pastors in this community.

COMPUTER DATABASES

One of the more interesting findings in this study dealt with pastors' use of another non-print-based information source, namely the computer. Before examining the use of computer databases as information sources, the use of computers themselves will be briefly noted. Nearly three-fourths (71%) of the sixty-two ministers interviewed in this study used a computer regularly in their ministry.

One might have suspected that those ministers whose formal education preceded the advent of the personal computer during the last decade--and they constituted nearly two-thirds of these pastors--would be much less inclined to use computers, since they had learned their profession without them. Quite the opposite was true. It was a sixty-two-year-old minister who said, "Thank God for the computer." And it was a minister with nearly thirty years of pastoral experience who referred to the computer on his desk as "one of God's greatest gifts." In fact, it was the younger pastors, more than the older ones, who usually did not have a computer, and the most frequently cited reason was cost.

In terms of quantitative data, the only statistically significant demographic variable that was related to the use of computers among these pastors was education, a finding that was significant at the .02 level using the Pearson Chi-Square test. Of those pastors with less than a master's degree, 71% (10 of 14) did not use a computer. Among the other pastors, only 17% (8 of 48) did not.

Besides cost, which was really only a reason for not *currently* using a computer, the reasons given for refusing a computer were more matters of personal preference than anything. One pastor, whose wife was a systems analyst and who had only a rather ancient manual typewriter on his desk, de-

clared: "You will never see me with one of those [computers].
I like things simpler than that." Another minister, who had a
rather dusty-looking Commodore computer in the corner hooked
to a portable television set, said: "Oh, that's just to keep my kids
happy if they are over here with me when I study. I'm not a
computer person. I would just as soon use a book."

This preference for print was also expressed by three
other pastors. One older pastor admitted somewhat sheepishly:
"We have this big, fancy computer at home, which I bought for
my children, because I really don't know how to use it. I'm
ashamed of this, but I'm computer illiterate." Another was quite
proud of his refusal. When asked if he used a computer, this
pastor, who had talked fondly of his earlier profession as a
librarian working with an 18th-century theological archive,
responded, "Oh, no. Never. Remember, I'm 18th century."
Part of these pastors' lack of use of computers may also be
related to the oral bias that many clergy bring to their profession
(see Chapter 4).

Not all of the pastors who refused to use computers were
anti-computer. One minister had encouraged his support staff to
use them, but he did not want to learn. As he explained, "I
guess I'm the old schooler, but I just find myself more comfortable writing things out long-hand. My staff keeps trying to teach
the old dog new tricks, but..." For several pastors, the issues of
convenience and comfort were the stated reasons: "[The com-
puter] is just not where I usually am when I'm working on a
sermon." Another had made a concerted effort to try to learn to
use his secretary's computer but gave up "mostly out of fear."
When asked for an explanation, he replied:

> Back in 1988 [my secretary] tried to teach me to
> use it. I got started on it, and one day I was
> working on it by myself without her. I did
> some commands, and it didn't do what I thought

it was supposed to do. So I got mad and walked away, and I haven't sat down at one since.

However, the overwhelming majority of the pastors in this study used a computer. Most were owned by the church, though a few either brought their own into the office or were given one by a generous church member. The use that these pastors made of their computers was of two basic types.

On one hand, the computer was used simply as a sophisticated word processor that allowed pastors to compose their sermons more efficiently. In the strictest sense, this use does not treat the computer as an information-gathering tool since it does not include the use of computer databases as sources of information. One older pastor's comments typified this use:

> I went to a seminar several years ago for ministers with long pastorates. Of the 21 who attended, there were only two of us who did not use a computer. So, I immediately purchased one when I came home from that seminar, and I just love it. It allows me to sit down and type my sermons and get them just like I want them. I can do spell-check. I can move blocks of text around. I can use the thesaurus right there on the computer. I can stare at my sermon on the screen and get every word just right before I print it out.

Most ministers mentioned this word-processing ability for sermon preparation as the major reason why they used computers. Not only did the computer allow them to compose more efficiently, it also allowed them to store their sermons in a more organized manner on disk (floppy and hard) for later retrieval and use.

On the other hand, the computer was also used as a means of gathering information in new ways by using purchased or self-created databases. The self-created databases were usually versions of electronic filing programs that allowed the pastor to access pertinent data about the church's members. In some ways this use of computers merely resembled a sophisticated Rolodex, but in other ways the data were able to be combined and new information acquired that was not feasible without automation. Membership interest inventories that could be combined with attendance records, giving statements, and demographic data was one example of this level of sophisticated filing and searching.

Seven churches had even networked the personal computers in their offices so that pastors and secretaries could share data instantaneously. One large church required all their pastors to be able to type "at least 50 words per minute" because each pastoral office had a computer that they were expected to use and also because the secretaries "do not type for people; they are project managers."

The purchased databases were of two types. The first type of off-the-shelf databases were Biblical in content. The most common example was a computer program that included all of the English text of the Bible with automated indexing features. Many versions also contained such supplementary data as the Greek and the Hebrew testaments, Greek and Hebrew lexica, and automated versions of older commentaries and concordances. One pastor, who was the editor of a computer newsletter for ministers had even helped write some of these kinds of programs. The impact of these Biblical databases on ministers' information-gathering habits was evident in several areas.

For example, the use of a Biblical database sometimes influenced how pastors used Scripture in their preaching. When one pastor was asked why he used the New International Version

of the Bible in his preaching, he simply said, "Because that's
what I have on my computer." When another was asked about
his frequent use of Biblical quotations in preaching, he acknowledged that he did that more than he used to since he got a
computer program because that database allowed him to search
the Scriptures for verses relevant to his topic and "easily download those into my sermon manuscript." Another pastor, who
had a set of Biblical reference works on computer--concordances,
commentaries, theological dictionaries--talked about the
computer's impact in these terms:

> It has made my sermon preparation so much
> easier. It's just like anything else in that I used
> to become careless in looking things up, and
> after three or four hours of looking for stuff I
> would just get too tired to do it like I should.
> But now my research is so much more because
> I have all this stuff at my fingertips. It is a lot
> easier than trying to remember, "Well, what
> book was that in?"

His reference to more efficient "research" raises the second use
of computers for these ministers, that involving non-Biblical
commercial databases.

The second type of commercial databases, in addition to
the Biblically based ones used by these pastors, was also
religious in nature. The most prominent one mentioned was
InfoSearch, used by five of the pastors in this study.

InfoSearch is a database manager program produced by
the same publishing house that publishes *Current Thoughts &
Trends*. The program accesses four different databases: one on
humorous illustrations for preaching and teaching, one on general sermon illustrations, one on hymns (complete with musical
accompaniment of the melody), and the automated version of

Current Thoughts & Trends. All four databases allow for Boolean searching and downloading into a variety of word-processing programs. Most of the items indexed in these four databases contain bibliographic citations and copyright notices.

Another commercial religious database used by at least one pastor in this town was the CD-ROM version of *Religion Index*, produced by the American Theological Library Association. This database was owned by a local university library, where a pastor doing research for his Doctor of Ministry project had used it.

One of the more sophisticated uses of the computer to gather information was found in an interview with a pastor also working on a Doctor of Ministry degree. When asked about his use of a local university library, he responded negatively, citing the problem of finding parking. He continued:

> Actually, I haven't needed to go there lately because I just call them up on my computer. I can access them through my modem. It's a local call so I can be on the line as long as I need to. And they've updated their computer system so I can look for articles as well as books. Even the local public library is on computer so I can access that as well. It's gotten to the point for me where if a library is not on a computerized system, it is very difficult to use. It's just so much easier to sit here at my computer and do searches. And it's so much quicker. You can do two, three, or four searches at the same time. For instance, one subject I wanted to do for my doctoral work was congregational health, so I just plugged in both names in the subject search, and it eliminated so much junk that I didn't want.

While this pastor's information retrieval techniques may not have been as sophisticated as traditional information professionals', his use of the computer to access university library databases was the most advanced use of the computer encountered in this study. It was no wonder that his closing remark to me was "I'd be lost without my computer." This focus on immediate access that the computer provides was also an important aspect for the next source of information mentioned by pastors, their own libraries.

PERSONAL LIBRARIES

The pastor's own library was the highest-rated item on the written questionnaire, scoring a 4.63 out of 5 possible points. The 4.63 score also had the lowest standard deviation value (0.517) of any of the 25 items, indicating that ministers were fairly uniform in their high opinion of the value of their own libraries as information sources.

This was not the case when asked about their use of other, institutional libraries. The use of institutional libraries by these pastors rated only a 3.03 on the written questionnaire, above the median but lower than all but nine other items of the twenty-five on the list (see Table 2 above). Ministerial use of the institutional libraries in the community, which included a public and two academic libraries, will be discussed after evaluating these pastors' use of their own personal libraries.

Not surprisingly, the single biggest reason given by these clergy for using their own personal libraries was access, as Soper (1976) also noted in her study of academic professionals. This was mentioned by several of those interviewed, but it was made most clear by this pastor:

When I'm researching some topic for a sermon

or whatever, I immerse myself in reading. And
I don't want to have to go and hunt for it. I
want it right there. So, you know, if I died and
went to heaven, where heaven would be, I'd be
in the middle of a library. And the stuff I
needed would all be there right at my finger-
tips.... So a lot of journals that I subscribe to,
for instance, even though I might not get everything read in them, I know that the articles are
there if I need them. I know I've got them on
my shelves and I can just reach up and get them.

This instant access was demonstrated by more than one
pastor during the interviews. When asked, for example, about
their church's position on a certain issue, two pastors reached for
official church policy manuals that were shelved next to their
desks. One pastor, in response to several critical incident
questions about his provision of information on certain occasions, repeatedly reached for books on his shelves to show where
he had gone to answer each question.

In many cases the pastors kept only a "core collection"
of ready-reference tools (Bible, commentaries, counseling books,
exegetical or lectionary aids) in their office, with the bulk of
their personal libraries housed at home. As one explained, "This
is an office. My study is at home. I can't do any reading here.
This is Grand Central Station so most of my books are at home."
There was something of that sentiment, as well as an emphasis
on access, in the comment of the minister who, when asked if he
ever visited other libraries in town, replied: "No. My library is
at the house."

This multi-site nature of ministerial libraries was one
reason why it was not possible to provide an accurate count of
the size of ministerial libraries in this community. A mean count
of 727 books per library was based solely on linear shelf space

and included only books in the pastor's church office.

There were also seven pastors whose libraries were quite substantial, numbering anywhere from 2,000 to 10,000 volumes. Somewhat surprisingly, there were few commonalities to these pastors. They were old, young, highly educated, not highly educated, long-term pastors, and short-term pastors. The only common thread was the size of church, i.e. pastors at larger churches had larger libraries. This correlation may be indicative of the larger salaries typically paid these pastors, which in turn provided them the economic means to build large, private collections. The lack of other common factors serves to further underscore the diversity of this group of information gatherers.

Another reason for not being able to provide a comprehensive measure of the size of these ministers' libraries was that most pastors said they were not able to estimate the total number of items they owned, partly because their collections were so varied--books, pamphlets, journals, individual articles, audiocassettes, videocassettes, and photocopied items--and partly because many had either boxed up items or loaned so many that had never been returned that they weren't sure what was actually on their shelves.

At least five pastors mentioned that they had recently begun to give away parts of their collections because "I just don't use them anymore" or because "my books were becoming too much a source of pride." On a slightly different note, one pastor, when asked the size of her library, merely said "hundreds," then glancing around at the few books in her office, continued: "This is just to let them know I have brains."

The primary use that the pastors in this study made of their libraries was either for sermon preparation or for counseling. My observation of their office libraries confirmed that the composition of these collections was mostly Biblical study aids for sermons and books on counseling. There was also evidence, to be sure, of some of the individual variety that was discussed in the sections on book and magazine reading.

Sometimes the stated rationale for using their personal collections was less focused: "I have quite an extensive library, both books and tapes in my office and at my home, that I use just to kind of stir myself a little bit." When asked about her use of other libraries in the community, one pastor said that she had never felt a need because she felt her own library provided her with the information she needed to function in her profession, but she also added, "And besides we have a decent church library that I can always use."

This comment about the pastor's use of the local church library was conspicuous by its rarity. Only five other pastors even mentioned that their church had its own library. Of those five, one "apologized" for its meager holdings. Two spoke well of their church's collection, but admitted that they rarely used it. Two others both spoke well of them and cited instances of using them. One of these two noted that when he referred to a book in his sermon that he knew was available in the church library, he mentioned that fact in his message. He also mentioned that the volunteer director of the church library, a retired university librarian, sometimes created a display of books on topics on which he was preaching.

While I did not investigate every church to see if it had a library--usually because of time--of the thirty-two where I did inquire, about half did and half did not. Among the half that did, I found only six that consisted of more than a few hundred "donated" works and that showed evidence of regular use. All of these six also collected children's works and videocassettes as well. In two other cases, churches had "replaced" their libraries with bookstores. An interview with one of the bookstore managers suggested that the "upscale" members of his congregation would rather "own" a book than borrow it. The pastor at the other church mentioned that all of the pastors on his staff took turns trying to read new items in their bookstore and "share" that information with their congregation.

Overall, however, ministerial use of church libraries was extremely limited. The pastors in this community, if they used any library other than their own personal collection, were much more likely to use one of the three institutional libraries in the area that were available to them.

INSTITUTIONAL LIBRARIES

While not a single pastor in this study denied regular use of his or her own personal library, fifteen of those interviewed said they did not use any of the institutional libraries in the community. The data from the written questionnaire highlight this contrast even more: forty rated their personal libraries at a 5 score, only seven did so for other libraries. The "other libraries" in this community consisted of a public library (228,000 items with annual circulations of 950,000), as well as two university libraries with combined holdings of nearly two million items--both of which were also open to the ministers in town and one of which had a very respectable religion collection.

Before examining how and why pastors used other libraries, the non-users will be dealt with briefly. Of the fifteen who expressed no use of institutional libraries, nine cited reasons of "no need" or "no time." While these could be two separate motivations for non-use, the context usually indicated that these ministers were, as one said, "just not interested in going there."

There was no demographically related variable to explain these pastors' lack of library use. Non-users were found among the older and younger, the more and the less experienced, those with college education and those without, and among theologically liberal and conservative ministers. This latter finding is not consistent with the earlier research by Porcella (1973), who found that "doctrinal viewpoint is clearly the most important of the independent variables for predicting use of libraries" (p. 67). This inconsistency may be due to the smaller size of the group in this study, the change of locale, changes in the ministry over time, or to some other unknown factor.

Of the six remaining non-users of institutional libraries, two who were new to the area expressed an interest in doing so. They just had not yet become users. The other four evidently had been users at one time, but quit for personal reasons ranging from "too noisy" to anger, i.e. one pastor had stopped using an academic library because they had "mistakenly" charged him for an overdue book and that had made him mad. One even offered this rationale: "I haven't read everything in *my* library yet."

Among the majority of ministers who were library users, three major reasons for visiting institutional libraries were given. First, the library was used as "a quiet place of refuge" to which pastors could retreat regularly from their busy offices. One minister "guarded" one day a week as library time so he could get away from the church building to think and read reflectively. Another was going to increase his library visits to two days a week so he could "get more done."

> I like to have most of my day at the library free
> to just read in a broad way. Actually, it's kind
> of a retreat day. It's a quiet day. I really enjoy
> it. I feel it's beneficial to me, and I hope it's
> beneficial to my congregation in the long run.
> I'm thinking of taking another day and protect-
> ing that too because it is good for my soul and
> good for my body.

In some ways, this use of the library is more geographic than substantive. In fact, one fairly well-known pastor in the community who used to use one of the academic libraries in this manner had now shifted to the campus computer lab because "not as many people know me there so I'm not interrupted as much." Yet, the reflective, meditative aspects of library use are not outside the scope of traditional library service either. This use of the library as a private retreat also provides evidence of the highly internalized nature of information acquisition among these clergy, a feature discussed by Dervin and Nilan (1986).

Second, the library was used as a source of general reading--either recreational or current events. "I love to sit and read the magazines when I drop my kids off for story hour," was how one pastor explained his use of the local public library. One of the two ministers in this study who had once been a professional librarian went to the library "just to browse." Another stopped in the public library "at least once a week to read the newspapers." One pastor, emphasizing her recreational use of the library, said she currently had "20 books checked out right now--pure junk."

Third, the library was used to meet a particular infor-mation need that a minister had. This use of the library also indicates not just why, but how, the pastors in this community used institutional libraries. When asked if he used the library, for example, one pastor replied:

> Oh, yes.   And I'm not just saying that because
> you're a librarian. I really do use it, at least
> once a week. Recently, I was doing some read-
> ing on the Amish, for example, and I wanted to
> know more of their background, how they were
> related to the Mennonites in this community, and
> their connection to Apostolic Christians. So, I
> just went to the public library and they had

reference books there on religious groups.
Now, they won't let you check those out so I
had to read them there. And from that I got the
names of five or six authors and titles. I just
went to the bookstore then and ordered them.

He later stated that "if the library had an illustration library for
my sermons, I'd be in there every day." Actually, a number of
ministers used the library to gather sermon material. "Just last
week I was at the library because I needed some statistics about
labor for a sermon I was working on," was one example of this
kind of library use.

Another pastor had heard about a product that he wanted
to use as an object lesson in an upcoming sermon, so he called
the public library reference desk to see if they could provide him
with an address for the company. They did so, and he was
"thoroughly surprised." The following pastor, new to the
community, noted his use of the library for sermon preparation
in a slightly different manner:

I was just at the library. I had to look up some
data for a couple of sermons that I'm working
on. Actually, I just wanted to make sure the
information I had was correct information.
When you're using illustrations, you want to
make sure.... Let me put it this way, we have
a lot of college-trained people in this church
who do a lot of reading and that type of thing.
That's a lot different than my former church.
They didn't read anything.

For him, the library was used not just as a means to gather new
information, but as a resource for corroborating known data.

Other ways in which pastors used the library to meet

specific information needs were often bibliographically related. One had viewed a video on sexual abuse which had referred to a particular book. He went to the public library to see if they had it for checkout, which they did. Another used the public library as an interlibrary loan channel for obtaining titles related to his Doctor of Ministry project. One pastor who had written several books on ministering to youth had frequently visited the state university library specializing in education to follow up bibliographic references he had seen in the books in his own library. Six pastors made specific mention of the "wonderful religion collection" at the private academic library. Explained one such pastor:

> Generally, what I do is take the lectionary along with me to [named this academic library]. I'll go through their religion books looking for material that I can use to preach those texts, commentaries and that sort of thing. They also have a good theological section at their library. Sometimes I'll just find things there that I wasn't looking for like the book I'm reading now on the Apostles' Creed.

Serendipity evidently also played a role in ministerial use of institutional libraries. Incidents of known-item searching, however, were mentioned much more often by these pastors. The pastor with computer access through his own modem to two of the three libraries in town gave examples of both subject and author searching, commenting that he often "felt like a detective" trying to find the particular work he wanted. One used the public library to read those titles he was interested in, but which he did not wish to purchase "until they come out in paperback."

Finally, one pastor who admitted to being an infrequent library user noted again the two tensions felt by these pastors in gathering information. When asked if he had "any opportunity to use the libraries in town," he replied somewhat frustrated:

> Opportunity? I have opportunity to use them,
> but I don't very much. Time is a factor, I
> suppose. Actually, I'm a people-oriented
> person. I love people. One of the tensions I
> work with is pulling away from people. I want
> to spend more time in the library. So one of my
> goals this year is to get together some men in
> the church and help equip them to minister to
> and with more people so I won't have to spend
> all my time with people.

This tension over "paper and people" and the pastor's professional inclination toward the latter underscores the importance of looking at the information-gathering behavior of the pastor from the standpoint of both formal and informal channels.

While formal channels were rated quite highly by these clergy, that is only part of the picture of how they gathered information. For these pastors, who tended to display a professional bias toward oral media (see Chapter 4), informal channels were also highly used. Though the formal channels of books, periodicals, audiovisuals, computer databases, and libraries were significantly used as information sources, informal channels were even more noted as information sources by the pastors in this study.

Informal Channels

The pastor who described himself as an "information junkie," with over 10,000 volumes in his personal library and with subscriptions to 101 periodicals, was just as dependent upon people as paper in providing him with the information he needed. This became clear listening to him describe where he found source material for his preaching:

> You know, I am always amazed at colleagues
> that can talk about their own personal experi-
> ences in their sermons. Now, on one level I
> don't think my life is boring, but I don't seem to
> have some of the great moving experiences that
> other people do. You know, I was at a meeting
> last week, and a guy talked about an airplane
> ride that he had had with somebody. How this
> woman had just been a refugee and was coming
> over to this country. How he took that story
> and just tied it in with his whole theme.
> Amazing. Now Bill lives and dies for preach-
> ing, so he really has the gift for doing this kind
> of thing. I don't. So, I depend on the Bills in
> my life who can share that kind of thing with
> me. And I will go ahead and share that with
> others, you know.

"Depending on the Bills in one's life" is an apt description of
how many of the pastors in this study relied upon personal, informal sources of information in their profession.

By "informal" is meant those channels of information
that are people oriented. Unlike formal sources, they are not
documentable in the sense that one can copyright or publish or
sell the information they provide, as one could with a book or
periodical or audiocassette or computer database. While there is
no precise definition of what constitutes an informal source, the
focus on a personal interchange with other individuals was a
distinguishing characteristic used in this study. In that regard,
such "informal" channels as prayer and divine revelation--though
cited in this study--are not included in this discussion.

The categories chosen at the beginning of this study were

those six informal sources listed on the written questionnaire: church members, local ministers, associate or co-ministers, denominational colleagues, church meetings, and denominational meetings. These six sources were given a composite rating of 3.75, significantly higher than the 2.83 rating given to the formal channels of print and audiovisual sources (see Table 2 above). In fact, the second highest rating of all 25 items on the questionnaire was given to members in the minister's own church (at 4.41). Only the pastor's personal library rated higher (at 4.63). These six sources were supplemented by questions and comments raised during the interview process.

The data from the interviews suggest that these pastors tended to classify informal sources into one of three categories: professional conferences, ministerial associations, and other personal networks. Though these are my categories, not theirs, they are useful labels for describing the kinds of informal sources that these ministers utilized. They are certainly representative of the major types of informal sources that the pastors mentioned during the interviews.

PROFESSIONAL CONFERENCES

Professional conferences are treated in this study as informal sources of information, even though in other professions they are treated formally (see, for example, Pandit, 1992). The reason for treating them informally here is because of the nature of such conferences among clergy. Unlike conferences among many other professional groups, ministerial conferences do not typically include the formal reading of papers which are later published in book or article form. Nor are formal "research projects" discussed as a means of disseminating cutting-edge information. Only one of the professional conferences mentioned by the ministers in this study included the reading of formal papers. Though this particular pastor had read "an exegetical paper" at one such conference, it could not be described as research-oriented nor was it subsequently published.

Instead, the professional conferences cited in this study usually focused as much on inspiration as information. This is not to imply that such conferences were not informative. Quite the contrary, leading theological educators and professional practitioners in the country were often on the program of the conferences cited, and the lectures they delivered were found by many to be very helpful in giving these pastors professionally relevant information. Yet, the lectures were often in the context of a worship service, and much of the information interchange that these pastors talked about took place outside the lecture hall in informal meetings and question-and-answer sessions.

The nature of the professional conferences mentioned in this study were quite varied, although most had a ministerial focus. Conferences on church growth from Fuller Theological Seminary were the most frequently mentioned, followed closely by conferences on preaching and counseling issues. Most were sponsored either by theological seminaries or by denominational headquarters, but others were under the auspices of such organizations as the ecumenically based Alban Institute of Washington, D.C., or the evangelically oriented Foundation for Biblical Inerrancy, also of Washington, D.C., or professional associations, such as one for campus ministers and another for youth ministers. A few were sponsored by local health professionals or academic institutions. The pastors in this study cited such topics as clergy malpractice, sexual abuse, alcoholism, death and dying, and professional self-esteem as representative of the content of the professional conferences they had attended.

The importance of professional conferences as informal sources of information may be found in one surprising statistic: only seven of the sixty-two ministers interviewed in this study said they did not attend them. And of these seven, four had only temporarily suspended their attendance because of the cost and time involved in their current Doctor of Ministry programs. The only other reasons given by ministers for not attending professional conferences were cost and time.

The reasons given for attending such conferences were many. For some, the ostensible reason was that attendance at professional conferences was required by the denomination. As one said, "It's expected of us to keep our ministry alive." For others, including those who also gave "required" as the reason, the motive for attending professional conferences centered on two issues: the informal manner in which the information was shared (rubbing shoulders with experts and peers) and the quality of the information presented. One pastor related the following incident as a means of explaining these twin values that he attached to professional conferences:

> I go to conferences, partly because it's a break and there are lots of times when you just need a break, physically and emotionally. But more importantly I feel that if we are striving for excellence, we need to be with peers who are excellent in what they are doing. That's inspirational, motivational. You are learning from them how they got to where they got. Or how you can become better at what you're doing. I don't have a big conference budget, so I try to stay with nationally held conferences that are going to have prominent persons there.
>
> I remember a couple of years ago during a budget meeting someone brought up the question of why the pastor gets so much for his conventions. My response was that I knew that these particular conferences were the ones where the top people were at. That's the kind of

shoulders I want to rub. Those are the kind of
people I want to be with and listen to. We had
one young fellow on the board who is a respected professional at one of the big companies
here in town. He finally stood up and said, "I
think we should give Pastor this allowance.
What we've budgeted for him, I'll spend in
three months at my professional conferences."
That's all he needed to say. There hasn't been
any criticism since.

For him, the need for informal, quality information in the
ministerial profession was closely akin to similar needs that his
church members recognized and approved of in the business
profession. This blend between informality and quality is also
evident in the following comments by another pastor:

Well, the primary reason I go to conferences is
either to gain new knowledge or a new skill.
The relational thing of sharing with others
personally is the other reason. Of the ones I
could attend I try to choose those that I think
will combine those two. For instance, I attend
[named a conference] because I can have both
the relational interaction as well as the
knowledge base. I usually go to these conferences with the hope of picking up other ideas
and bibliographic data. I also get to interact
with other ministers.

For some the quality of the information is more telling.
One pastor said that the material presented at professional
conferences was "the single most important source of information" for him. For him, attendance was not even the key issue
since much of his material was gathered by listening to tapes of
professional conferences "at least two hours a day." For

another, attendance helped him focus on the quality of the information. The essence of his argument for preferring conferences to reading books was that he could ask questions and dialog on what he was learning at the conference, but that he could not do that with a book.

For still another, attendance was absolutely crucial because it was the way in which the information was presented that added to its value:

> I go to a lot of conferences. I feel like workshops, seminars, and conferences are probably some of the best tools for information that a pastor has because instead of just information there is motivation and inspiration. And I can leave a conference just pumped up and ready to put into action what information's been given at that point. I'm going to one this month as a matter of fact. It's on dysfunctional families.

The focus on people over paper is evident in his remarks. He, like many of the pastors in this study, desired the personal touch in information gathering. The way in which the information was presented was just as significant to him as the information itself.

This focus on the informal is at this point very reminiscent of the concept of information as process, not merely product (see discussion in Appendix). The information acquired at professional conferences was, for most of these pastors, just as dependent upon the process they went through to acquire it as it was upon the actual data they obtained. As one minister summarized it: "If all I wanted was content only, I could just order the cassettes and listen to them. But there is so much more going on that that just doesn't touch."

MINISTERIAL ASSOCIATIONS

This pastoral focus on people-oriented informal sources was also evidenced in the frequent mention of these pastors' participation in local ministerial associations. Only nine of the sixty-two ministers interviewed were, by choice, not members of some type of ministerial association, and two of them talked at some length about how "lonely" their profession was when discussing this issue.

Seven different local ministerial associations were discovered during the course of this study, only two of which were widely known among the clergy in the community. The two that were well known were an evangelical ministerial alliance and a county-wide clergy ministerial association. The former had about twenty-five evangelical pastors who met monthly for lunch and for "informal sharing of ideas." The latter was in some transition during the time of this study. Before discussing these two larger groups, the other five will be briefly mentioned.

The other five ministerial associations in the community were much smaller in scale and focus than the two groups mentioned above. Three of these were the "book review" groups mentioned earlier in this chapter, of which two were denominationally oriented. A fourth group of ministers who met regularly in the area also had a denominational membership, but did not meet to review books. Instead, they met to "improve ministerial skills" by such methods as peer review of members' sermons and inviting other professionals (such as pastoral counselors) to talk about their role in the ministry. The fifth group was composed of the black ministers in the area, though not all of the black pastors attended. In fact, none of the three full-time black ministers interviewed in this study seemed to know much about it other than its existence.

Of the two larger ministerial groups, the most controversial and difficult to study was the county-wide clergy
ministerial association. The controversy and difficulty were
evident in two ways. First, five different names were given to
this association by the clergy supposedly involved in it. Second,
the interviews revealed that some pastors thought it had "died,"
others thought it had been "revived," and still others didn't know
if it was currently functioning or not. Only five pastors were
interviewed who said it was still operating and that they were
fairly regular attenders--two of those five were current officers.

Reasons cited for the "death" or "low profile" of this
ministerial association were its "theological liberalism" (cited by
some evangelical pastors), its lack of professional focus ("a
theological dog-and-pony show"), the nature of some of the
churches ("They're too competitive for this kind of cooperation"), and its inability to impact the community ("They didn't
deal with real community issues").

Unfortunately, the time frame for this study did not
permit further study of why this particular ministerial association, which met only quarterly, occasioned such diverse
opinions. It was learned that the association's current expression
was the result of a recent merger with one of the local hospital's
chaplaincy groups. The topic of discussion, for example, at a
recent meeting to which members of the local medical profession
had been invited concerned the question of whether the physician
or the pastor should inform dying patients that they were
terminally ill. There were mixed opinions among both groups
of professionals.

The evangelical ministerial alliance was much more
active in this community, but only within the last few years.
One of the officers of this group was of the opinion that "God
called me to this town to help bring pastors together." In fact,
this pastor was not only actively involved with the monthly

alliance meeting of ministers, but also participated in a very informal mentoring program for area pastors which will be discussed more in the last section of this chapter. Though I was not able to attend any of the meetings of this group, the participants that I interviewed had uniformly positive opinions of its value as an informal source of information.

The informational role of this ministerial association was clear in an incident related by the following pastor. When asked what books, if any, he was reading, he replied that he just didn't have time to read. Since he seemed genuinely "down" about that, I suggested that perhaps he had learned other ways of getting the information he needed. His response:

> That's interesting that you should say that. Just last week I was at our evangelical ministerial meeting. We always take the time to go around the room to see if anyone has any questions to ask or things to share. And I said that our church was in the process of relocating and that we could really use some help in knowing how to go about that. I even asked them if anyone there knew of any books on the topic that I could read. Well, none of the ministers there knew of any, but one spoke up and said that he knew of a minister friend who had just gone through relocation so he gave me his name to call. Then another said that they knew of a minister in town who had just relocated. I later talked to him, and he was very helpful in sharing the experiences they had had. So I was able to get a number of personal contacts that I could just sit down and talk to.

"Just sitting down and talking to" another person was found to be a major part of the information-gathering behavior of the ministers in this study, and a finding not unlike what some have suggested for the future of one of the traditional information professions, the field of library and information science (cf. Lancaster, 1990).

PERSONAL NETWORKS

When asked if he was a member of any ministerial associations, one minister who pastored a congregation belonging to a somewhat separatist religious group, whose members frowned on such affiliations, responded that he was not. He added, however, that he had begun "building my own personal network" with two local ministers.

Another pastor, in response to my question about his attendance at professional conferences, related that there weren't any in his special area of expertise (ministering to the "baby bust" generation of twenty-something-year-olds) so he had called a few professional colleagues "just to see if we could get together and talk about common concerns." These were only two of the many examples that the clergy in this community cited concerning their need and desire for personal networks.

One pastor who did not experience such networking locally wondered why it seemed to be so absent among the ministers in the community, adding that "I make up for it by spending time on the phone with distant colleagues." However, her experience was not typical. In fact, most all of the pastors in this study noted some form of personal networking, both with ministerial colleagues and with others, usually church members. This preference is not surprising given the oral bias that seems characteristic of the pastoral profession. The importance of these personal contacts is underscored by the results of the written questionnaire, which ranked all such informal sources well above the median score of 3 (see Table 2 above).

The most highly ranked personal network sources were church members (at 4.41) and other ministers on staff (at 4.29). Church members were often mentioned in the context either of discovering "news" information (who was in the hospital, who had had a baby, who was moving into the parish) or of preparing sermons ("I often use what my people say in my sermons"; "people sometimes give me articles that I get sermon ideas from"). The growing use of church-based support groups found in this study was another indication of the emphasis that the churches, not just the clergy, in this community placed on the value of personal networks.

On a clergy-to-clergy level, contacts with other ministers were the most frequently cited type of personal network. This often involved co-pastors on staff. However, nearly half (30) of the 62 respondents were solo pastors so such opportunities were non-existent for them. For them, as for most ministers in this study, the building of personal relationships with other pastors, local and distant, was mentioned frequently. One pastor, who had developed a collegial relationship with several other pastors in the state, spoke of how helpful their regular meetings had been, "holed up in a hotel somewhere" for professional interchange. He spoke in the past tense because, "My network has now all moved, and I miss them." Though a primary purpose of these networks was "fellowship," other reasons of a more direct informational nature were also observed or stated.

In four cases, for example, pastors had developed contacts with colleagues who were more computer literate than they in order to receive assistance in using their own computers in ministry. One was on the phone with his informal contact, a minister across town, when I arrived for the interview because he couldn't get his software to boot. Another was on his way to a "computer whiz" friend after the interview so he could get help on a new program he had just purchased.

Besides information on computers, counseling was another area mentioned frequently as a catalyst for using personal networks. One of the directors of a local pastoral counseling agency stressed this importance of networking when counseling. He always encouraged pastors who were doing a lot of counseling to enter into a personal relationship with someone more experienced so that they could "talk through things professionally."

In the earlier discussion of the pastor as equipper/ reference librarian, mention was made of the pastor who often phoned local contacts to help him with counseling cases. The presence in this community of a 24-hour telephone information referral center was also noted as an informal source by several ministers. Interviews with the two directors of this agency confirmed that clergy often called them to find out where to direct certain potential counselees. People in the community also sometimes used it to establish a personal contact with clergy. The day before my interview with the directors of this agency, for example, a man had called wanting to "talk to a gay priest."

In fact, the phone was frequently mentioned by several of the pastors in this study as an information-gathering device when using informal sources. One had called the airport to find out what "attitude" meant as an aviation term while doing research in that area. Another had called all of his campus minister colleagues when his parish membership had dropped off to see if they had noticed a similar decrease and how they had handled it. One pastor noted that he did "a lot of counseling over the phone," but that was more in an information-provision role than an information-gathering role.

Often the type of information desired when personal networks were used was related to the pastor's preaching role. "I often call my Dad, who's a preacher, to talk about a sermon I'm working on," was one example of this use of personal net-

working. Another pastor was delighted that a retired seminary
professor of preaching was considering joining his church
because then he "could pick his brain" about homiletical issues.
One younger minister said he always spent some time each week
talking to his church members at their places of work so that he
could set his sermons in a more accurate context. An older
pastor had surveyed his congregation informally at one point to
see what topics they wanted him to preach on. One submitted
copies of his sermons to minister friends for their comments so
he could "improve my preaching."

     One of the somewhat surprising findings in this study
was the increasing use of the mentoring model as an expression
of personal networking among ministers. Six of the sixty-two
pastors mentioned their participation in a mentoring partnership
with either older or younger pastors. One campus minister had
just set up a mentoring program at one of the universities for
young black men, using area ministers and church members as
mentors. One of the participants in this study was mentoring a
black student in this program, but they had just begun and he
had little to share about the experience. Another pastor talked
nostalgically about a minister from Virginia who had mentored
him early in his ministry. One minister, frustrated with the slow
growth of his church's membership, spoke of how helpful an
area pastor had been in these terms:

> [Named his name] is a friend of mine. He and
> I talk a lot. He's almost been kind of a--I don't
> want to use the word savior--but he has been a
> mentor to me. He knows what I'm going
> through.

     The importance of mentoring and of building personal
networks for pastoral professionals was highlighted during a
conversation with the following minister. As a middle-aged
minister somewhat new to the area, he had been frustrated that

other means of developing personal networks had not developed for him. He then talked of the need for mentoring among ministers if they were to function fully as professionals:

> When I moved here I was really looking forward to becoming an active member of the county ministerial association. I have been disappointed in that this group is really struggling to the point where we're in the middle of trying to find out if there's any life left in it. There is a cluster of my denomination's ministers that try to get together once a month, and I meet with them.
>
> There is also another group. I am kind of the mentor for two younger pastors in the area. This is their first pastorate out of seminary, and I meet with them regularly. We form a resource group, and that's probably the most important group to me.
>
> Our denomination was finding that new graduates were going out to churches and just being eaten up in their first pastorates. Church members' expectations are so much higher now, even than when I began pastoring. It's a professional society, and it's tough on new ministers. People are used to experienced professionals. The mentoring model is desperately needed now.

Echoing the need for ministerial mentors was another middle-aged pastor (five of the six pastors involved in mentoring were middle-aged; one was in his sixties) who was himself mentoring ten younger pastors. His rationale for his rather extensive involvement in this area was this:

The challenges and pressures for today's
minister are enormous. There is always [the
denominational headquarters], but these young
pastors need "front-line guys" who know personally what's going on. There are just so many
questions that a pastor has to wrestle with.
There are so many hats he has to wear. I'm
talking about philosophy of ministry and authority and the basic issues that churches are
struggling with. Whew!

This model of the minister as mentor was for the pastors
in this study an expression actually of their role not only as
information gatherer (what is going on with those they mentor),
but as information disseminator as well (how can I help them).
The personal touch was also quite pronounced in the pastor's
role of information dissemination, the subject of Chapter 4.

Summary

The focus on people over paper highlights the tension
that the pastors in this study faced in their role as information
gatherer. In this regard, the information-gathering behavior of
the clergy in this community was expressed in two ways:
through the use of such formal channels as books, periodicals,
audiovisuals, computers, and libraries, and through the more
informal channels of professional conferences, ministerial
associations, and other forms of personal networking.

The needs that precipitated their information-gathering
behavior may be viewed from four perspectives: point of origin
(self-generated or generated by others), utilitarian or instrumental
needs that were focused on a particular incident, current awareness needs that were not occasion-specific, and the perception of
information overload that characterized several of the pastors in

this study. The next chapter will look at what these pastors did as a result of their information gathering, the role of the pastor as information disseminator.

4. THE PASTOR AS INFORMATION DISSEMINATOR

In his 1964 Terry Lectures at Yale University on the role of religion in science and philosophy, Ong (1967) discussed three major communications media, each of which, he argued, has had a significant impact upon the way Christianity promulgates its message. These three are oral, print, and electronic media. In this study of pastors as information disseminators these three media are also important considerations in discussing how clergy communicate the information that they gather.

This chapter will look briefly at the influence these three media exercise upon pastors as disseminators of information before examining particular dissemination roles. The primary roles that will be examined in this chapter are those of the pastor as healer (counselor) and the pastor as herald (preacher). These two are highlighted because they were the ones most often mentioned by the pastors in this study. Four other, less-frequently cited roles will also be studied briefly, those of the pastor as teacher, writer, media personality, and community spokesperson.

The purpose of this introductory overview of the influences that media exercise over information dissemination in the ministry is not to cover exhaustively this large body of literature. Rather, the goal is to touch upon those salient features of print, electronic, and oral media that help explain the information dissemination process as observed in this particular study of pastors.

The Influence of Media in Ministers' Dissemination of Information

The interviews conducted with the clergy in this community, as well as a number of studies investigating the role of media in religious communication (e.g. Ong, 1967; Ellul, 1985; Postman, 1985; Fant, 1987), suggest that the way in which modern ministers disseminate information is influenced by the media they use. For example, Ong asserted strongly the natural bias of historic Christianity for the spoken word--"Faith comes by hearing" (Romans 10:17). However, he also noted the natural affinity of the ministry to electronic media. He included among these media the communication technologies of the telephone, the radio, the television, the cinema, and the computer (pp. 87-88). This affinity is a consequence, he argued, of the re-involvement of the senses in electronically based communications, particularly that of hearing, which was lost in print media.

Ellul, on the other hand, argued that only the oral is ultimately compatible with the Christian message and that the Church and the clergy "humiliate the spoken word" [small and capital "w"] when they utilize image-based electronic media. His rationale was that visual media present only distorted "reality" whereas oral media create a universal "truth" that is not limited to what the eye sees (p. 22). For Ellul, seeing is not believing in that such media as television not only often present a distorted view of reality, but they elevate the image over the real or true (cf. the irony, he suggested, of the phrase "pretty as a picture").

Postman differed from both Ong and Ellul in that he elevated print media over both oral and electronic ones, something they did not do. Though he wrote of the power of, and the rekindled need for, oral discourse in the public life of America, his focus was upon print. In his review of certain features of American history, Postman observed that this country "was dominated by a public discourse which took its form from the products of the printing press. For two centuries America declared its intentions, expressed its ideology, designed its laws, sold its products, created its literature and addressed its deities with black squiggles on white paper" (p. 63).

In a chapter on the ministry's use of electronic media, Postman (1985) denied that religious information could be conveyed correctly by electronic media, especially television. He based his argument on the inability of the television medium to be "sacralized."   What he meant was that television has no "sanctuary" in which the sacred may be separated from the secular.   A televised sermon, for example, may often be sandwiched between a fishing show and a rerun of a Sherlock Holmes movie.

Regardless of the futility of any of these arguments for or against one set of media over another,[22] the interviews with the pastors in this study indicated that many ministers exhibited a preference for one of these three media and that this preference exercised some influence on how they chose to disseminate information. The tension among these media for ministers appeared to be based on three realities.

First, most of these pastors were trained in seminary in a very print-oriented culture. As seminarians they read books, conducted library research, and wrote papers as part of their professional degree programs. Even the field-based Doctor of Ministry program that many of these ministers had either finished or were pursuing consisted primarily of print-based assignments--reading books and writing papers, as these pastors noted during the course of the interviews.

Second, these clergy ministered to congregations that were very electronically oriented, especially in the relatively affluent community in this study. Many of their parishioners watched television, viewed videos, or used computers every day.

Third, these pastors functioned professionally with communication patterns that were decidedly oral oriented. Nearly every pastor in this study delivered a weekly oral address, counseled people face-to-face, attended professional conferences to hear speakers and talk to colleagues, and otherwise engaged in oral modes of information dissemination. By contrast, print media were used primarily for information gathering, with very few pastors engaged in regular writing (except for preparation of sermon "notes" for oral dissemination). Electronic media were used even less, though the few who did were doing so in some creative and apparently successful ways. The next section will examine more closely how the pastors in this study interacted with these three media.

Print Media

Eisenstein (1979) has demonstrated the profound influences that print media have had upon the way people gather and disseminate information. Among the influential trends she noted were the rise of the library researcher, the spread of the solitary writer, and the popularity of the published author whose works could be read and critiqued.

These influences are also present in contemporary seminary education. Ministerial candidates are trained to use the library (the use of which is stressed in one of the thirteen criteria for accreditation by the Association of Theological Schools). Seminarians are also expected to write research and position papers, which are critiqued by peers and professors. While such oral modes of address as preaching are part of "skills" courses, there appears to be a print bias in seminary education, though further study is warranted to substantiate the degree to which this may be true. One pastor in this study noted this print emphasis negatively when he criticized the "book knowledge" that many seminary-educated pastors brought to the ministry.

Another fundamental factor in examining the print media utilized by pastors is the historical description of the Christian church as a people "of the book."[23] In this study, for example, frequent references to the printed text of Scripture in the sermons of these pastors was the most visible manifestation of this phenomenon. Of the 48 sermons I heard (39 in person, 2 on video, and 7 by tape) during the course of this project, the most-frequently cited source during preaching was the Bible (185 [33%] of the 552 source citations; see Table 8). It was often the case that pastors would begin their sermons by reading from the Bible ("Our text for today is...").

Theologically conservative ministers were especially prone not only to read long sections of Scripture during their sermons, but also to have the congregation follow along in their Bibles. One such pastor observed that his goal in preaching was to "stimulate people to do what the Bereans did and search the Scriptures" (a reference to Acts 17:11). On numerous occasions at these churches, I observed members of the congregation "following along" in their Bibles, whether the pastor had requested them to do so or not. These examples suggest that the prominence enjoyed by the "Written Word" was sufficient to overcome the otherwise oral bias of the sermon.

It was not surprising, then, to discover a preference for print media among many of the pastors in this study. It was surprising to find this preference limited almost exclusively to how pastors gathered information (note the pastor's comment cited earlier, "reading strengthens my ministry"), not to how they disseminated it.

The one noteworthy exception, besides the use of Scripture in preaching and the few pastors who were published authors (discussed at the end of this chapter) was the pastor whose sermon manuscripts, which were distributed at every service, read like published articles. The print media features he utilized included such devices as homophones (e.g. a play on the words "I'll" and "aisle" which made little sense orally), frequent citations of other sources, the consistent use of quotation marks which were not noted orally, and the use of complete citations for quoted materials, including publisher, date, and page number. Journal and book titles were even underlined. While two other pastors in this study distributed printed manuscripts of their sermons, none was as print-oriented as this pastor.

The only other major use of print media to disseminate information was the pastor's column in the church newsletter. I read more than fifty such articles, but they amounted to little more than either brief devotional "opinion pieces" or recounting of news items to keep the church informed of internal current events. On a few occasions, these columns were used to notify parishioners of new policies or of church board decisions, but these "published notices" were always supplemented with oral announcements.

The only prominent use of the church newsletter to disseminate information in any substantial way was the practice of a church which had called a "parish nurse" to assist in "holistic ministry." She wrote regular columns on health and wellness tips, e.g. how often to have one's blood pressure checked, the symptoms for mild depression, and how to start an exercise program. Overall, however, the only significant writing that these pastors did was by way of sermon preparation. Yet, the "oral" nature of these writings was very pronounced, as shall be shown below.

Several reasons were given by the pastors in this study for this lack of preference for print media in information dissemination. For some, the solitary nature of this form of media was not amenable to the people-oriented profession of ministry. Even the necessary "writing" of sermon preparation was a professional conundrum for this pastor, whose comments were also cited in Chapter 2 in a discussion of the pastor as wounded healer:

> I'm too much of a people person to like the time I have to spend by myself working on the sermon. I'd much rather be out there with the people than by myself reading and searching and studying. So, I still struggle with that aspect of ministry.

For others a professional preference for non-print media sometimes combined with a personal proclivity that was often ambiguous. For example, one pastor loved to read, but hated to write. For him preparation, not publication, was a driving force in his use of print media, unless the "publication" was oral.

> Writing is very difficult for me, because part of my personality temperament is that I can never get it well enough prepared and get it done well enough. So you constantly postpone or pro-crastinate or you read more to get ready. My writing is geared more toward research projects and not books. I can head up research teams [for my denomination], create documents, and do the research kind of stuff, but just the idea of writing the product doesn't appeal to me. It's not my gift. And preaching is no different. Now once my sermon is prepared and I'm in the pulpit, I thoroughly enjoy it, but that is a blood-sweat-and-tears process.

As with many pastors, print media were used by this minister to gather information, but not to disseminate it. Several pastors noted a preference for print media in gathering information. As one observed when asked if he would rather read a book or attend a conference on the same topic:

> I'd rather read a book. You can skim a book to get only what you need. You can scan the table of contents and read the first sentence of each paragraph without reading the whole thing and still get a good feel for the information in it. I like to write notes in the margin too and photocopy sections for my sermon file.

Another commented that he would rather "flip the pages" than "hit the F10 key" on his computer to search for the information he needed. Yet such comments were quite rare among the pastors in this study. Any preference for print media exhibited by these ministers was limited primarily to acquiring, not disseminating, information. And even this proclivity to print was tempered by a strong reliance upon more personal, informal sources of information, as was shown in Chapter 3.

My observation of these ministers suggests that printed forms of information dissemination were not highly used for at least three reasons. First, there were few professional incentives for using print media to disseminate information. For these ministers, it was "preach or perish," not "publish or perish." There were no local church boards nor denominational judicatories demanding that the pastor write as part of his or her job description, which was not true of oral forms of communication.

Second, dissemination of information in printed form was perceived as requiring more time than dissemination in oral form. Such print practices as multiple source citations, precise verbatim quotations, and peer review demanded a schedule that was rarely possible in ministry, given that oral dissemination was required on an almost daily basis.

Third, writing was a solitary discipline that did not fit the temperament of most pastors (cf. Oswald and Kroeger, 1988, whose research indicated that nearly two-thirds of pastors in America are extraverted). Even given the preference for print that some of these pastors displayed in their information-gathering habits, they still preferred to disseminate that information through non-print media. The need for "eye contact" and "audience participation" that was noted by these pastors in communicating what they found were features that simply were not possible using print media.

For example, one pastor noted the considerable "research" he did to prepare his sermons, using a number of books in his own library. Yet, he brought only a few written notes to the pulpit so that he could be "free to hear" the responses of his listeners and adjust his "written" sermon accordingly as he went. Without these oral reactions, he said, he could not "preach at all."

Electronic Media

Another form of media used by some of the pastors in this study was electronic. By this term is meant those media that utilize such modern communication technologies as the tele-vision, the cinema, and the computer (cf. Ong, 1967, pp. 87-88). A distinguishing characteristic of these media for this study is their visual orientation, combined with an emphasis on audio in the case of the former two especially (note also this distinction in the Fall 1982 issue of *Daedalus: Journal of the American Academy of Arts and Sciences* that was devoted to "Print Culture and Video Culture").

The focus here is primarily upon television, not so much the computer, as an example of electronic media. The body of literature on the influences electronic media, especially television, exercise in the communication of information is quite large, beginning with McLuhan (1962). This discussion is limited to only one instance of such influence in terms of how that influence was demonstrated among the pastors in this one community. Further research outside the scope of this study is needed to examine all of the relevant issues regarding electronic media.

For some of the pastors in this study the preference for electronic media was limited to information gathering, not dissemination, as was pointed out in Chapter 3. A number of pastors noted their need to watch television and movies, for example, because their parishioners were doing so, and, therefore, they needed to be able to "speak the same language." Some preferred televised news to news magazines because of "the time factor." Another pastor refused to use libraries that were not "computerized," a rare instance in this study of a marked preference for electronic media other than television.

However, for some of the pastors displaying a preference for electronic media, their use of such media was prominent in their role as information disseminators as well. In particular, there were four churches in this community who utilized electronic media rather extensively as a means of information dissemination. The case-study method was utilized at three of these four churches as a means of discerning the direct and indirect impact that the use of electronic media had on how these ministers disseminated information.

For one large church, the use of electronic media, particularly television as a medium, was quite indirect. The pastor's message was not televised nor disseminated in other electronic media, though he and every other pastor on staff used computers extensively in researching and preparing their weekly messages. Instead, the electronic "bias" of this congregation was felt most clearly in the overall ambience that characterized the communication methods of the Sunday morning worship service.

For instance, the newly constructed sanctuary of this church was decidedly non-traditional in architecture, built "to attract the baby-boomer generation" who grew up on television. Not only were there no stained glass windows, no pipe organ, and no large wooden pulpit, there were no hymn books, no pew Bibles, and no printed programs (save for a brief outline). The focus was clearly upon something other than print media.

In the place of print media were mood lighting, a so-phisticated sound system, and a fifty-foot screen onto which were projected the words of various hymns. The church library had been replaced by a bookstore featuring audiocassettes of the preacher's sermons and contemporary Christian video programs. Dramatic presentations, both live and on videotape, were featured in the worship service, and they were used not only as "entertainment," but to introduce the content of the morning message by touching on the same themes.

The one-hour service was divided into several short sections, much like a television program segmented by com-mercials. The sermons themselves were delivered in a style reminiscent of television news anchors--clearly enunciated, softly spoken, minimally gestured, read from a computer-generated script placed on a stage podium lit by high-powered spots.

For this pastor, the use of electronic media was quite indirect but nonetheless real in his manner of disseminating information. One of the phrases he kept repeating in describing his preaching style was "economy of words," as if to reinforce the time-sensitive nature of television. In fact, a distinguishing feature was this church's appeal to an audience raised on tele-vision. Five of the fifteen references to television in the forty-eight sermons observed in this study were by this one pastor, whose age marked him as a member of the "television generation." The information in the music, the drama, and the sermons was couched in the electronic terms and framework congenial to the "baby-boomer television generation" that came by the hundreds to this church's services.

At another church, roughly two-thirds the size of the church discussed above, the use of visually oriented electronic media was even more pronounced. This congregation, though a traditional Protestant denomination, had begun to experiment with newer forms of communication since the arrival several years earlier of a new senior pastor. Part of the transition was felt to be in keeping with the "high church liturgy" that characterized the congregation, since they were already "very visually oriented--vestments, banners, candles, live manger scenes in the sanctuary."

This church featured a musical nightclub for teenagers in the community, complete with a large-screen television for showing musical videos. Average attendance was running 600 young people per week, each of whom paid a fee to enter. The youth minister's office looked like an electronic showroom, complete with television, stereo, compact disc player, videocassette recorder, and computer. Several hundred videos used in various programs in the church sat on his shelf.

The pastors' offices were all equipped with computers which were on a local area network, and pastors were not hired unless they were computer literate. The computer program, InfoSearch, mentioned in Chapter 3, was used extensively by these pastors in sermon preparation. A new addition to the church building was being built, and part of the remodeling was to include video monitors at every entrance so that information about church events and programs could be conveyed in electronic format, complete with video snippets illustrating various church news items.

The visual orientation of the electronic media being used by this church was quite pronounced in discussions with three of the church's five pastors. One associate pastor had just presented a dramatic monologue in full costume the Sunday prior to the interview, and had, in fact, been hired because of her expertise in drama. The senior pastor, who had given a similar dramatic presentation that I had not been able to observe, when asked for an audio recording of his sermon, replied, "Well, it wouldn't mean much unless you can see it." A third pastor had originated the Christian nightclub for teenagers and had pushed for the increased use of videos and computers.

The senior pastor of this church talked at length about the "electronic bias" of the modern church member ("We have people with master's degrees who can't read simple instructions"). That bias was a reason for his use of electronic media in disseminating information. The following interchange with this pastor indicates that the key issues that these pastors were wrestling with in the use of electronic media, especially television, were such things as the "bias" and "monopoly" of this form of media in American culture (cf. Carey, 1967, and his discussion of these two terms) and the ways to use and not to use these media, primarily television, in the church. The discussion of electronic media began with this question about preaching:

> Interviewer: Let me ask you how your preaching differs now from what it did 25 years ago?
>
> Pastor: Well, in many ways. For example, the old code language of preaching [which he further describes below] is out of date and doesn't work anymore. It doesn't connect with our culture and our people. I think we're in an incredible time of transition with how language is used. It's images now. We just invested again in more video-editing equipment because

we believe that's the only way we can do announcements in church anymore.

In the new building that we're beginning, when you come in here in 18 months, at every entrance there will be a monitor on, an information monitor. It will list the activities for the week in the parish as well as video snippets of what we've planned, showing you what these things look like. Okay? For Sunday morning, we are going to be heading very quickly to, instead of the pastor giving three or four minutes of announcements, having two to three minutes of quick video clips showing people what's going on.... Just look at MTV. They're the ones that are doing the really creative things with television, with images. That's where we are headed and if you want to reach this younger generation, you have to do it through images, to speak their language.

Interviewer: How has this affected your preaching?

Pastor: I prepare my sermons in images. How can I describe it? I'm highly visual, but I'm very right-brained. What I do is when I prepare to preach a sermon, I literally see the sequence of images, and then I visualize the sermon and I preach the images I see. Now when I preach, it comes across as very logical because people can follow the images....

I honestly believe that preaching as we now know it is a dying art form. TV is the problem, and I believe that it is a problem. Now, prob-

lems are things for me that you work with. It
doesn't necessarily mean it's a negative, but it
takes a tremendous amount of energy to make
the transition. I experience younger people who
are increasingly value programmed in terms not
only of their values, but even in terms of the
media itself in terms of how they learn. I believe, I'm convinced that the attention span is
down to 12 seconds. Unless you can create images in your storytelling, you lose people. I
probably lose people a lot.

Interviewer: Do your plans regarding the
increased use of video mean you will begin to
televise your services for those in the
community?

Pastor: No, we are convinced that we are a
community of worshipping Christians, the body
visible. We won't televise because I don't want
people to think they can watch church on TV
and believe they can get the same experience.
We would rather people in the community hear
that incredibly neat things are happening here
and then be invited by someone to check it out
for themselves, than for us to put it out there
and have people make a judgment based on what
they see on the tube.

Plus, I'm convinced that when people turn on
the television set they are so accustomed to
professional editing and good quality, that when
they turn on a local cable channel [in any
community] to see a church service what they
see is an arcane embarrassment.

The "bias" of television was evidenced by this pastor in his comments about how young people learn ("to reach the younger generation, you have to do it through images"). The "monopoly" of television was reflected in his remarks about "preaching as we now know it is a dying art form" because of its non-image base (contrast Ellul, 1985).[24]

This pastor had chosen to deal with these twin issues of bias and monopoly by deciding to use television in limited ways. For example, it would be used as an information delivery channel within the building and as a mental model for preaching (two very different uses), but it would not be used as a public relations device nor as a substitute for corporeal, corporate worship. However, the last limit was tempered somewhat by this pastor's criteria concerning the quality of televised church services. It would be helpful to do a follow-up study to determine the results of this church's experiment.

Two other churches in this community had decided to use electronic media in precisely the manner that the first two churches did not, namely by televising their worship services. Both churches were relatively affluent, downtown congregations who owned their own video camera and editing equipment and had lay volunteers in the church who had some professional experience in video production. Both services were televised over local cable television on a weekly basis.

Interviews with the ministers of these two congregations, coupled with extensive observations over a six-week period, revealed two impacts that such use of electronic media had had on their information dissemination. First, information was dispensed in a more carefully planned and rehearsed manner than would have been the case with oral modes of dissemination. For example, the length of the sermon was timed rather carefully to conform to the time slots allotted them on local cable. In addition, both ministers had their second service televised, not their first, so they would "have a chance to practice" during the first non-televised service.

Second, information was delivered in a media-sensitive manner, i.e. the style of delivery was cognizant of the camera. The two ministers occasionally stared into the camera lens. They sometimes made mention of "you folks at home who are watching." They appeared, like the pastor of the first church mentioned above, to present themselves as television news anchors, reading or reciting (one used a full manuscript, the other memorized his text) their "scripts" for the camera in measured, professional tones.

However, I was not able to detect any impact of the electronic media upon the topics they chose or the sources they used. Both used religious "jargon" that the non-churched person might have difficulty understanding. Both preached with their particular denominations in mind. Both cited names that only the members present would be expected to know. Somewhat surprisingly, even the topics were not "toned down" for the "user friendly confines" that Postman (1985) argued were characteristic of television and that made use of such media by ministers problematic. For example, one televised sermon featured a message on God as a consuming fire, a topic not likely to attract high viewer ratings (cf. the discussion near the end of this chapter on the pastor as media personality).

These four churches were the most prominent users of electronic media in disseminating information. One other pastor had served as a television scriptwriter for a religious program, but that had been some time in the past and he was not able to recall any specifics. Another pastor spoke frequently on the radio, but that was only partly related to his profession as a pastor and will be discussed later in this chapter under "The Pastor as Media Personality." Some used videocassettes as part of their premarital counseling, but that too will be discussed later.

Perhaps part of the reason electronic media, especially television, were so little used by other pastors to disseminate information has to do with the "moral baggage" that this medium carried in many of their minds. These pastors, like Postman (1985), may not have believed that television could be sufficiently "sacralized" to be a "worthy" medium for such an "otherworldly" message. One pastor, for example, noted how his viewing of a video produced by a nationally known preacher had convinced him how "television is selling us a world view that is un-Christian."

According to the literature, some modern ministers view electronic media as having a negative effect upon preaching. Willimon (1990), for example, argued against the image-based orientation of many contemporary sermons because of their tendency to entertain rather than to inform and their preference for storytelling over theological discourse. Shepherd (1990) correctly critiqued this view by noting that neither has to be the case and that storytelling can be both entertaining and informative, as Jesus demonstrated in his use of parables.

What this study did reveal was a strong trend among many pastors to use storytelling in their preaching. This trend, which is discussed near the end of this chapter in more detail, may be due to the dominance of electronic media, particularly television, in American society, where the storytelling form appears to predominate.

Oral Media

By far the most commonly used forms of media to disseminate information by the ministers in this study were oral. Carey (1967) noted this natural "bias" that oral media have toward religion and sacred traditions in their conserving, communal, and celebrative aspects (also noted by Goody, 1977; McLuhan, 1964; Olson, 1977; and Ong, 1967 and 1982). Oral media include dialog, group discussions, public address, and other forms of verbal interactions between people.

The earlier discussion of the informal sources used by pastors in Chapter 3 has already shown how prevalent oral media were in gathering information, but these media were just as prominent in the pastor's role as information disseminator. The interview data and questionnaire results indicate that there were two major oral means of communication among the pastors in this study regarding their roles as information disseminators: private conversations in a counseling context and public preaching in the pulpit. Both of these roles will be discussed in some detail below, but in this section the nature of oral media will be viewed briefly as a background to that discussion.

The pastor's propensity for oral media is not surprising. Several studies of orality and ministry have confirmed this relationship; see, for example, Lawless (1985) who studied the oral aspects of the chanted sermons of Southern women preachers, and Niles (1984) who examined the oral addresses of black religious leaders.

The witness of the Bible is also relevant. From such Scriptural sentiments as "Faith comes by hearing" and "In the beginning was the Word," the church and its leaders have recognized the centrality of the spoken word. The "Written Word" itself displays oral characteristics: Psalm 119 is an acrostic, the Beatitudes are mnemonically structured, Paul asked for his epistles to be "read aloud" to the church recipients, prophetic visions were spoken by God to the prophets. The emphasis upon preaching, especially in Protestantism, has served to underscore this emphasis.[25] As one pastor observed about his communication of Scripture to his congregation, "I want people to have a new hearing of this ancient text." He did not say "a new reading."

For the pastors in this study, the oral bias of their profession became clear in several instances. For example, the interview process itself suggested that these pastors were quite at ease with the oral nature of the interviews. Most of the interviews lasted at least an hour, with twelve extending to more than ninety minutes. One pastor even generalized that "pastors can't give short answers." Long pauses and "I-have-no-idea" answers were relatively rare. These ministers seemed orally facile and ready to respond.

On a number of occasions pastors noted how they often "ad-libbed" when preaching by inserting illustrations or citing quotations that came to them extemporaneously. Observations of these pastors' preaching, coupled with follow-up interviews, indicated that quoting Scripture from memory during the sermon was quite prevalent. This reliance upon memory is further evidence of these pastors' orality. In fact, the publicly preached sermon was the most prominent evidence of how orally oriented these pastors were.

For example, only six of the sixty-two pastors interviewed prepared a full manuscript for their sermons, and of those only three brought the written text to the pulpit. As one explained, "I prepare a complete manuscript so I know what I want to say, but I don't take it to the pulpit because that is too confining. It's too tempting to just read it." Two of the three ministers who did bring a manuscript to the pulpit usually did not read from it--they had it memorized, but they brought it because it was "like a security blanket"--a rare deference to a print bias.

Most of these pastors preferred an outline to a complete manuscript because they were freer to adapt their message to the need of the moment, an extemporaneous style characteristic of orality. A few pastors used no written notes at all in their preaching. One particular example of this practice of using no written aids in the pulpit was found among the pastors of the church that used electronic media so extensively in their ministry (the second church mentioned above). They used only "visual word pictures" in their heads from which to preach.

The sole exception was a sermon by the senior pastor of this church on the need for the congregation to accept his authority as senior pastor. On this one occasion the pastor read his sermon from a full manuscript because "I wanted to make sure that the sermon was exactly the same at each service and that I not delete any points that I had carefully thought through about the present and hidden congregation." His comment on "the present and hidden congregation" referred to the rhetorical device he employed in this message of talking about a previous, similar congregation he had served while, in fact, making it quite clear that he was really referring to the current congregation. This double entendre was clear to me as an observer even though I was not aware of the particular issue of authority with which this church was dealing (it was confirmed during a follow-up interview with the pastor).

Even the pastor of the electronically oriented "baby-boomer church" (the first church mentioned above) who "read his script" actually used only an extensive outline which he color-coded to indicate different kinds of material, e.g. illustration, Scriptural quotation, Greek word. In listening to his sermon at earlier and later services on the same day, it became apparent that he often altered his message, in response to audience reaction, even though the printed outline remained the same.

The sermon was too much of "an auditory event," as one minister observed, to be susceptible to the standardization prevalent in print media. This difference between orality and literacy was evidenced in this pastor's comments about how he used sources in his preaching:

> I need to be very careful with this, but I'm
> going to go ahead and say it [a possible refer-
> ence to his perception of my role as a print-
> oriented researcher and librarian]. If I go
> through one of these [sermon illustration books]
> and I find an illustration that doesn't quite fit,
> but if I could change certain words in it or re-
> write it, I'll do it. Now, if it's a quote from
> somebody, I won't do that. I won't do anything
> like that. But if it's just a fictitious story, I
> might be able to change it with a different
> sentence or two or update some of the really old
> stories.

This tendency to "change certain words" is entirely in
keeping with oral media, but is not usually associated with print.
It is a telling example of how these pastors often reshaped
information during the process of disseminating it. Another
pastor, who was very print oriented in his information-gathering
role, said that he often "made up stories like Jesus did in the
parables" because he did not need to worry about citing sources
or quoting them accurately when he preached.

The preference for oral media was noted as well in the
counseling role of these pastors. Representative of this oral
approach to information dissemination was the comment, cited
in Chapter 3, of the pastor who no longer gave people printed
resources when they came for counseling. His rationale stressed
a pastoral preference for "people over paper," using the vocabulary of communal ("care"), personal ("their pain") orality
("hear" and "talk about it"):

> That is not what [people] want.... They are
> more interested in having somebody else hear
> their pain and at least talk about it and care, than
> read about it.

The conversational nature of oral media was particularly well suited to the role that many of these pastors played in their counseling. Though printed instruments (such as the Taylor-Johnson Temperament Analysis test) were used in counseling, the pastors were much more likely to describe their counselor role with orally biased phrases. Content analysis, for example, revealed these relevant phrases spoken by the pastors in this study: "Pray together," "They want a listening ear," "I try to get them to talk," and "I share with them from my own experience."

This section has shown that the media that these pastors used--print, electronic, and oral--had some impact upon how they disseminated information. The solitary nature of print media (cf. Eisenstein's [1979] discussion of the lonely reader) was probably a factor in the little use made of these media by these pastors, beyond their widespread use in information gathering. The popularity of electronic media had encouraged some pastors to utilize these forms of media in ministry as means of disseminating information. The "moral baggage" of television, however, coupled with the high cost of this technology and the theological concerns for the elevation of the "image" over the "word" may have been reasons for their rather limited use.

For most of the ministers in this study the media of preference were clearly those associated with orality. The communal and interpersonal aspects of oral media were no doubt major reasons, as was the historic affinity between orality and religion. The next section will look at how the pastors in this study disseminated information, primarily orally, in terms of the particular professional roles that they filled.

The Minister's Two Major Roles as Information Disseminator

The two most-frequently mentioned roles that the pastors

in this study filled in terms of information dissemination were that of counseling and preaching. Other roles that involved information dissemination, such as that of teacher and author, were either mentioned much less or not at all; four of these lesser roles will be considered at the end of this chapter. Roles that did not involve information dissemination in any substantial way, e.g. administrative tasks that were essentially routine in nature, are not within the scope of this study and are, therefore, not included in this discussion.[26]

The prominence of the healer (counselor) and herald (preacher) roles were not too surprising given the nature and needs of the modern minister. For example, regarding the need for pastoral care in contemporary society, Bellah and his associates have noted in their book *Habits of the Heart* (1986) that Americans are living in a "therapeutic culture." The clergy in this community echoed again and again this theme. It could be summarized in more than one pastor's comment that "my counseling load could overwhelm me if I let it."

In fact, one of the most popular specializations among Doctor of Ministry programs in this country is the pastoral care and counseling track (Carroll and Wheeler, 1987). In this particular community, a pastoral counseling center in existence only fifteen years had grown from one counselor with a few clients to more than forty pastoral counselors seeing nearly 5,000 patients--over a third of whom had been referred by local clergy. One of the directors of this agency did not seem to overstate the case when he observed that "counseling is one of the pastor's biggest needs."

The prominence of preaching in information dissemination was also noted by these pastors. Given that perhaps as few as 15% of church members see their pastor regularly outside of the pulpit (Oswald and Kroeger, 1988), the emphasis on the preacher as herald, as much as healer, was not surprising. On the questionnaire, a plurality of pastors (38%) listed preaching as their most time-consuming task in ministry, and a majority (77%) listed it in the top three. No other ministerial task was rated so highly by these pastors. The priority of preaching, particularly in Protestant churches, has had a long tradition (cf. Holland, 1969), and even among Catholic congregations there has been a renewed emphasis upon the homily (see, for example, Healy, 1988, and Greely, 1989).

While the distinction between counseling and preaching is a valid one, in the minds of some of the ministers in this study a necessary or at least desirable overlap also existed. When a pastor with a professional doctorate in pastoral counseling was asked about his counseling role, he replied, "Well, I do most of my counseling when I preach." His emphasis, like many in this study, was upon what was often termed "preventative counseling."

Twenty-five of the forty-eight sermons observed during this study had a counseling theme for their topic, e.g. depression, family relationships, co-dependency, broken relationships, dysfunctional families, contentment, and death and dying. In a review of contemporary American preaching, Averill (1988) observed that "for most [parishioners], the sermon is the only pastoral care they'll get" (p. 29).[27]

For some of these pastors, the two roles overlapped because of time constraints. "I have to do preventative counseling in my preaching or I could easily become overwhelmed in my counseling," was how one pastor explained this need to bridge both roles. After one case study involving observation and interviews with one pastor over a five-week period, I noted that counseling vocabulary (co-dependent, dysfunctional, bondage) was frequently used by this pastor in his sermons. His response was that these sermons had "taken their flavor from my recent counseling."

Still, there are important distinctions between how these pastors disseminated information privately in their counseling roles and publicly in their preaching roles. Therefore, these two roles of the pastor as information disseminator shall be looked at separately.

The Pastor as Healer

The role of the pastor as healer is a longstanding one, which may be traced to the model of Jesus, who, according to Matthew 4:23, "came teaching, preaching, and healing." Among most modern ministers this healing role is usually translated into a counseling context, a "healing of the soul," as McNeill (1951) has noted in his history of pastoral counseling.

This section will examine the information that pastors disseminated in their counseling role from three perspectives: the questions being asked of pastors, the answers they were giving, and the answers they were not giving, i.e. the issue of referrals as it bears on professional competence. It is important to emphasize here that the content of the information is not the key concern here. Rather, the extent and intent of the information sources used by these pastors are more central to this discussion. In addition, my focus in analyzing the counseling role of the pastor is only upon the informational aspects, not upon everything that counseling entails.

One of the most surprising findings in this study was the tension that the pastors in this community felt over their role as counselors. On one hand were those pastors who said, as did this one, "ministry is counseling." On the other were ministers who refused to do any. The tension often centered on the professional competence needed to do pastoral counseling, but the reasons given for doing and not doing counseling were somewhat more varied. Before discussing the three perspectives, this tension over care and counseling will be examined briefly in order to set the later discussion in a proper context.

THE TENSION OVER CARE AND COUNSELING

An important distinction in this tension over the role of counseling was often drawn by these pastors between pastoral care and pastoral counseling. Pastoral care was usually perceived as something every pastor does--visiting the sick, comforting the bereaved, giving advice to parishioners about routine personal problems. I found no one in this study who did not willingly and frequently perform pastoral care in those terms. However, pastoral counseling was viewed by these pastors as a situation involving two key criteria: it was long-term and it was relatively deep-seated, requiring more than personal or spiritual advice. In those kinds of situations demanding pastoral counseling, the pastors in this study were divided in their opinions into four groups.

The first group of pastors were those who refused to do any pastoral counseling primarily because of a perceived lack of ability.[28] A frequent explanation given was "It's not my forte" or "I'm not gifted" in that area. On one level such explanations were merely statements of personal preference, i.e. I would do it if I liked to do it. But on a deeper level, these explanations suggested that counseling required a level of competence that they did not believe themselves to possess. As professionals, these pastors were admitting that they did not have access to the information needed to counsel professionally.

For some, such competence may have been viewed as divinely available (note the supernatural reference in the comment "I'm not gifted"). However, even for fundamentalist pastors the issue of professionalism (note the discussion on this topic in Chapter 2) was a key concern in their ability to disseminate information correctly in such counseling contexts. The following comments by the pastor of a quite conservative church typified this view:

> It's been quite a learning experience for us. We have learned that, strange as it may seem, the Word of God does not seem to be able to set these people free.... And it's been strange for us because I came into this area of ministry with the idea, well, so who needs a psychologist? The Word of God will set you free. And all I have to do is tell them the Word of God says this and just have faith and believe and trust God and everything will be fine. Well, that's not true. It's true, but it is more complex than that. You are dealing with people's emotions and stress and anguish and bitterness and resentment and all those things that have got to be straightened out before the Word can ever take effect.... There have been times lately when we have told people that we are not able to reach [them]. "You need to seek professional counseling."

His ability to disseminate only Biblical information was viewed by this pastor as inadequate information. He could dispense information that was accurate ("It's true"), but not sufficient ("it is more complex than that"). His readiness to refer to professional counselors was a typical response for this first group of pastors. Since they did not feel competent to counsel, they quickly referred to those deemed more qualified when such situations arose. The issue of referral will be considered in more detail at the end of this section on the pastor as healer.

The second group of pastors were those who did not counsel, not because of a perceived lack of professional ability, but because of other professional concerns. A chief concern for

many of these was time.[29] These pastors felt they could disseminate accurate and sufficient information because of their formal
training in this area, but that doing so was too time consuming.
One pastor, for example, with considerable experience in counseling had recently had his church begin a formal relationship
with a local pastoral counseling center so that he could automatically refer potential counselees to them. With this move
came an accompanying change in his professional job description
to exclude counseling because:

> my counseling load had begun to overcome me,
> overtake me. The time involved was incredible.
> I now do only strictly entry sessions. I do not
> refuse to see people, but I quickly refer. The
> way I can explain it is I moved from counseling
> to pastoral care. I can do about ten times the
> pastoral care that I used to do in counseling.
> It's just amazing.

The time factor was noted also by another pastor who recounted
the more than forty hours per month that he and his staff spent
in counseling. The demand had become so great that he also had
adopted a new policy of referring all but a few marital cases.
Another church had implemented a similar policy based on frequency, i.e. the pastors would counsel people for a maximum of
three sessions and then refer. The senior pastor explained that
though some of his staff were trained to do such counseling, that
was "not what they were called here to do--we're pastors, not
counselors."

This emphasis on pastoring over counseling was made by
another minister who had completed a professional doctorate in
counseling. The conclusion of his doctoral research was that
pastors should not do counseling "because of the problem of
transference." By that term he meant that he could "not be their
pastor and their counselor." He noted that the "purity of the

counseling room" was too easily tainted by the many social encounters between pastor and parishioner. He also observed that the pastor could be "ambushed" because it was too tempting to use such interchanges as sermon illustrations. Even if the use was indirect or nonexistent, the public perception was still there that "he's talking about me." As another pastor observed in light of these perceptions, "It's hard to be someone's pastor and counselor. People don't want to tell their deepest problems to someone they see all the time."

The third group of pastors were those who did some counseling, both because they felt they were professionally equipped to do so and because they limited their counseling to specific kinds of cases. The most prominent situations were those that involved marital or premarital counseling. Many pastors in this study, even those who said they were quick to refer, acknowledged that they usually did their own marriage counseling, usually in the context of counseling a couple preparing for marriage. Such cases were often quite time consuming with sessions averaging one hour in length and four to six in number, but they were also often cyclical in nature, occurring usually in spring or summer. Though specific strategies of information dissemination will be discussed below, these pastors frequently used such psychological instruments as the Taylor-Johnson Temperament Analysis or the Myers-Briggs Type Indicator to gather and disseminate appropriate information for these couples.

Another church, whose senior pastor had previously had his own professional practice as a pastoral counselor in a large metropolitan area, continued to do some counseling "just to keep my fingers in it, to stay exposed to that area of expertise." This same church had also hired a "pastor to the community" who, though paid by the church, worked at a local counseling center to which the members of the church were often referred.

The fourth group of pastors were those who felt quite competent to counsel a variety of cases and rarely referred. As discussed in Chapter 2, the professional image of these pastors was most closely akin to that of the pastor as expert, at least in terms of counseling. This group of clergy was quite small, only four could be safely described in these terms, and shared two common characteristics. They were all trained professionally in counseling and they all said they enjoyed the counseling role. One, in fact, was in the process of resigning her position as pastor to become a full-time counselor. Another had received a professional doctorate in counseling and was used as a referral source by several pastors in the community. One, however, appeared not to have demonstrated sufficient competence as a counselor and was being asked to resign, partly due to a poorly handled counseling incident that had resulted in accusations of sexual misconduct. However, the details of this case cannot be discussed because of a promise of confidentiality.

The presence of these four different views on the role of the pastor in counseling underscores the complexity and diversity that existed among these clergy regarding the nature of the information that these ministers attempted to disseminate as counselors. The next section will look at this type of information dissemination from three perspectives: the questions being asked of pastors, the answers being given, and the answers not being given, i.e. the issue of referrals as it bears on professional competence. Since the dividing line between pastoral care and pastoral counseling is often either thin or moving, this discussion will include both aspects of the pastor as counselor.

THE QUESTIONS BEING ASKED

One of the limitations in studying how these pastors disseminated information was that direct observations of private counseling situations, unlike public sermons, were not possible.

The issues of privacy and confidentiality simply made such methods nearly impossible in this type of study. Therefore, the data presented here are confined primarily to reports made by these clergy during the interview process.

One other source of data was found by interviewing and obtaining records from a community information referral center. Started by a campus minister in conjunction with a local university, this center had grown in its twenty-year history to become an independent, not-for-profit agency with a full-time staff of six, a pool of 120 volunteers who averaged 80 hours of training each, and a bank of ten 24-hour-per-day telephones.

In 1991 this center received more than 50,000 phone calls, up from less than 20,000 five years earlier. While these calls dealt with such diverse needs as employment information, housing needs, utility bill payment assistance, and medical problems, including the fastest-growing category--AIDS information--the largest share (48%) of the calls this center received were counseling related.

For example, more than 2,000 of the 50,000 telephone inquiries were questions about "relationships," another 1,800 were incidents of depression or anxiety, and 1,500 were serious enough to be classified as "suicidal situations." One staff member summarized the nature of these kinds of information needs in the community this way:

> We get a lot of emotional, listening, problem-solving, and referral-type questions as far as Where can I find counseling? What's the number of the family counseling center? or Connect me to the crisis center. The most frequent kind of request we get is for counseling. When a volunteer answers the phone, it might be a runaway, it might be domestic violence, or suicide.

While research into how this information referral center handled these issues would make an interesting study, the present project is limited to the kinds of questions asked of the clergy in this community, to whom the callers to this center were often referred. The center referred calls to clergy either when ministers were specifically requested or when the center's volunteer staff deemed such referrals as most appropriate, though no particular criteria were noted in the latter case. The data from this information referral center are intended only to emphasize both the frequency and the diversity of counseling-related questions in this community. As one pastor observed somewhat simplistically, "People here have a lot of holes in their pockets."

Part of the reason for the frequency of counseling-related questions may be found in the remark of a pastor who had been in the community for more than ten years. When asked why he felt so many people were asking their pastors for counseling, he responded, "People are more likely to seek counseling period than they once were. There is more openness now about counseling." He also mentioned the surfeit of "pop psychology books" on such topics as co-dependency and how these materials seemed to make the public more aware of and sensitive to counseling issues. Another pastor noted this same trend in terms of the increase in his counseling load:

> I wouldn't say there is any change in the sort of problems that people are having today. I would say that there are probably more people having problems than there were, say, ten years ago. Ten years ago, if somebody came to me, things were really bad already. I think people's consciousness with respect to their needs-- emotionally, relationally, so forth--I think that consciousness has been increased. I think people are just more relational now than they were ten years ago.

Regardless of the historical accuracy of these cultural assessments, the perception existed among these pastors that there was a greater willingness currently in the community to seek information from pastors relative to a particular counseling need. Only a few pastors cited counterexamples, and these were discussed in Chapter 2, e.g. the tendency of some "yuppies [to] take care of their own problems" or the reluctance of older parishioners to admit such needs.

The range of the counseling needs cited in this study was quite large. At one end of the scale were such traditional religious topics as questions related to grief and bereavement that were frequently cited. Questions by elderly parishioners about death and dying were also mentioned often, as were marital problems such as divorce. At the other end of the scale were questions by parents about raising a chromosome-deficient child, by a teenage girl who did not want to have an abortion despite her parents' insistence, by a woman who claimed her house was haunted and wanted the pastor to find out how to "un-haunt" it, and by a woman who was "married to Jesus" and wanted to know how the pastor could help her "meet the President." In the middle of this scale were the many less-traditional and less-bizarre questions for which the pastors in this community were being asked to provide information.

One theme that emerged from the interviews was the increasing number of questions about new kinds of family problems. While family issues have long been a staple of pastoral counseling, the pastors in this study also noted how the trends in this area represented new problems for them. When asked about his counseling role, for example, this pastor replied:

> I don't see myself as a professional counselor. I'm not qualified in terms of certification. But any minister today that has any direct respon- sibility to people can't help but be very heavily

into some kind of counseling at some level. We've seen a tremendous increase in dysfunctional families, broken families. The fact that so many children... This is the first generation in the history of the human race--in the past 20 to 25 years--where the vast majority or at least a significant part of it, perhaps a majority, are being raised without the presence of at least one parent. It's pretty much a time when both parents work, and we still have no idea what the consequences of that will be. There hasn't been a generation of the human race where that's been true.

This pastor continued by noting that the lack of family support systems was one of the two main reasons for the depth and volume of the counseling problems that he encountered. The other was "the devaluation of family stability in our culture," by which he meant the lack of sufficient role models portraying "healthy families" both inside and outside the church. The problems associated with the increase in single-parent families was also noted by several pastors as a new trend in the kinds of counseling cases they had.

Sometimes the questions clustered around issues of domestic violence, which the directors of the information referral center said was one of the fastest-growing types of calls in this community. Questions about domestic violence were also noted by the directors of the local pastoral counseling center as particularly troublesome for area clergy.

This problem was compounded by recent state laws that had mandated the reporting to law enforcement officials of such situations--even when only suspected--by professional pastoral counselors, but not by clergy, who were exempt. The legal distinction made in these statutes concerned whether information was being disseminated for free or for fee (cf. the fee–vs.–free access of information debate in the library field), an issue that will be discussed in the section "The Answers Not Being Given."

Several pastors talked in quite generic terms about the rise in these kinds of questions, but seemed reluctant to say much more, perhaps because of these very laws. One pastor did mention a case of a daughter sexually abused by her father that had later been the subject of a network television program, but no other details were provided.

The pastor of a church traditionally associated with pacifism said that he had recently attended a workshop on domestic violence and had used that material in his counseling because "pacifists have not always found good and effective releases for anger and frustration and have repressed it, with families [having] borne the brunt of that repression." A fundamentalist pastor whose church held a very high view of the family also indicated he was seeing more cases of "sexual abuse from a parent to a child" in the last few years than at any other time in his ministry of more than twenty years.

If there is any summary term to describe the kinds of questions most frequently asked of these pastors, it would be "relationship"--at least that was the term used most by the pastors in this study. Broken relationships, dysfunctional relationships, co-dependent relationships, family relationships, marital relationships, parental relationships. As this campus minister commented:

> Relationships. Those are the kinds of questions
> I get. Dating relationships. That may involve
> religious questions if they are from different
> religious traditions. There are quite a few like
> that. Some have relationships that are just not
> healthy and are causing pain on one or both

parts. Relationships that have broken up.
People who are trying to understand why. I
have a lot of students who are dealing with
family of origin problems--alcoholism, with one
or both parents, physical and sexual abuse,
illness of a parent, death of grandparents. Those
become issues. It is usually the first time that
this age group has experienced death in the
family. A lot of students dealing with illness,
cancer, AIDS. Those kinds of issues on top of
just the regular religious questions and students
preparing for marriage.

His comments, though focused on college-age students, demonstrate the range of the questions being asked: from the "regular
religious questions" to the newer issues of abuse and AIDS. As
for their role in providing AIDS information, most pastors admitted little involvement. This could have been due to a very
active and public effort by one of the local hospitals to fill this
role, or it could have been due to these pastors' reluctance to
discuss such cases.

       One of the rare firsthand glimpses into how pastors in
this community provided information dealt with questions of
family relationships. The incident involved a local professional
pastoral counselor, who was also a pastor, and his delivery of a
"guest sermon" to a church in the community. His approach
was to use the passage in the Gospel of Luke on Jesus' three
temptations as a stepping stone to relate three case studies of
family relationship problems that he had recently seen.

       The pastor's dissemination of information in this one
incident was rather indirect in that, other than oblique references
to the Biblical text, he cited no sources beyond the data in these
three cases. Instead, his recounting of these three incidents
indicated that he used his formal training as a non-directive

Rogerian counselor to elicit from the families involved information about how they perceived their relationships. He then relayed this information in the context of these three stories as a means of enabling his listeners to understand how other family members might be perceiving them. My limited observation of this one incident suggested that it had some effect in that several couples in the congregation nudged persons whom I took to be their spouses at key points and whispered such comments in my hearing as "Now I understand" and "I didn't realize."

Most of the data in this study relative to how pastors disseminated information in their role as counselors were self-reported in the interview process. In light of the diversity and complexity of the questions being asked of pastors in this community, what answers did these pastors say they provided? The issue here is not specific pieces of information, but the strategies and goals that were utilized in disseminating the information. What answers were being given to these questions?

THE ANSWERS BEING GIVEN

The answers that the pastors in this study gave to the questions they were being asked about counseling needs will be considered generically. My concern is not over particular answers, which were typically not observable, but over the general patterns or categories of communication strategies that emerged from what these pastors reported. This is consistent with the definition of information given elsewhere (see Appendix), the focus of which is not on content, but on communication channels and how they are used by pastors. As noted earlier, this discussion of counseling is limited to the informational aspects of this role, not to everything involved in counseling.

The information that the pastors in this community disseminated in response to the counseling questions they were being asked may be grouped into three categories of communication strategies. These categories are not mutually exclusive in that many pastors indicated they employed multiple methods. Two of these information-dissemination strategies are comparable to communication modes that other professionals, such as librarians, might be expected to utilize, while one had no parallel outside the pastorate.

The first type of information dissemination employed by these pastors in response to questions about counseling needs may perhaps best be described as "divine communication" or prayer. This type of information dissemination clearly has no parallel in the field of library and information science. Among these pastors, however, prayer was one of the most commonly cited strategies in terms of how clergy answered counseling questions.

It should be pointed out that prayer here does not refer to the pastor's own silent prayer for "wisdom," but to the use of spoken prayer by the pastor during the counseling session. In this context, prayer refers not so much to the source of information as to the delivery system or channel. Though both elements were present in the examples cited by these pastors, the emphasis here is upon the "packaging" or form that information took as it was disseminated by clergy to counselees.

For example, one pastor recounted how he had met recently with a couple experiencing marital difficulty and that his answer to them was to "pray with them, sharing Scriptures and experiences that the Lord brought to my mind." While I was not privy to the encounter, it seems clear that this pastor, like others in this study, utilized prayer as a medium for communicating information--Biblical texts and personal experience. Though the information could have been disseminated in other ways, the use of prayer as an information channel brought components of "authoritativeness" and "sacredness" to the information that would not otherwise have been so obvious. In such cases the pastor's "divine authority" (see Chapter 2) was quite pronounced.

Another pastor related that he often used prayer at "the altar" to address counseling questions. By that he meant that at the close of the worship service, he would invite parishioners with counseling needs to come to the front of the sanctuary and "kneel at the altar." There the pastor would talk to them and give them counseling advice couched in the form of prayer. In one reported incident at another church, a separated couple contemplating divorce came forward--one kneeling at one end of the altar and the other at the opposite end. The pastor's strategy was to pray first with one and then the other, "sharing Scriptural principles and spiritual insight" until they finally came together in the middle of the altar. Such "altar calls" were typically followed by more formal counseling appointments. However, as one pastor insisted regarding such sessions: "If they haven't been to the altar, I can't do anything for them in counseling."

Though somewhat extreme, this example underscores how prominently many of the pastors in this community used prayer as a means of disseminating counseling information. Less vivid examples were noted by many of these ministers. The particular pieces of information became secondary to the channel by which they were delivered, and the information channel served to underscore the validity and importance of the data being disseminated.

A second type of information disseminated by these pastors in response to questions about counseling needs was the distillation of printed material delivered orally. This kind of approach is much more comparable to what any information professional might provide. Using this strategy, pastors would often draw from their own reading in counseling texts, then summarize this information for the counselee. Unlike standard library reference practice, however, these pastors relied primarily on a narrow range of theologically compatible materials found in their own libraries. In addition, they rarely furnished the "patron" with the original or primary source, preferring instead to summarize the printed information orally.

Eleven pastors, for example, showed me their "shelf" of counseling materials when asked how they responded to counseling questions. Five pastors pointed to their "book" on counseling in response to the same query. As one noted, "Anything I don't know, I've got that...encyclopedia of psychology." Several pastors noted that the information they gave to counselees was mostly summarized material from one or two authors, particularly Gary Collins, a noted evangelical psychiatrist teaching at Trinity Evangelical Divinity School. One of the criteria used by pastors in selecting certain books or authors was "practicality" or as one minister explained, "I read some [counseling] books by Crabb and Adams...but Gary Collins, I think, does a great job of making it practical; he's the most practical." In these cases, intellectual access appeared to be the chief concern.

The following response to a question about counseling strategies is another example of this approach:

> The first thing that comes to mind is that you've got a tremendous number of people with severe problems. Usually it goes back to broken families or troubles at home, there is lots of that. So you have to... You either have to send them somewhere or you have to learn up on those kinds of issues and then help them.

What this pastor meant by his expression "learn up on those kinds of issues" was that he would buy and read "three or four" books on a counseling topic so that he could convey that printed information orally with the counselee during a private session in his office. Many of these pastors, unlike reference librarians, for example, tended not to seek out a variety of sources with which to satisfy others' information needs.

The oral dissemination of information distilled from printed materials is another example of how pastors differ from traditional information providers. Rarely would a pastor simply refer a counselee to a printed source for the information he or she needed to address a particular problem, e.g. depression, marital communications, job-related stress. Instead, the pastor almost always distilled the information for the counselee and delivered it orally in an intermediary role.

This approach to information dissemination allowed the pastor to maintain the personal nature of ministry inherent in oral media, while gathering the information from print media. The comment cited earlier of the pastor who had decided not to refer people to the books he had read that addressed their counseling needs typifies this approach:

> I might say, "Well, I remember reading such and such..." but not to say, "Here, you read this." That is not what they want to do. They are more interested in having somebody else hear their pain and at least talk about it and care, than read about it.

This pastor disseminated the information in these books, but he did so orally with tones and gestures that suggested personal involvement and caring--features not as pronounced in print media. The inability to observe any counseling situations firsthand made it impossible to discern how or whether the printed data were altered or adapted by this pastor or by others. However, it seemed likely that certain changes in the information-transfer process did occur, especially condensation.

This approach to information dissemination also allowed the pastor to serve as an information "filter," a role also suggested for librarians by Ortega (1961), though his suggestion was based on the volume of materials available to patrons, while these pastors' filtering role seemed more related to their professional preference for oral media over print.

Several pastors, however, did remark that they often "took [their counselees] through a book" by having them read certain passages together in the pastor's office or by completing questionnaires in certain books. The strong preference for oral media in delivering counseling information did not preclude entirely the use of print media. Even pastors who relied heavily on "divine communication," for example, noted their use of such standard publications as the Taylor-Johnson Temperament Analysis in both collecting and disseminating information in cases where personality assessment instruments were of value.

Besides prayer and oral summaries of printed material, a third type of information-dissemination strategy employed by the pastors in this study was the use of electronic media. The sole example of this strategy to disseminate information involved the viewing of videocassettes designed to assist clergy in premarital counseling. Frequently, these video programs included dramatic portrayals of various marital situations. About a dozen of the pastors interviewed said that it was their standard practice to have couples considering marriage view videos on the topic of marriage. This pastor's comments were typical:

> We do a lot of premarital counseling. If someone wants to get married, they must consult with us at least four months in advance. We meet with them once a week for this kind of thing. We have videos that we show them. We watch them together, and afterwards we discuss what is in them. We also have them answer

some questions based on the video programs.

This use of electronic media, though not that widespread among the clergy in this community, was mentioned favorably by those pastors using it. Its advantage appeared to be the medium's ability to create vivid life-situation scenarios, including problematic ones, to which the counselees could relate without making the pastor the focus of the situation. Since the pastor did not have to "create" the situation by storytelling or role playing, he or she could then act as "impartial judge" in pointing out to the counselees what the "video couple" did right or did wrong. In these cases, the electronic media allowed certain kinds of information to be disseminated vividly while enabling the pastor to function as intermediary between the information and the recipients.

In addition to these three approaches, one of the most frequently mentioned strategies for answering counseling questions was not to answer them at all, i.e. to refer to professional counselors or other agencies. Since this approach differed greatly from the other three by making the pastor only an indirect disseminator of information, it shall be considered separately.

THE ANSWERS NOT BEING GIVEN

Wilson (1983) noted that one of the distinguishing features of a professional is that he or she knows what questions not to answer. This aspect of limited knowledge, discussed in Chapter 2, is central to the discussion of the pastor as healer or counselor.

The most visible demonstration of the pastor's "limited knowledge" in this study was the common tendency for most of the pastors to refer people with questions that these clergy deemed beyond their expertise. As information disseminators, these professionals frequently struggled with the roles they should and should not fill in answering certain kinds of counseling questions in light of their professional training and expertise. The question of competence has become particularly acute in contemporary ministry because of the recent rise in religious litigation.

As noted in Chapter 1, clergy malpractice was listed recently by the American Bar Association as one of the new frontiers in American legal practice. Six of the sixty-two pastors interviewed in this study spoke at some length about this issue and the need for their churches to carry extensive malpractice insurance. Though none of the pastors in this community had been the subject of such suits nor knew of any who had, the directors of the local pastoral counseling center knew of at least six clergy in the community in recent history who had been dismissed because of ethical misconduct in their role as pastoral care givers.

The sensitivity of these pastors to the problem of clergy malpractice and religious litigation was quite evident in the following interchange with a pastor who had been in the community for a number of years:

> Interviewer: Do you ever refer people to other agencies for counseling?
>
> Pastor: Oh, yeah. Most of the time.
>
> Interviewer: Why is that?
>
> Pastor: I refer them to the agencies that are professionals in those areas. I stay away from there [because] we have to be wise enough to know that in this day and time there is a lot of

suing going on, even in the church, even ministers being sued. So the church has to carry
insurance, counseling insurance on the pastor
because someone might get devilish enough to
sue him, you know.

Interviewer: Is that something fairly recent in
your ministry?

Pastor: Well, twenty years ago it wasn't even
thought of. That's why now I have a lot of
people who are not members here and when they
call, I refer them right on. I do not counsel
people that do not have their membership here at
this church. I do not counsel them. I've got to
keep my church out of legal problems, and our
insurance agent advises us to do that.... You
want to do the Lord's work, but you have to be
careful.

This interchange raises several issues that are involved
in the pastoral practice of referring. First, there is the issue of
professional competence; "I refer them to the agencies that are
professionals in those areas." Second, there is the issue of legal
ramifications; "I've got to keep my church out of legal problems" resulting from "ministers being sued." Third, there is the
issue of individual church policies; this pastor, for example, did
not counsel people who did not "have their membership" in that
church. In this section we will look at each of these three issues
in turn as they relate to fairly new caveats being placed on the
clergy as information disseminators.

The first issue involved in knowing what questions not
to answer is that of professional competence. As one pastor with
considerable experience in both ministry and counseling noted,
"It is a stereotype to think that all pastors are competent to

counsel, and if they are not knowledgeable, they can hurt someone." Another pastor, who had practiced professionally as a counselor in a large metropolitan hospital before entering the ministry, said he always referred "open-ended cases" because they were "best left to the experts." A pastor who was himself undergoing counseling for stress remarked that he was quite quick to refer because he knew firsthand the advantages of "seeking professionals." The pastor of a large congregation whose special focus was on preaching was quite candid about his readiness to refer: "I tell people, hey, I work on sermons, they counsel, for eight hours a day. They are professionals."

The presence of a large, well-known pastoral counseling center in this community also contributed to these pastors' willingness to refer. When asked why he did not mention this counseling center as one of the agencies to which he referred, one pastor responded, "[The center] is so well known in this area that by the time they come to me they've usually already been to [this center]." Well over two-thirds of the pastors interviewed in this study mentioned this particular counseling center as the one to which they usually referred. "They are the only ones in town I trust," was how one pastor described the reputation for professional competence that this pastoral counseling center had earned locally.

Not all pastors, however, shared this same enthusiasm and respect. The one common characteristic among this smaller group of pastors was their lack of "theological trust" in this center. The center's appeal was ecumenical, which resulted in its lack of appeal to these pastors who were all quite theologically conservative. Phrases such as "too worldly," "secular," "liberal," and "lack of grounding in Scripture" were used by these conservative pastors to explain why they chose not to refer to this particular counseling center. The only other reasons cited for not using this center was a perception on one pastor's part that it relied "too much on drugs" to help people and the concern of another pastor to refer "poor people" because of the expense involved.

The question of expense raises the second issue involved in pastoral referrals, clergy malpractice. The legal foundation for clergy malpractice appears to be based on two considerations. According to the directors of the local pastoral counseling center the first consideration concerned whether pastors did or did not charge for the counseling they provided. If they did not charge, as was the practice of the pastors in this community, then clergy could not be held legally liable for the information they disseminated. In the legal sense of the word, such pastors were not advertising themselves to the public to be "professional [i.e. paid] counselors." [The historical precedent of exempting the "spiritual counsel" of clergy from malpractice cases was also noted in the 1984 *Nally v. Grace Community Church* discussed in Chapter 1.] The fee-versus-free distinction in the dissemination of counseling information is an unusual extension of the fee-versus-free debate that has existed in the library and information science field.

A second consideration in the legal basis of clergy malpractice concerned the use of professional vocabulary. This is how one pastor in the community, who had recently conducted a workshop on clergy malpractice for pastors in his denomination, explained this new development:

> I did some studying about counseling for a workshop I just recently completed. I discovered through a lawyer friend of mine that [a nearby state] has enacted a new law that lumps clergy in with all therapists, and that we are liable for bad advice or sexual misconduct along with all. No clergy have been prosecuted so far, but under this new law they can be prosecuted like any other psychiatrist or psychologist....

What the law focuses on is that if clergy use
terms found in psychology and psychotherapy,
they are liable along with other therapists. If
they stick to religious issues or Biblically based
counseling, then they are not liable.

Unfortunately I was not able to confirm the existence of this law
through other sources, but, if true, it does appear to introduce a
new criterion for defining malpractice.

At any rate, the legal ramifications were being taken
seriously by many of the pastors in this community. Several
mentioned new provisions in their church insurance to cover
malpractice. One pastor had had his church join a Christian
legal association as a precautionary measure. Since actual cases
of malpractice either did not exist or were not known in the
community, no further inquiry into this issue was possible. Still,
the increasing awareness among these clergy over malpractice
appears to underscore the importance of professional competence
and the increased understanding on the part of these pastors
regarding knowing what questions not to answer. This concern
over malpractice, coupled with other professional concerns, had
led a number of ministers and churches in this community to
adopt policies regarding the practice of referrals.

The third issue involved in limiting the information
dissemination role of the pastor in answering counseling
questions concerns individual church policies. Seven of the fifty-
eight churches represented by the sixty-two pastors interviewed
in this study had recently adopted formal or informal policies--
none were found in writing--limiting the counseling role of the
pastor and encouraging more referrals.

Said one pastor, "We have a church policy here: three
and out." The pastors on staff at this church could see a person
up to three times, but then they had to refer. In addition to the

need to lighten pastoral time demands, this policy was also intended to prevent pastors from becoming involved in cases deemed beyond their competence as clergy. Another church had "an understanding among the staff" that the pastors would refer "any deep-seated problems." One pastor made special mention of an "unspoken church policy" that the minister could see no one more than "three or four" times.

Even among those churches where no such church-wide policies were cited, there was frequent mention of the pastor's individual decision to refer often. A pastor who rarely saw people more than once or twice saw one couple eight times, but "only because they would not go" to the agency to which he had tried to refer them. Several pastors, trained in counseling techniques, mentioned that they only did "diagnostic interviews." "My goal is referral not repair," is how one pastor described his role as pastor. "I talk to them, I refer them, then I disengage," was another's explanation of his practice. Several pastors noted that they continued to see counselees who were clients of professional counselors, but only "as their pastor" or "when they just need a listening ear between sessions."

In all of these situations, ministers were not neglecting their pastoral *care*, merely delegating their pastoral *counseling* to those better trained. In such cases, the professional image being portrayed was that of the pastor as generalist, as discussed in Chapter 2.

SUMMARY

This discussion of the pastor's role as information disseminator in the context of counseling has been limited by the inability to supplement any of the interview data with direct observations of this kind of information transfer. It was not possible to cite and analyze specific examples of how information

had been used by these pastors to meet the needs of their counselee patrons.

Instead, this discussion has focused on three more
indirectly observable aspects of this kind of information
interchange. First was the tension over pastoral care and
pastoral counseling, with the preference for the former tending
to limit the amount and kinds of information given. Second was
the influence that various media had upon the information
disseminated, particularly in terms of prayer and the oral
distillation of printed material. Third was the diversity and
depth of the counseling-related questions being raised in this
community, which partly accounted for the frequent practice of
referring.

The pastor's role as healer, however, was not the only
significant occasion for the pastors in this study to disseminate
information. The pastor as herald was an even more prominent
platform for the dissemination of information by ministers.

The Pastor as Herald

The ministerial task that the pastors in this study cited as
being the most important and most time-consuming was that of
preaching. Like the Biblical "kerux" or herald, these pastors
saw themselves primarily as preachers who stood before the
people of God and delivered a message from the Word of God.
Though long a priority among Protestant pastors, even among
Catholic clergy the importance of the sermon is being re-
emphasized (cf. Healy, 1988, and Greely, 1989). As one pastor
in this study commented, "My offering to God is what I do on
Sunday morning."

Among the sixty-two pastors interviewed for this project,

more than three-fourths (77%) listed preaching as one of their top three areas of ministerial responsibility, with most of those listing it first, in terms of the time they devoted to the task. Only administration was rated so highly, placing second, but it was not viewed by them as requiring any significant dissemination of information. Furthermore, when asked on the written questionnaire to list an area of ministry in which they did the most reading and studying, the overwhelming choice was preaching, cited first by thirty of the sixty-two respondents. By comparison, counseling finished a distant second with only seven pastors listing it first.

This pastoral focus upon preaching is emphasized here not only because of the high priority that these pastors placed upon it, but also because of the possible public perception that the sermon is simply a twenty-minute event on Sunday morning that is only one equal task among many for the modern minister.

In this section, the pastor as information disseminator in the pulpit will be considered from three perspectives: the purpose of the sermon, the role of the messenger, and the information in the message. The last perspective will consider the impact of the sermon topics chosen, the use of sources, and the styles of delivery.

Unlike the discussion of the pastor as healer or counselor, this section on the pastor as herald relies not only upon the interview data but upon the observation of 48 sermons preached by 23 preachers at 20 different churches during the ten-month course of this study. Seven of those churches were chosen as case studies, where I was able to attend several Sunday morning services and conduct multiple interviews with the pastors about the sermons they had preached.

Table 6 below provides a summary overview of the representative nature of these churches. These seven churches were chosen because of their reflection of the diversity of the churches in this community in terms of their size, the educational level of the pastor (last column), and their theological position (as judged by me). The column in Table 6 marked "# of Visit" refers to the number of times that I attended the Sunday morning services of these churches. The total of 29 visits to these seven churches accounted for 28 of the 48 sermons I observed during this ten-month project, since on only one of my visits to these seven churches was there no sermon delivered.

Table 6
An Overview of the Seven Case-Study Churches

Name of Church	Atten-dance	Theological Position	# of Visit	Inter-view	# of Staff	Highest Degree
Church 1	1,400	Moderate	7	5	2	Bachelor
Church 2	1,100	Liberal	6	4	3	M.Div.
Church 3	1,000	Conservative	4	3	1	Master's
Church 4	800	Liberal	4	4	2	D.Min.
Church 5	300	Moderate	4	4	2	D.Min.
Church 6	100	Conservative	2	3	1	Bachelor
Church 7	20	Moderate	2	2	1	M.Div.

NOTE: The numbers in the column labeled "# of Staff" refer to the number of staff I interviewed, not to the number employed. The actual numbers of staff at these seven churches were (in order from 1 to 7): 5, 5, 2, 4, 3, 1, and 1. My goal was to interview only those staff who regularly preached.

Though not noted in Table 6, the preaching pastors of these seven churches also reflected a variety of age groups: two were in their thirties, three were in their forties, and two were in their fifties. One of the seven churches chosen for a case study was actually a campus ministry that functioned for all practical purposes as any parish church might.

One of these seven churches' services was also televised weekly on local cable, which provided an opportunity for a more detailed examination of this use of electronic media in information dissemination. The pastor of another of these seven churches also broadcast regular radio messages, which will be discussed at the end of this chapter.

The interviews with the pastors of these seven case study churches typically lasted one hour, ranging from a maximum of two hours and a minimum of fifteen minutes in the case of some non-initial interviews. The emphasis in these case studies was upon the sermon, so the observations were focused upon that event.

In addition to hearing these pastors' sermons, I was also able to obtain the written materials that they took to the pulpit, which usually consisted of extended outlines or sometimes full manuscripts of their message. These materials, coupled with the interviews, allowed me to gain a better understanding of how these pastors and, by extension, the other pastors in this study disseminated information in the pulpit.

The data from these seven case studies will be presented in this section along with the data from the interviews of all sixty-two pastors, as well as with my observations of the twenty other sermons I heard. Thirteen of these twenty other sermons I directly observed while visiting thirteen other churches on single visits. Seven sermons I observed by either viewing video-tapes (in the case of two) or by listening to audiocassettes (in the case of the remaining five). However, these combined data will be presented in such a way as to maintain the anonymity of all of these churches.

This section on the pastor as information disseminator in the pulpit will fuse these case studies with the other examples. The goal is to maintain both the depth of data that the case studies offered and my obligation to preserve their anonymity.

THE PURPOSE OF THE SERMON

One of the questions I asked of most of the pastors in this study was a query about their philosophy of preaching. The purpose of this question was to discover in these pastors' own words what it was that they were trying to do in the pulpit on Sunday morning.[30] This was deemed important since the sermon is viewed in ministerial circles as something more than simply an oral discourse on a religious topic.

The sense of sacredness, in particular, with which the sermon was imbued by these pastors became clear in one of the first interviews I conducted. When asked about the amount of preparation that he devoted to his sermon on Sunday, this pastor noted, as did most other ministers in this study, that he spent more time on this one task than any other in the pastorate. His rationale for treating the sermon so seriously was this:

> I'll never forget my homiletics professor in seminary, an outstanding black homiletician and pulpiteer. He told us students once that if we ever found ourselves on Saturday night trying to put together an outline of a few things we'd like to say on Sunday morning, that quick as we could, we should call the local radio station and have it announced over the radio that Sunday morning church was being cancelled because we had no right going into the pulpit being un-prepared. I'll never forget him telling us that God expects and God demands more than that.

The uniqueness of the sermon became apparent at several points in this study, particularly in considering the connectedness between the message and the messenger, a point to be discussed in the next section. In this section, my goal is to provide a brief overview of the sermon's purpose in relationship to the role of the pastor as information disseminator. Some of these pastors' descriptions of the sermon's purpose have already been discussed in Chapter 2 under the section dealing with the pastor as interpreter.

It became quite clear in this study, however, that not everything that was said in the sermon was related directly to information transfer (using the definition of information provided in the Appendix). The following comment by one pastor provides perhaps the most succinct summary of what many pastors expressed in less direct terms relative to the multiple purposes of the sermon, only one of which is specifically focused on information dissemination. When asked his philosophy of preaching, this pastor responded:

> My approach to preaching is this. What do I want my people to know? What do I want them to be? What do I want them to do? I try to include all of that in each sermon. Some sermons are going to be heavier on one than the other. Some of them are going to be more of what I want them to know, so I concentrate on teaching them certain things. Others are more motivational, focusing on the doing.

His focus on knowing, being, and doing is a fair summary of what many of the pastors in this study were attempting to do in their preaching. While all three purposes have components of information dissemination, the issue of "knowing" is most relevant.

The point to be made here is that, though all sermons disseminate some information, not all, or even most, things said during any given sermon were so directed. Many times during the sermon a minister would spend considerable time inviting people to do certain things, e.g. repent or pray, without conveying any new information or repackaging in any substantive way old information. Sometimes entire sermons were used to motivate people or to encourage them, without any significant dissemination of information other than quoting a Scripture verse or two and recounting it over and over.

Therefore, in discussing the interview data and the analysis of the forty-eight sermons that were observed, this multiple nature of the sermon needs to be kept in mind. The focus of this discussion will be only upon the information disseminated in the pulpit and will consider other features of the sermon only insofar as they bear on this focus. In considering the purpose of the pulpit sermon, the concentration in the present study on only the informational role of the sermon must be constantly kept in mind.

THE ROLE OF THE MESSENGER

"When someone asked me once after one of my sermons how long it took to prepare, I told them, '38 years.'" This preacher's comment highlights an important distinction between the pastor's role in the pulpit as information disseminator and the role of traditional information professionals. To this pastor, who had been in ministry for 38 years, the preparation of the messenger as a person was just as significant as the preparation and delivery of the message in the pulpit.

In explaining, for example, his philosophy of preaching, a black pastor made this comment about the importance of his personal history and heritage in his preaching:

> I am not a hellfire and brimstone preacher. It is
> more sustaining and encouraging. I do preach
> with feeling and emotion, but my goal is to
> relate how I see a particular Scripture speaking
> to the people for today. I want to help them
> with their daily living, and *I do that through
> some of my own history as an African American*
> [emphasis mine], as well as through some of our
> shared history.

My observation of one sermon preached by this pastor seemed
to bear out this affinity between his own experiences and his
message. For example, he frequently used the language and
experience of the black community to illustrate his points and
was careful, though he preached primarily to a white audience,
to include black authors and sources in his sermons, e.g. Martin
Luther King, Jr.

While one could argue that the personal experiences of
librarians and other information professionals also bear
significantly on their ability to disseminate information, for
pastors--particularly in their roles as wounded healers and
interpreters of sacred text--the interplay between messenger and
message was nearly inviable. It was not merely a matter of
using life experiences anecdotally in the sermon. The line
between the disseminator and the information being disseminated
was nearly invisible at times.

Part of this interplay is probably due to the component
of trust so essential to the pastor's authority in dispensing
information. The importance of the personal authority of the
pastor, discussed in Chapter 2, is vital at this point, as Aristotle
and Quintilian have noted in their emphasis upon *ethos* and
pathos, as much as the *logos* or content, in public speaking. The
classic definition of preaching by Phillips Brooks (a noted
American preacher of the 19th century who was "university

preacher" at Harvard), in fact, stresses this connection between who the pastor is and what the pastor says: "Preaching is truth delivered through personality." The pastor's comment in Chapter 2 about his changed perspective on information in ministry is appropriate to repeat here:

> My whole thinking on information changed after I went to a right-wing, anti-abortion conference.... I was prepared not to listen.... But then...I found myself really listening. Not because of all his facts, but because I found myself starting to really like him as a person.

It is not possible to discuss the information disseminated in the pulpit without looking also at the importance of the one doing the disseminating and his or her personal involvement in the message. For example, several pastors mentioned during the interview process that they could only preach on topics with which they themselves were "struggling." One pastor explained his need to identify strongly with the sermon in these terms:

> You asked in your letter how I go about preparing a sermon or choosing a topic. I'll tell you. I choose an area where God is dealing with me. If it's not genuine with me, if it's not something that I'm wrestling with in my life, then it does not come across as genuine. And if it's not genuine, then people are not going to listen; I don't care how much you've prepared.

For him, as for many of the pastors interviewed in this study, the acceptability of the information being communicated was in large measure dependent upon the believability of the communicator of that information. Unlike the traditional information professional, the "genuineness" of the pastor's personal life is almost always "on display" in the ministry, and the importance of integrity and "practicing what one preaches" becomes particularly acute and expected. In other words, the sermon in this study was not viewed merely as an oral delivery of factual information. The consistency between what was said and what was lived was quite pronounced.[31]

This interplay between messenger and message was evidenced, for example, in the way in which many of these pastors relied on prayer in preaching. For many, preaching was essentially predicated upon prayer. In contrast to the use of prayer as a "divine communication" channel in counseling, prayer in this context was used by these pastors to mean the private request for some type of wisdom or assistance. As one pastor said, "I always pray before I step into the pulpit." Another noted that she always prayed, "You, not me, God" as she began to preach.

Several pastors mentioned that they had not originally planned to become ministers because they disliked public speaking. Yet, even in these cases they noted their reliance upon "asking God for spiritual help" in overcoming such an obvious obstacle to the pastor's weekly need to publicly disseminate information in the pulpit. On a more routine note, the prominence given to private prayer in the public sermon was noted by many ministers, including this one:

> I spend a lot of time in prayer when I'm work-
> ing on a sermon. That is a major part of my
> preparation. I probably spend more time in
> prayer than I do in study. [Pause.] Yeah, it's
> at least 50/50. I spend a lot of time in prayer....
> Part of the reason also is that I think presenta-
> tion is so important. Timing and presentation in
> preaching. I can say the right thing at the
> wrong time with the wrong spirit. So, I have to
> make sure my spirit is right. A few months

ago, I was frustrated with people and it was
coming through with whatever I preached. It
would come through, and I didn't realize it until
I got away to just pray and just seek the Lord.
He began to deal with me, and we had a significant turnaround from that point on.... God
began to deal with me in how to present the
message.

This pastor used prayer in one sense as a means of ad-
justing his delivery of information in ways that would be more
acceptable to his audience. In a deeper sense, his need to pray
"to make sure my spirit [was] right" suggests that preaching
could not effectively occur without the proper person in the
pulpit. This technique is without parallel in traditional
information provision, and these pastors were at a loss to
describe their use of prayer in terms that permitted analysis.

On another level, however, prayer sometimes amounted
to little more than the "quiet reflection" in which any public
speaker might engage prior to an oral address. "I usually lock
myself in the bedroom on Saturday evening and meditate on my
sermon," was how one pastor described the use of solitude to
help him improve his delivery. Another said he usually "prayed
and meditated for at least a week" on any given sermon topic so
that he could better understand how to talk about it to his
congregation. On an extended basis, this reflection even took
the form for some pastors of summers off or of sabbaticals so
that they could spend time preparing messages as well as
preparing themselves for the next year's series of sermons.

The point of prayer and meditation in this discussion,
however, is not that these devices merely helped pastors "think
more clearly" about what they wished to say in the pulpit. The
significance of these techniques is that they served to underscore
the importance of the person in the pastor's dissemination of

information. Note the comment cited above by the pastor whose prayer resulted in "God [beginning] to deal with *me* in how to present the message" [emphasis mine]. Prayer and, to some extent, meditation also reinforced the sense of "divine authority" and the important uniqueness of the information in the sermon.[32]

THE INFORMATION IN THE MESSAGE

The information that these pastors disseminated in their sermons will be considered in this section from the standpoint of three key issues: the choice of sermon topics, the use of sources in sermons, and the style in which information was delivered in the sermon. As before, it needs to be pointed out that the "information" under discussion here is not so much focused on the substantive content, but on the sources and channels used to disseminate the data.

The Choice of Topics

As an information disseminator in the pulpit, the pastor's first power is in deciding the topics on which he or she will preach. Unlike the role of the pastor as healer where the choice of topics is largely up to the other party, the pastor as herald allows the preacher considerable power to choose his or her own subject areas.

In the discussion in Chapter 3 on the information needs generated by others, it was noted that even outside the pulpit the pastor has the power to create an environment conducive to only certain kinds of questions by virtue of his or her openness to and practice of discussing only certain topics. This latent power is perhaps most prominent in the pulpit in that the pastor is the one who chooses the issues to address, and by extension, the information that will be delivered. To be sure, the wide use of the lectionary and its fixed, three-year cycle of Scriptural readings exercised some controlling influence in this regard, but even those pastors who used the lectionary had considerable freedom to develop a particular Biblical passage as they saw fit.

The topics of the 48 sermons that were observed during the course of this study tended to cluster into five different kinds of categories. The first four of these five categories were limited to topics that focused almost exclusively on Biblical information: Biblical characters, Biblical books, Biblical doctrines, and the Christian life. Other sources of information were used in discussing these topics in these four categories, but the substantive source in nearly all of these sermons was Scripture. Only the fifth category--counseling issues--included a rather broad range of resources, from the Bible to books on popular psychology. The topics of the 48 sermons observed in this study are presented according to these five categories in Table 7 below.

It should be noted here that this analysis of sermon topics is limited to the major themes addressed in the 48 sermons observed. On some occasions, pastors would raise other topics only tangentially related to the major subject of the sermon. In such cases, the use of information sources was noted and examined below, but the discussion in this section is limited to the major topics of these sermons, as summarized in Table 7.

The tabular arrangement also allows for these data to be presented in terms of two other important criteria, relative to the use of information sources in the sermon, textual sermons and topical sermons. The difference between textual and topical sermons is significant, in that many pastors typically prefer one form over the other, and this preference has a bearing on the kinds and extent of the information presented.

Textual sermons rely heavily upon one or more Scriptural texts to provide much of the substance of the sermon, while topical sermons are much more open-ended in terms of the kinds of data presented. To be sure, a topical sermon may be based ostensibly on a particular text of the Bible, but the text is used only as a stepping stone to other information or sources. For example, while 35 (73%) of the 48 sermons observed in this study cited at least one Biblical passage, only 18 (36%) used the text in any substantive way in the sermon. The numbers of textual and topical sermons are listed in Table 7 below according to five different categories of sermon topics that were found in the 48 sermons analyzed in this study.

Table 7
Categories of Sermon Topics Preached

Topic by Category	# of Textual	# of Topical	# of Total	Percent
1. Biblical Character	2	2	4	8%
2. Biblical Book	2	0	2	4%
3. Biblical Doctrine	3	5	8	17%
4. Christian Life	2	7	9	19%
5. Counseling Issue	9	16	25	52%
	---	---	---	----
	18	30	48	100%

The four sermons on Biblical characters included one on the Apostle Paul, one on Elizabeth (the mother of John the Baptist), and two on Jesus. The two sermons on Biblical books were on I Samuel and Paul's Epistle to the Philippians. The eight sermons on Biblical doctrines included topics on faith, prayer, love, and resurrection. The nine sermons on the Christian life were an amalgam of topics on encouraging people to "live more like Christ." By far the most frequent topic among the sermons in this study was that of counseling. These twenty-five sermons provided information on everything from depression and disappointment, to co-dependency and dysfunctional families.

The emphasis by the pastors in this community on counseling topics in the pulpit is consistent with the earlier discussion of the pastor as healer. Counseling issues were perceived by these ministers as being important information needs to address. This pastor's statement summarized this perspective:

> I remember a preaching professor say to us, "What are you going to say in your sermon that is going to make someone get off the bus and want to come in and sit down to hear you?" What am I going to say to the 250 people in my congregation that will help them with the last argument they had with their spouse or their worrying over their kids? ... I'm very reactive, but I think a pastor has to be sensitive to what is going on in the community and where the people are.... Just picking up the newspaper and reading you can tell that dysfunction is prevalent in our society and culture and families.

His perception of widespread dysfunction and family problems in the community was an important factor in choosing the sermon topics that he did.

Another pastor, who frequently preached on counseling or relational issues, said that he would much prefer preaching through books of the Bible as he used to do, but that the needs of his congregation would not permit him to do so. He quoted as supporting evidence "a statistic from a recent book" that he had read which suggested that "75% of the people coming through the church door today are addicted, co-dependent, or dysfunctional." The pastoral staff of one large church had even chosen to "preach through" a popular book on co-dependency, written by a Christian psychologist, because "that's what our people are reading." Said one pastor of a small church, "I try to feel the needs of my people so I preach on relationships often because that's what they need."

It should be noted that much of the counseling information that was observed being disseminated in sermons dealing with these topics was Biblically based, though not necessarily drawn from one particular text of the Bible. It was very common for the preachers of those sermons to draw principles from a variety of Scriptural passages that they "applied" to a given counseling problem.

For example, one pastor used the Old Testament prophet "Nehemiah as a case study to help us understand how we can deal with disappointment." He read several passages from the book of Nehemiah and then drew principles from those passages which he offered as "suggestions" for how the parishioners could deal with similar situations of disappointment. The information he cited was limited primarily to Old Testament history and to his own personal testimony in handling disappointment. Another pastor, who had a professional doctorate in pastoral counseling and who had decided to address several counseling-related issues in a series of sermons, chose an epistle of Paul as the narrative framework from which he then addressed such issues as co-dependency and marriage. The strong use of Scripture and the constant emphasis on Biblical principles were particularly prominent in these kinds of sermons.

There was one sermon on depression that I observed, however, in which the pastor frequently used the technical vocabulary of psychology, e.g. manic depressive, psychoses, endogenous depression, and reactive depression. Since this pastor had not had formal training in pastoral counseling, I felt this was a significant opportunity to determine the degree to which his preparation for this sermon, which consisted of some rather extensive reading in books and articles on the topic, had enabled him to speak authoritatively on the subject.

In order to assess the accuracy of the information being conveyed by the pastor in this sermon, I provided an audio-cassette recording to a graduate professor of pastoral counseling, who also had his own part-time counseling practice, and asked for his written opinion. Among his comments were these:

> [This] sermon provides basically accurate overview data on depression. While [there were] some problems with the five categories of depression that he mentioned, he wisely limited his clinical response to reactive depression, leaving the door open for people to ignore his recommendations if their depression does not seem to be reactive depression.... From the standpoint of being helpful to the general Christian who is sometimes depressed, I would say it is a helpful message.

It should be noted that this sermon is only one instance of using such a high level of technical information in the pulpit that was not of a theological nature. However, since it was the most prominent example of this kind of information dissemination, this single case does at least suggest that such data could be conveyed from the pulpit accurately and appropriately by even "non-experts" in the field. It would be helpful to do further study with a number of such sermons by a variety of pastors to determine if this one instance represents a pattern or not.

The pastors in this study, however, mentioned other factors besides counseling-based information needs that influenced the topics on which they chose to preach and the information they chose to disseminate. Sometimes, an event or situation in the community was the catalyst for a sermon. One pastor had preached a sermon on Jesus' encounter with a non-Jewish woman (from John's Gospel) because of "the issues of racism that our neighborhood is dealing with," a reference to several race-related incidents in the community. The information he conveyed in this sermon was limited, however, to Biblical data with only oblique references to the local context.

Another pastor mentioned that he often used the newspaper as a way of discovering issues that he felt needed addressing from the pulpit. Similarly, two ministers commented that they had recently preached sermons on evil because of the publicity given in the local paper to a particularly heinous crime committed in a nearby state.

Many pastors noted that they had preached at least one sermon related to the Persian Gulf War a year prior to this study because of the involvement of local citizens in that military event. A campus minister's message on this issue had been deemed sufficiently useful that the university had requested copies to be made and distributed to the students and faculty. Unfortunately, this minister could not find any extant copies for me to analyze.

Sometimes, the calendar was the catalyst for choosing a sermon topic. Certainly the advents of Christmas and Easter determined the sermon topic for many pastors at those times of year. One campus minister had preached a sermon on stress prior to my interview of him in December because he felt it was a significant issue for university students at that time of year as the semester drew to a close. The pastor of a church with many young adults had preached a series of sermons in the fall that he had entitled "Christianity 101" because many new students and other new members were coming back to church after the summer months, and he felt they needed a basic re-grounding in the faith. The anniversary of the Supreme Court's *Roe v. Wade* decision had also provided the opportunity for three of the pastors I interviewed in January to preach a sermon on abortion because it was "National Right to Life Sunday."

One of these pastors talked about his sermon on abortion and provided me with a copy of his detailed notes that he took to the pulpit. Most of the information he provided was taken from his interpretation of Jesus' parable of the Good Samaritan in Luke 15. He felt that babies were the modern equivalent of the "man who fell among thieves" and needed help similar to that provided by the Good Samaritan. He quoted from three contemporary Christian authors to support his stance against abortion, but the most substantial use of information outside of Scripture was his citation of some abortion statistics from a 1985 booklet on abortion. He had even photocopied the first page of this booklet and pasted it into the introduction of his sermon notes with a marginal gloss listing the author, title, and date of publication. His rationale for using--in his words--"this one outdated source" was that "someone sent it to me several years ago in the mail so I had it handy in my library."

Other researchers have noted the importance of access in how professionals use information (e.g. Allen, 1987; Lancaster, 1990; Soper, 1976; and Wilkin, 1977). The fact that the ministers in this study rated their own personal libraries as their most important source of information (see discussion in Chapter 3) also suggests that these pastors likewise placed a high value on the accessibility of information. Certainly, this pastor's use of this information source in his sermon on abortion supports this perception.

However, the topics chosen for the sermons preached by the pastors in this study are only part of the picture to be painted of how these ministers disseminated information in the pulpit. Though the choice of topics exercised some controlling influence on the range of information presented, what is at issue is how these pastors actually used the various sources in their sermons.

The Use of Sources

Unlike the traditional information professional, two sources unique to the ministry accounted for nearly half of all the sources that I observed being used in the 48 sermons preached by the pastors in this study. These two sources were the Bible and anthologies of sermon illustrations. The use of Scripture has been discussed in Chapter 2 under the pastor as interpreter.

In this section, the Bible will be considered in the context of how it was used publicly in the Sunday morning sermon. The use of illustration digests has also been discussed briefly in Chapter 3 in the section on abstracting services, which such digests resemble, but they too will be presented here from the standpoint of how these preachers used them in the pulpit.

Before looking at sources, some overview data demonstrating the range of sources used in the 48 sermons observed during this study is provided in Table 8 below. The second column indicates how many times a particular type of source was observed during the 48 sermons that were analyzed.

In the table below, "personal illustrations" are, strictly speaking, more content oriented than my definition would allow. They are included here, however, in order to present a more complete picture of the various kinds of information used in these sermons. Also, "current events" in this table refer to local, regional, national, and international news events known through a variety of sources.

Table 8
Frequency of the Sources Used in the 48 Sermons
(N = 552)

Type of source used   Frequency Percentage

1. Scriptural citations   185   33%
2. Personal illustrations   83   15%
3. Illustration digests   76   14%
4. Biblical commentaries   36   7%
5. Books on religious themes   34   6%
6. Current events   26   5%
7. Books on secular themes   24   4%
8. Religious magazines   20   4%
9. Television programs   15   3%
10. Greek and Hebrew language tools   14   3%
11. Secular magazines   12   2%
12. Unknown   9   2%
13. Radio programs   7   1%
14. Musical selections/singers   6   1%
15. Movies or films   5   1%
                                         552   100%

        In interpreting the data presented in Table 8, it needs to
be made clear what is meant by the term "use." "Use" does not
necessarily mean "cite." The sources analyzed in the sermons
preached by the pastors in this study were not always carefully
or even directly noted by these pastors in the pulpit or even in
their notes.

        Sometimes the use was obvious, such as those instances
where the pastor specifically mentioned a particular author or
title. At other times, the use was inferred, for example, when
the pastor referred to "commentators on this Scripture." Insuf-
ficient data were found to allow any observations regarding the

circumstances under which a pastor did or did not cite a source. One pastor did note that he did so only when he thought it would "mean anything" to his congregation.

The 552 sources used by the pastors in the 48 sermons observed during this study were not always directly cited as is common practice in print media. On only two occasions did I observe such wholesale lack of attribution that the sermon could have been described as plagiarism. Both pastors were quick to acknowledge privately the sources from which the majority of their sermons had been taken, but this was not done publicly in the pulpit.

Part of this failure to cite may be due to the oral bias of the pulpit sermon. In a tradition at least as old as the Puritan preachers, many pastors have a tendency to view all non-Scriptural texts as mere commentary on the Bible. In a pioneer study of preaching and religious culture in Colonial New England, for example, the Yale historian Stout (1986) offered this important insight in his book *The New England Soul*. Based on his examination of more than 2,000 Puritan sermon manuscripts and handwritten sermon notes, Stout (pp. 35-36) observed:

> Despite the wide reading...that went into preparing a sermon series, extrabiblical names rarely appeared in the notes. The minister's intent in eliminating such references from the sermon was not to plagiarize their sources; strictly speaking there was no human "original" to steal or copy. The only original was God's Word, and all commentaries were part of a derivative common enterprise. When people listened to the sermon, they expected to hear God's Word--and only God's Word--made comprehensible to their limited capacities. As

Dover's John Rayner warned, "If any minester
will preach trash and toyes, traditions of men
instead of the puer word of God, theire workes
shall be burnt."

A similar insight has been applied recently by Miller (1991) to
the black church and to the preaching of Martin Luther King,
who has been posthumously accused of plagiarism in his doctoral
dissertation. The highly oral tradition of black preaching, Miller
argues, is a linguistic genre that is also viewed as a "derivative
common enterprise" not susceptible nor amenable to attribution.[33]

Therefore, in discussing the sources "used" by pastors in
these 48 sermons it is important to keep this consideration in
mind. It should also be noted that the 552 sources listed in
Table 8 do not include anonymous references whose source cannot be known nor common maxims that have, in effect, passed
into the public domain. For example, neither statements such as
"They say time heals all wounds" or "A stitch in time saves
nine" nor jokes or fictional stories were included, unless the
pastor noted either publicly or privately a particular source for
that usage. The category labeled "unknown" in Table 8 was
used to cover such references as "I read somewhere once that
62% of the ...". With these observations as background, the
individual categories listed in Table 8 will now be discussed.

As stated above, the source most frequently used by
these pastors in the pulpit was Scripture. Fully one-third of the
sources used in these sermons were from the Bible. As pointed
out in Chapter 3, among some of these pastors the frequent use
of Scripture in preaching was due in part to the easy access
provided by their computers. One pastor frequently read Scripture from the pulpit because "it's so easy to download these texts
from my Bible search program into my word processor."

Another pastor quoted frequently from a version of the

Bible that was not his personal favorite "because it's on my computer." The nearly constant use of Scripture in the sermons of one pastor whom I observed over a several-week period led me to ask him about this practice:

> Interviewer: Have you always quoted a lot of Scripture in your preaching?
>
> Pastor: Yeah, I have always used the Bible a lot, but I think my computer has probably encouraged me to use even more Scripture. It has made me aware of Scriptures that I didn't have in my mind by memory. I make a lot more references to Scripture now because my on-line Bible program has got so many cross-references, almost 600,000 for the whole Bible. It's a great program. So when I do my sermons...I can call up those references and put them right into my word processor. I even print the Scriptural references in condensed print so I can get more of them into my sermon notes.

In these cases, the electronic media exercised an otherwise hidden influence in terms of the amount of Biblical information that pastors disseminated from the pulpit. The influence here, however, was one of degree. These pastors would undoubtedly have used Scripture prominently in their preaching, but the computer allowed them to do so to a greater degree.

The importance that the pastors in this community attached to the use of Scripture in preaching was highlighted by this pastor's comment regarding the advice given to her by a homiletics professor, "I don't care what your source is when you preach, even if it is the telephone book, you make sure you bring them the Biblical message of Good News." Hyperbole notwithstanding, the prominence given to the Bible as the source of sermonic information was not surprising.

What was a little surprising was to find the use of Scripture fairly evenly divided along the theological spectrum, from conservative to liberal. Only two sermons among the 48 had no Scripture in them at all. One was by a liberal minister whose congregation had "no more than 10 to 15% who were Christian," and the other was by a rather conservative pastor who ironically noted that his pet peeve was "preachers who didn't ever use the [Biblical] text" in their preaching. One theologically liberal pastor attributed the emphasis he placed on Scripture in his sermons to a childhood experience:

> I am theologically liberal, but I have a strong
> passion for the Scriptures.... I credit a Sunday
> School class for that. When I was in sixth grade
> in [named the place], one of the courses that I
> had was about the Bible and how it came to be.
> That laid so strong a seed that ever since then
> I've just loved to study and use the Bible.... In
> fact, when I interviewed for this position, one
> woman who heard me describe myself as a Bib-
> lical preacher felt sure that she had a rabid
> fundamentalist on her hands. Really, you can be
> liberal and Biblical at the same time.

Unfortunately, I was not able to observe any of his sermons to determine the manner in which he used the Bible as an information source in his preaching due to a recent illness that had kept him out of the pulpit during the time of this study.

The primary use of Scripture in the sermons I observed was to lend a sense of divine authority to what was being said. A conservative pastor noted this use of Scripture in preaching in these terms:

> My sermons usually begin with a topic or
> thought in my head, but I always try to find a
> [Biblical] passage that deals with that idea....
> I've found out that even though this is my
> sermon, it is good for people to know that it's
> Scriptural. While I may not always give exact
> verse references, I'll say things like, "As it says
> in Matthew" or "As John says" so they'll know
> that it's not just me talking.

His need to support his own thoughts with Scripture was
an attempt to provide "divine support" for his words, which, of
course, he believed to be in full agreement with Scripture. The
use of Scripture as an authoritative source (using the source-
based definition of information provided in the Appendix) was
made explicit in this pastor's response to a question about what
sources he relied on in preaching:

> From a philosophical standpoint, my major
> source is the Word of God. I don't mean that to
> be trite.... I was visiting a church recently
> where the sermon was just illustration after
> illustration and no [Biblical] text. The sermon
> never referred back to Scripture. I believe if
> that is what we are going to do, we lose our
> authority. I'm not standing up there to give
> them [my] thoughts.... The Bible is our first
> source.

As noted in Chapter 2 under the pastor's divine
authority, the importance of this use of Scripture cannot be
underestimated in the sermon. Some pastors even went so far as
to highlight Scriptural quotations in their sermon notes in red
because when they glanced down at their notes during delivery
the red text would stand out and they would be less likely to
forget to use this source during their oral delivery. For one, the

red markings were his clue to introduce the quotation with "The Bible says...," much in the same way that Billy Graham does in his preaching.

My observation of one pastor's monolog on the Biblical character of Elizabeth suggested that nearly the entire sermon was taken from Scriptural texts, and this was confirmed by interviewing the pastor and by reading her sermon manuscript. At least five pastors were observed quoting Scripture extensively during the sermon from memory, usually the King James version because of "the beauty of the language," as one commented. In fact, one pastor quoted fourteen different passages from the Bible from memory during just one sermon. He later explained that "we were trained to do that in school." Many pastors used Scripture much less frequently, but equally substantively. As one pastor noted succinctly, "All I have in the pulpit is one Scripture and one idea."

The heavy reliance upon Scripture in preaching, however, was noted by some pastors in this study as problematic. The difficulty was that they believed that more and more people in their audience on Sunday morning were less and less Biblically "literate." For example, when asked if they could refer to the Biblical prophet Jonah (he of "whale" fame) and assume a majority of their audience would automatically know to whom they were referring, most pastors replied that they could not. Typical of how these pastors said they would alter, but not abandon, the use of less known Scriptures was this pastor's comment:

> I'll usually go ahead and use the Scripture, but I'll introduce it briefly with some humor: "You all know the story of the big whale" or "The fish with indigestion" or something like that. So there is a connection that people will feel without feeling that you are talking down to them.

One particular example of how a pastor used Scripture without presuming awareness on the part of his audience was found in the case study of a church where the sermon was televised over local cable. In one sermon on the topic of "spiritual language," the pastor made a reference to the Biblical text of Genesis 11 in this way:

> You remember the Old Testament story of the tower of Babel in Genesis. It is rather interesting that these chaps there thought that all they needed to do was build a big tower that reached to heaven, and they wouldn't need God anymore. They could just simply climb the stairs, and they would be there. How futile their efforts were when God had to step down a long way, just to see the heights they had come. But it said the whole world was filled with one language, and somehow God confounded the language. And all the people found difficulty understanding each other. They could not understand each other.

Instead of asking people to turn to the text (which many presumably could not have located) or referring to it in passing (which presumably would have left many people wondering what it was that was being cited), this pastor spent some time rehearsing the Biblical story. However, he did so with phrases that were meant to inform, without insulting, e.g. "You remember the Old Testament story...in Genesis."

His use of repetition at the end of this Scriptural reference also appeared to be a conscious effort to help his audience remember the information: "God confounded the language," "the people found difficulty understanding each other," and "they could not understand each other." The time it took to recount the Biblical story and reinforce it through repetition was worth the use of Scripture as an authoritative source in preaching.

In addition to the Bible, Biblical aids were also commonly used. In Table 8 these sources include "Biblical commentaries" and "Greek and Hebrew language tools," which together accounted for 50 uses or nearly 10% of the 552 sources used in the 48 sermons. The wide use of these tools, including the lectionary and its accompanying aids, has already been discussed earlier in Chapter 3.

In this section, the public use of these sources in information dissemination in the sermon will be briefly noted. The use of Biblical aids in preaching was one of the more difficult sources to detect because of how these pastors used them. Their primary use was for background material, some of which was discussed publicly in the sermon and some of which served only to help prepare the pastor privately. Therefore, even though commentaries were observed as being used in public delivery on only 36 occasions, it is quite likely that the information contained in them made its way into these sermons more frequently in less observable ways.

Even the 14 uses of Greek and Hebrew in the pulpit were usually couched in such phrases as "the original language suggests" or "what this word really means is." As one pastor noted, "I don't do exegesis in front of my congregation." These pastors evidently assumed that they would convey a sense of "academic arrogance" if they were to pepper their sermons with "the Greek word here is *pharmaceia*" or "in Hebrew *sheol* means."

The one exception was the public use by several pastors of the Greek word for love, *agape*, which appears to have become a "Christianized" term in widespread use among church members. One pastor did underline in red the meanings of

Greek words in his sermon notes in order to "emphasize their importance," but I did not observe his mentioning the word "Greek" publicly when he preached these sermons.

The most vivid example of the use of Greek and Hebrew language tools in the sermon was the case of one pastor who regularly followed a lengthy exegetical guide that required translation of the text and extensive word studies in Greek and Hebrew lexica and theological dictionaries. However, in neither of the sermons that I observed him preaching did he make any direct mention of this exegetical preparation. As with many pastors, the use of Biblical reference tools was primarily kept in the study, not in the pulpit.

This practice of not noting more scholarly sources, such as Greek and Hebrew reference tools, is in rather stark contrast to what information professionals in academic circles typically do, where such scholarship is expected to be exposed, not hidden. Again, the lack of emphasis by the pastors in this study on the image of the pastor as expert, as discussed in Chapter 2, is relevant.

Another category of sources used in preaching was personal experiences, which was second only to Scripture in frequency, accounting for 15% of the 552 sources used in the 48 sermons I observed. One pastor noted that he had begun more and more to use his own life experiences as sermon sources because of a recent workshop on preaching that he had attended in which this had been stressed. In the following interchange, another pastor explained one of the reasons why personal illustrations were so popular among pastors:

> Interviewer: Are there any particular sources that you use in finding illustrations for your sermons?

Pastor: The bulk of my illustrations are from
my own life.... I've got a book here of 7,000
sermon illustrations, but I've found that most
people really don't want to hear what G. Camp-
bell Morgan [a noted 19th-century British
preacher] or some of the greats from the past--
Whitfield--have said about a particular passage
of Scripture that I relay to them. They've got
hurts, and they've got needs. And they want to
know how that passage works out in real life.
And who better to illustrate that than me.

Interviewer: How do you do that?

Pastor: I think if you asked someone from my
congregation, they would say that I'm extremely
vulnerable in the pulpit. I will share illustrations
from my marriage, from my family, you know,
that can be very tender and open. But if I'm
going to allow the Holy Spirit to minister, I've
got to model that kind of transparency.

Interviewer: Do you subscribe to any
illustration services? For example, several
ministers in town have mentioned InfoSearch?

Pastor: No. Those are fine. I've got no
problem with that. I've just found that the
instant bond, coming from the communicator's
perspective now, that you develop when you
open yourself up is just incredible. I mean the
room goes silent, bam, right now.

The sense of intimacy between information sender and information receiver was a major factor in this pastor's, and others',
use of personal illustrations and experiences.

One pastor used a number of sources in his sermon on persecution, but it was his reference to a traumatic incident involving himself that, in his words, "hushed the crowd so you could hear a pin drop." My observation of this sermon confirmed the effect that this one reference had on the audience. The image of the pastor as a wounded healer, discussed in Chapter 2, also testifies to the relationship between these kinds of very personal sources and the pastor as an information provider.

Some pastors also used the personal experiences of their church members as sermon sources, provided they had their permission and, in the case of some churches, the pastors did not "break the seal of the confessional." One pastor spent at least one day a week visiting parishioners where they worked not only so he could better understand them, but also so that he could "preach in their terms." Another said he often used in his sermons what was happening in the community relative to what his members were experiencing, which, he continued, "is why I try to visit at least five people a week."

Another pastor made a particular point of telling an otherwise unknown story about Albert Einstein by noting that it had been relayed to him by a personal friend who, while a student at Princeton, went Christmas carolling with several students to Einstein's home and was invited in to hear the scientist play a religious Christmas carol on his violin despite his Jewish heritage. In one sermon, a pastor read during his introduction a lengthy letter written by a couple in the congregation as a way of establishing rapport with his audience.

One of the most unusual uses of a personal source was by the following pastor. He recounted at the beginning of the sermon his own recurring nightmares as a way of introducing a message on the seriousness of worship. He introduced his sermon with these words:

> Let me tell you how I feel. Oftentimes it starts
> in the wee hours of a Saturday night. I'm
> getting restless, nervous. "Oh, no, not again,
> please not again." But still the nightmares
> begin.... I'm stepping into the pulpit--no
> sermon, no notes--where I had placed them just
> before the service. I look back to the choir, and
> it's always the same choir member, who will
> remain unnamed, waving my manuscript in the
> air, with a devilish smile on his or her face. I
> leave the pulpit and start toward the waving of
> the papers. Along the way I encounter deep
> crevices and chasms, fingers clawing at and
> ripping my robe. And the very worst: robed
> and hooded skeletons, which disintegrate at my
> slightest touch.

The longer he talked the quieter the auditorium became,
and it appeared that people were quite stunned by this rather
personal information. It did, however, seem to have the effect
he desired, that of communicating a sense of wonder and seriousness to the worship service. He did, in fact, continue in his
sermon to explain that the point he was trying to make with this
revelation was that the church auditorium could be, and should
be, a place of fear and awe when used seriously as a place of
worship.

In this and similar cases, the intimate aspects of personal
experiences were used by these pastors to elicit a sense of
"ownership" of the information. In other words, this happened
to *my* pastor so it must be true and important and worth noting.

On the other end of the involvement scale was the widespread use of illustration digests. These anthologies of stories,
quotations, and historical incidents were frequently used by the
pastors in this study to illustrate or reinforce points in their

sermons. Fully 14% of the 552 sources used in the sermons I observed were taken from what were often described as "encyclopedias of illustrations." Many pastors had even developed their own set, often copying them onto 3" x 5" cards for filing purposes.

The frequent use of these resources underscores an important finding relative to how these pastors disseminated information publicly in the pulpit. Most of the 76 instances of pastors citing such sources were actually derived from perhaps as few as ten different illustration resources. Yet, to the hearer it would appear that as many as 76 different sources were being cited.

For example, one pastor began his message by quoting Benjamin Disraeli. A later interview indicated that he had found that quotation, not by reading books by or about Disraeli, but by referring to an illustration digest. Another pastor recounted at some length a touching story about a 19th-century hymn writer, but it was apparent only to him and later to me that he had not read any primary sources on this man, only an illustration from an anthology.

While the use of anthologies or quotation digests is not unique to the pastoral profession, these tools do appear to be more than an incidental resource for information dissemination. The growing use of computer-based illustration services, such as the InfoSearch program discussed in Chapter 3, suggests that such tools are not decreasing, only finding newer and more efficient forms.

One possible problem that may be associated with the use of these kinds of sources is the tendency to use such material in isolation from its original context. Another concern is that many of the illustration books that these pastors gave me to examine appeared to rely on rather dated material, whose accuracy and authenticity were open to question.

For these reasons, there is the concern that the information disseminated from these secondary, abstracting sources may not be as reliable as would be primary resources. The use of these anthologies also creates the illusion that pastors are more widely read than perhaps is the case. At any rate, such tools did appear to be significant sources of information for many of the pastors in this study, though their influence was tempered by their general use as illustrative material, not as substantive points in the sermon.

Two other categories of sources used by these pastors in their preaching were books and periodicals. These will be considered here together because both types of sources appeared to be used in similar ways and with comparable frequency (ranging from 6% for religious books to 2% for secular magazines; see Table 8). The same diversity of reading patterns that was noted in Chapter 3 was also found in the use of these sources publicly in the pulpit. There were no particular authors or magazines that were quoted or referred to more than others.

Among the 48 sermons heard in this study, there were references to such authors as Charles Swindoll (a contemporary preacher), William James (a 19th-century philosopher), Dr. Seuss, Martin Luther, Thornton Wilder, and Vince Lombardi--all of whose works had been read--at least in part--by the pastors who cited them. Pastors quoted articles from *Leadership*, *Christian Century*, and *Moody Monthly*, but they also referred to articles in *Sports Illustrated*, *GQ*, and *National Geographic*.

The common practice was to cite only the author or the title (sometimes both), almost never was complete bibliographic information given as would be expected with information disseminated through print media. Sometimes the author's background or qualifications for writing were provided (e.g. "as David

Seamands, a noted Christian psychologist, has written..."), but such details were dependent upon whether the pastor thought they were necessary or relevant. This appears to be another instance of the pastor functioning somewhat as filter in terms of the amount of information disseminated publicly in the pulpit.

It was my observation that books and periodicals were used by these pastors for two purposes in terms of their information value. In several instances, they were used to provide numerical data, as was the case in the sermon on abortion mentioned earlier. In other instances, they were used because of the particular phrasing by the cited author. For example, in a sermon on marriage one pastor used the following source in the following way:

> In Thornton Wilder's play *The Skin of Our Teeth*
> the character of Mrs. Antrobus says to her hus-
> band, calmly, almost dramatically: "I didn't
> marry you because you were perfect.... I mar-
> ried you because you gave me a promise...."

The alliterative contrast between "perfect" and "promise," coupled with his use of the term "dramatically," enabled this pastor to make a memorable point about the importance of commitment in marriage. The importance of phrasing to these pastors is not surprising given the oral nature of the sermon, where such rhetorical techniques are prized. On one occasion, even the title of a sermon was borrowed directly from a book title because of its rhythm and cadence, "My Utmost for His Highest," after a devotional book by Oswald Chambers that was used by one pastor in a sermon on commitment.

Another, more ambiguous source was the use of current events. Unlike books or periodicals or other print-related sources, these sources were more focused on the content than the container. The 26 uses of such sources could not be isolated clearly according to their origin, but they are included here because they do represent a different kind of information being disseminated in the pulpit. The 26 references to current events noted in Table 8 were rather widely distributed in terms of content. Two of the more significant allusions were to the Thomas-Hill Senate hearings in the fall of 1991 and the Los Angeles riots in the spring of 1992, events which accounted for seven of the 26 references.

The sermon on persecution mentioned briefly above included four references to the Thomas-Hill hearings, all four of which were intended to help the audience understand what it was like to be "persecuted" in contemporary society. The information associated with this case appeared to be accurately conveyed from the pulpit, but it was equally clear that the pastor's focus was upon Clarence Thomas, the Supreme Court nominee, not upon Anita Hill, the woman who accused him of sexual harassment.

While this focus seemed to suggest that the pastor might be "taking sides" in the pulpit over this controversial issue, during follow-up interviews he assured me that his intention was only to call attention to the public perception that Thomas was being "persecuted," not upon the legitimacy of Hill's accusations, i.e. his focus was upon the accused, not the accuser. He was quick to stress the seriousness with which he treated allegations of sexual harassment, particularly in light of the number of professional women who were members of his congregation.

As for the references to the Los Angeles riots, one pastor used the incident to suggest how "we all as citizens are partly to blame" because of the injustice inherent in "the system," while another pastor used it to talk about his recent jury duty in a local homicidal case in order to demonstrate how difficult and serious it was for an individual to "prove beyond a reasonable doubt that presumably innocent people are really guilty." As with personal illustrations, the references to current events appeared to be employed because of their power to focus the audience's attention on what was being said, that is, the information was not new so the attention was on the pastor's interpretation of the data.

The last category of sources used in preaching by the pastors in this study include the electronic media of television, radio, and movies. Together these three types of information sources were cited 27 times, with over half (15) being television (see Table 8). Music may also be included here in that three of the six uses of this source were to theatrical productions, while the other three were to published hymns.

The relatively infrequent use of most of these electronic media publicly in the pulpit may perhaps be attributed to the oral "bias" (and to some extent, print "bias") that most of the ministers in this study demonstrated, as discussed at the beginning of this chapter. Five of the fifteen references to television programs, for example, were by one pastor. His church's electronic preference was noted in an earlier discussion.

When television sources were used, they were often intended to provide a common "story" with which the audience could identify. In one instance, the young pastor of a church of mostly "twenty-something" members referred to several situations portrayed on the program "Saturday Night Live," whose primary viewers fit this age group. Another pastor used the Bill Cosby program to talk about family relationships because he felt he could safely assume that most everyone in his congregation were familiar with that television program. The references made to radio were primarily by theologically conservative pastors who recounted stories told by Paul Harvey.

Only five movies were cited in the 48 sermons observed in this study. They were *The Dead Poets Society*, *Bill and Ted's Excellent Adventures*, *The Black Robe*, *Boyz 'N the Hood*, and

Backdraft). Like television, these sources were used to recount stories or events that the pastor expected the audience to know. This evocative nature of the more popular forms of electronic media may be used more and more by pastors in the pulpit as familiarity with Biblical stories is replaced by the "stories" on which the television generation has been reared. However, considerably more study is needed to substantiate this conjecture.

The Styles of Delivery

Before concluding this discussion of the pastor as information disseminator in the pulpit, one final area needs to be examined regarding the styles in which these pastors delivered the information they disseminated. At issue here is not just the topics on which these pastors chose to speak or how they used particular sources in their sermons. Though less evident, the manner in which these pastors disseminated information also appeared to have some effect upon the actual information dissemination process in the pulpit. The scope of this project did not allow for any detailed analysis of homiletical style or audience analysis, but two brief observations may be made about how pastors communicated in the pulpit the data they gathered in the study.

First, the prominent use of storytelling was quite evident in this study.[34] No sermon was observed in which this predominantly oral form was not employed in some manner. Part of these pastors' preference for this oral technique may be due to the perceived truth of Whitehead's observation that "in the real world it is more important that a proposition be interesting than that it be true," as Lischer (1984, p. 28) noted in his critique of the growing use of storytelling as a homiletical device.

What Lischer and others (e.g. Willimon, 1990) who have denounced this oral technique as providing entertainment at the expense of information have failed to note, however, is that storytelling can be used to provide information that is both interesting and true. As an oral device, storytelling exhibits no necessary exclusivity regarding the kinds of information that can and cannot be correctly conveyed, except perhaps complex theoretical concepts.

Homer's *Iliad*, for example, contains accurate political, military, architectural, engineering, and economic information, along with its religious myths, and yet this story was delivered in oral form for centuries before being committed to paper. Similarly, much of Scripture is in narrative form and was originally the center of an extensive oral tradition. Recent homiletical theoreticians (see Eslinger, 1987, for a convenient summary of five such advocates) have suggested that storytelling is a mode of delivery quite conducive to telling the Biblical story accurately and adequately.

Storytelling was used in two ways by the pastors in this study, in terms of the sermons I observed. On one level pastors told stories simply as illustrations. The framework of the sermon was basically propositional (introduction, major points, and conclusion), but stories were frequently used to support the propositions being made. Sometimes these stories were from the Bible, many times they were not. Several sermons used what the pastors termed "case studies," which were really extended stories used to demonstrate the points they were trying to make in their sermons. The information in these stories was quite varied, ranging from biographical data to counseling theory.

On a more complex level, the sermon itself was often the story. The dramatic portrayal by one pastor of the Biblical character of Elizabeth was entirely one long story told through her eyes. The pastor's explanation was that "this story is so powerful on its own." The pastor who recounted from the pulpit her own life story as an adult child of an alcoholic was another example of the sermon as story. In this case, the story contained counseling information that she deemed helpful to parishioners facing similar situations. The reported effect of this "story" was so pronounced that she viewed this one sermon as a turning point in her ministry in that she felt that parishioners thereafter began to accept and trust her as their own pastor.

The effect that storytelling in general appeared to have when used by the pastors in this study was that this style of information dissemination allowed listeners to grasp the information in digestible chunks (episodic stories), in a logically inductive manner (story, then moral), and with some sense of personal involvement in the information (identification with the story's characters).[35] Since the research design in this exploratory project was limited to interviews with pastors, not their parishioners, further study involving audience analysis is needed to determine what effects were actually occurring.

The second style of delivery noted in this study, besides storytelling, was the presentation manner of the television news anchor that appeared to predominate among many of these pastors. What is meant by this electronic image of the news anchor is that many of the sermons were delivered in calm, measured, professional tones associated with network news broadcasts. Most ministers stayed behind the pulpit, "read" from their script (written or oral), and displayed little of the emotional passion so prominent among televangelists, who appear to stand more in the tradition of the revival tent than the television medium.

While this image may be forced in some aspects, it was not foreign to some of the pastors I interviewed. Even among denominations often associated with a highly emotional style of preaching, one pastor acknowledged that "when it comes time to deliver the message [on Sunday morning], I'm the newsman; I report the news." To be sure, my observation of his preaching was that his style was quite emotional, even demonstrative, yet his mental image of himself was still that of the news reporter. Shelley (1986) also noted this trend among contemporary clergy to use the model of the television news anchor in their preaching.

One of the implications of this manner of delivery for the ministry is that the information being disseminated by the pastor using this style can be trusted in the same way that one can trust a Walter Cronkite or a Peter Jennings. A further implication, though quite untested in this study, is that a generation of church members raised on television are more likely to listen to that style of information delivery than they are to the styles associated with earlier eras of preaching in this country.

Here, too, further study is needed to establish definitive criteria that are characteristic of the television news anchor that could then be compared to modern preaching styles. If the comparison were to hold across cases, then this finding could serve as a key component in examining the information transfer process in religious communication.

SUMMARY

Among the findings that emerged from this study of the pastor as information disseminator in the pulpit, there are three that fairly summarize the significant issues. These three findings concern the purpose of the sermon, the role of the messenger, and the use of sources in the pulpit, particularly in terms of delivery styles. These three are summarized more completely in the conclusion to this study.

The Minister's Other Roles as Information Disseminator

The strong emphasis placed upon the roles of healer and herald, counselor and preacher, by the pastors in this study is not meant to deny that clergy sometimes occupy other roles in their dissemination of information. However, it was quite clear among these pastors that other roles were considerably less important in their estimation. Only four such roles of any significance to this study were mentioned during the interviews with these ministers. These roles were teacher, writer, media personality, and community spokesperson. The first two are terms that came directly from the interview transcriptions. The second two are labels that I have used to describe how some pastors disseminated information.

The Pastor as Teacher

One of the surprising findings of this study was how relatively little emphasis was placed upon the teaching function of the minister. Less than a third of the ministers I interviewed said that they taught formally on any regular basis. Many, instead, identified with the pastor who explained that "my teaching is my preaching."

In fact, several pastors who "taught" on Sunday evening or at some other public occasion during the week frequently used the sermon as the form of their delivery with some adaptations to the less formal aspects of these events, e.g. they stood on the floor rather than in the pulpit and allowed some questions to be asked. Some pastors did suggest that they would like to do more teaching, but they also noted that they did not have time to do so because of the demands of administrating, preaching, and counseling that were placed upon them.

Much of the teaching function of the church had been delegated by these pastors to lay leaders or to part-time pastors. Some of these pastors who supervised the church's teaching program were ordained and some were not, suggesting further evidence of the lack of professional emphasis placed upon this pastoral function. To be sure, there were many pastors who conducted home Bible studies but these were usually on a very informal basis and were frequently combined with the pastoral role of home visitation.

The lack of emphasis on adult education by many of the pastors in this community was illustrated most clearly by the following comments by a pastor whose church members included, ironically, a number of professional educators.

> One of the frustrations I've had here, absolute frustrations, is... a resistance here toward education, which blows my mind. A lot of Ph.D.s out in the congregation...including a doctor of education... They're probably my worst students in resisting. Adult education here has been low on the totem pole for a long time, and education in general has been. Right now we struggle each year to have a Sunday school.... There is one member who said, "I don't need to learn any more about religion."

While there may have been several reasons for the sentiments expressed in this church, the pastor's comments did reflect the relatively low priority accorded the pastor's role as teacher. Because of the limited role that these clergy said they played in teaching, few attempts were made to examine this aspect of the ministry in any detail.

In only one case was an unusually elaborate program of adult education in place, and the pastors on staff at this church often taught classes as part of this effort. However, most of the teaching was done by either lay people or professionals in the community with expertise in a given area. For example, a university professor of psychology taught a class in Jungian theory, while a counselor at a local pastoral counseling center taught a course on marriage enrichment. Persons enrolled in these courses for six weeks, paying "tuition" much as a university student would do when enrolling in a college class.

Unfortunately, I was not able to observe any of the teaching that occurred in this church's adult education program because of time constraints. In order to supplement the findings from the pastor's other two major roles as information disseminator, further study may be needed regarding how the pastor uses information in his or her role as teacher.

The Pastor as Writer

The pastor's role as writer was even less pronounced than the pastor as teacher. Only four of the sixty-two pastors I interviewed were published authors, not including another twelve who had had "brief devotional articles" that were derived from sermons accepted for inclusion in their denominational "publications."

One of the four pastors who were published authors had written a book containing his answers to religious questions commonly asked by Catholics, a work which had been favorably reviewed by *Booklist* and the Catholic Digest Book Club and which was discussed in Chapter 3. Another pastor had written four books on youth ministry which had been published by two nationally known publishing houses in that field. My interview with him indicated that he not only drew upon his own experiences as a youth pastor, but "read a lot of periodicals on research in adolescence and education." He also subscribed to several abstracting services in these fields and when he "saw something catchy" in them he went to a nearby university library specializing in education to locate those items for his research and writing.

A third pastor had written a book of devotions, but it had been privately printed by him and contained only personal and Biblical information. The last pastor among the four published authors had recently had an article, based on his doctoral research, accepted for publication in a refereed theological journal, but it had not yet been published and he did not have a copy readily available for me to examine (he was in the process of packing and moving to a new ministry). There was also one other pastor who had once reviewed books for *Christian Century*, but he also noted that "when Martin Marty became editor, he informed me that they were looking for reviewers with more name recognition."

Several pastors mentioned that they had submitted articles for publication to ministerial magazines, but had not had any accepted to date. One pastor had submitted his doctoral thesis to a denominational publishing house but had been rejected for "economic reasons," i.e. the publisher was experiencing some financial problems. Another pastor edited a newsletter for ministers who used computers, but it was distributed only infrequently and his articles were fairly brief, focusing usually on new product announcements. A third pastor had written and read an exegetical paper for a regional meeting of his denomination, but a perusal of that paper indicated it was little more than an extended, textually oriented sermon.

The only regular writing that the pastors in this study did was in terms of preparing sermon notes, but this practice and its strong oral emphasis was discussed earlier in this chapter. My observation of the lack of writing among these pastors suggests that the oral "bias" of ministry mitigated against the pastor as writer. Other than weekly or monthly church newsletter columns, which were only very limited examples of writing, these pastors were either not prone or not able to do any significant writing. Some acknowledged the first reason; they simply had no interest in disseminating information through

written means. Others indicated that they were interested, but
just had "no time" in their current ministry.

The Pastor as Media Personality

Only three of the pastors in this study could be described
as media personalities, but they are included here because of the
uniqueness of their roles as information disseminators in the
community. The term "media personality" in this context refers
to pastors who publicly disseminated information to the larger
community via either radio or television. Two of these three
were pastors of churches whose services were televised weekly
over a local cable channel. The third was one of "ten opinion
leaders" in the community who were invited by a local radio
station to give biweekly addresses on "any issue affecting our
citizens."

The "radio" pastor, unlike the television preachers, did
not "preach" on the air. His topics were often more of a political or civic nature. As the pastor of a large conservative
congregation, he admitted that his role, however, was to "represent the conservative voice in the community." Though these
radio spots were limited to three minutes in duration, they
generated a fair amount of discussion in the community, at least
according to this pastor. In particular, his radio messages were
often rebutted by a rather liberal local Jewish rabbi, but this
pastor said that that was part of the intent of this radio program,
to show the diversity of views on various issues.

This pastor graciously supplied me with the written
transcripts of eleven of the addresses he had given over a recent
several-month period, since I was not able to hear them firsthand. Three of his radio addresses were devoted to local efforts
by a citizen's group to combat pornography, one spoke out
against a proposed off-track betting site in the community, one

was on the need to wear seat belts, two were on adolescent problems of drugs and suicide, one was on a town-gown controversy that had recently occurred, one was on the issue of insensitivity (precipitated by a recent incident where an impatient driver had honked impatiently at a funeral procession), and the last two were on the "true meaning" of Thanksgiving and Christmas.

In these eleven messages, this pastor used a total of seventeen different sources, but only four were identified in any way: a recent article in *Sports Illustrated*, two editorials in the local newspaper, and "the National Highway Traffic Safety Administration." Most of the information that was disseminated was either historical (especially the spots on the two holidays) or of a personal nature, i.e. the pastor's own opinions. My reading of these eleven transcripts suggests that the information was quite general and definitely focused on supporting politically conservative causes. This, of course, was the role he felt he was asked to play by the radio station.

The other two "media personalities" were the pastors whose sermons were regularly televised over local cable. My observation of these sermons in person and on videotape did not reveal any significant differences between the two forms of delivery, other than the two issues mentioned earlier in this chapter related to the need to practice and polish the delivery and the need to be cognizant of the camera and the viewing audience.

The videotapes I observed were not on a par with network television for obvious financial reasons, but there were some attempts to do minimal editing. The pastor's face was sometimes put on a split screen in the corner of a wide-angle shot of the audience, but the effect of such editing was one of disproportion. The standard shot was of the full figure of the preacher standing behind the pulpit with portions of either the choir or the audience also visible, as well as architectural aspects of the sanctuary (altar, communion table, banners, etc.).

These video techniques of minimal editing and wide-angle shots appeared to lessen somewhat the otherwise negative impact that Postman (1985) argued televised sermons carried. Postman's concern was that most preachers were filmed in such a way as to have only their faces typically filling the screen. This close-up technique, he argued, gave the impression that the message was purely personal, involving neither the audience nor the deity as represented in the religious artifacts present in the sanctuary. Presumably, the authority of the information in the message would be sacrificed at the expense of the pastor's overwhelming screen presence. This criticism, however, was not apparent in the two examples under discussion here.

Both of the televised pastors in this study were, in fact, quick to downplay any major impact that television played, either internally or externally. The primary viewing audience was elderly members who were home-bound or resided in "nursing homes." On occasion, a wider impact was felt. For example, one pastor talked about his own media *persona* in these terms:

> I think we are in our third year now [of tele-vising locally over cable]. We get just all kinds of responses from that, particularly in the nurs-ing homes and people confined to their homes or to the hospital. I'm surprised sometimes at the number of people who... I went to [a local] rental place sometime last year to get a power saw, and I walked into the barn where you pick up your stuff. I heard this man say, "Well, you're [named the pastor's name]. I watch you every Monday night." Really? "Yes, I work seven days a week so on Sunday I'm just wiped out, but I watch you on Monday night." He did go on to say, though, that he didn't watch me during football season because of *Monday Night Football*.

At least on a local level, the televised services had enabled this pastor to become somewhat better known in the community. In neither case, though, did these television programs appear to have drawn more people into their congregations since attendance figures had remained on a level comparable to pre-televised services. The reluctance of other churches in the community to engage in similar programming has already been noted earlier in this chapter under the section dealing with electronic media.

The Pastor as Community Spokesperson

The last significant role that the pastors in this community appeared to occupy in disseminating information was that of community spokesperson. This role was played out in many ways by the pastors in this community. Some pastors, for example, took a fairly active role in local politics and civic issues. While none held or even ran for political office, many reported that they often engaged in voter registration drives, addressed the city council on such issues as pornography and legalized gambling, spoke out publicly on both sides of the abortion issue, invited politicians to address their congregations, or, in the case of the "radio" pastor discussed earlier, used the local media to focus attention on community concerns they felt were important.

Other pastors used the media as well, but in less prominent ways. The local newspaper, for instance, featured a weekly column on religion in which five of the pastors interviewed during the course of this study were quoted on issues ranging from time management to community building projects. One pastor's funeral sermon for a prominent local educational leader had been broadcast on radio and reprinted in the newspaper, with the result that she had become known as *the* female pastor in town.

Other pastors' information-dissemination roles in the community were much more indirect, but apparently nonetheless significant. At least twelve of the pastors I interviewed served as volunteer chaplains to the community police department, and this allowed them access to a part of the public that they otherwise did not reach. One of these pastors' work had become so well known that local judges sometimes referred delinquents to him and his church to perform "community service." While four pastors' churches were in the midst of relocation moves from the poorer parts of town to the more affluent suburbs, three pastors had decided to remain, partly in order to "provide a voice" for the economically disadvantaged.

One minister had organized a mentoring program in the community for young black males who attended an area university and had received state funding to duplicate his efforts at other academic institutions in the region. Another minister served as a trustee for a local university, a forum which provided him an opportunity to address the religious and educational needs of students. Two pastors served on the boards of local Habitat for Humanity agencies. One was active in MADD (Mothers Against Drunk Driving). Added to these pastors' influence were the active involvement of the Salvation Army and a mission for the homeless in the community, both of which were frequently cited in the local newspaper when articles were written on issues related to the recession or to poverty.

In summary, the pastors in this study were active in disseminating information not only in their congregations, but in their community. A limiting feature of this project, however, was the inability to assess accurately the extent to which this involvement was effective in addressing community concerns and problems. Interviews with directors of an information-referral center in the community suggested that clergy were frequently relied on to provide help in many of the questions they received, but further research is needed to provide more detailed data.

5. CONCLUSION

Overview of Findings

The Research Questions

This exploratory study of the ministers in one Midwestern community has sought to provide a descriptive analysis of how and why pastors use information by answering the three research questions that guided this study. The three questions, outlined in Chapter 1, are these: 1) To what extent do pastors function as information professionals? 2) Why and how do pastors gather information as part of their professional duties? And 3) In what ways do pastors disseminate the information that they gather as part of their professional duties? Given the prominent role that pastors play in our information society, what ministers know and how they share that knowledge are issues worth addressing.

The first of the three questions begs an earlier question: What is an information professional? In this study, the definitions and descriptions suggested by Asheim (1978), Abbott (1988), and Mason (1990) have been used. Mason's summary definition of an information professional as one who possesses specialized knowledge about knowledge that he or she uses to improve the intellectual state of others suggests the extent to which pastors function, and do not function, as traditional information professionals. Pastors do not primarily possess "specialized knowledge about knowledge" nor are they concerned only with their clients' "intellectual state." Yet the pastors in this study certainly possessed specialized knowledge--ranging from factual, to religious, to relational--which they used as professionals to help people understand certain areas of their lives more fully, particularly those areas related to emotional and spiritual problems.

It may have been less confusing to have avoided the term information professional in favor of "information provider," but I chose not to do that in this study for three reasons. First, the professional component was very pronounced in the ways that these pastors provided information, particularly in terms of their professional authority. Second, the focus of this study was on more than just these pastors' *provision* of information; the *acquisition* of information (what ministers know) was equally at issue. Third, the particular value in using the term "information professional" was that it allowed me to examine the areas in which pastors were both similar to and different from such traditional information professionals as librarians. This comparison was deemed important in studying a group of information users that has not often been examined in the field of library and information science.

The three questions centering around the pastor's role as information professional were occasioned by such studies as Porcella (1973), George et al. (1989), and Tanner (1991), as well as by recent public opinion polls (see Chapter 1). These studies suggest that the profession of the pastorate occupies a significant role in the provision of information in this country, in some ways second only to the medical profession. A review of the relevant literature in this field (see Appendix) provides further evidence of this role, but also emphasizes how little is still known about the use of information among pastors, not to mention the difficulty even in defining the term "information." The only major examination of this topic has been the one by Porcella (1973), which is now more than twenty years old.

In keeping with Dervin and Nilan's (1986) call for a "new paradigm" for user studies that is sensitive to the complex nature of information and its users, this study employed naturalistic methods--primarily multiple interviews, case studies, and participant-observation. In particular, 84 personal interviews were conducted with 69 different individuals. This number includes 62 pastors at 58 of the 64 churches in this Midwestern community of nearly 100,000 that had full-time preaching pastors. The seven non-pastors who were interviewed included two directors of a local pastoral counseling center, two public librarians, two directors of a local information referral agency, and a church bookstore manager. Their responses enabled the findings to be set in a somewhat larger community context.

The pastors were contacted by means of a letter of introduction, and 91% of the full-time ministers who preached on a regular basis agreed to participate. The interviews were conducted using naturalistic methods, with most averaging fifty minutes in length. My role as a seminary professor and former minister allowed me to develop a fairly immediate rapport with most of the interviewees. Consequently, I found most of these pastors to be quite willing to share even very personal and sometimes negative information, as was pointed out in earlier chapters. The answers they provided to my questions, coupled with the size and diversity (educationally, theologically, and demographically) of the population under study, as well as the high response rate, indicates that the data and consequent findings of this study are at once broadly based and deeply felt.

In addition to the interviews, seven case studies at seven different churches were conducted over a ten-month period, focusing upon the role of the pastor as information disseminator in the pulpit. As noted in Table 8 in Chapter 4 and the surrounding discussion, these churches and their pastors provided rich and extensive data to supplement and corroborate my preliminary findings from the single interviews. The multiple interviews employed in the case studies provided numerous examples of the value of follow-up questions to issues raised in the first encounter.

For example, most of the findings about the pastors' use of sources in sermons would not have surfaced without several interviews subsequent to hearing these pastors preach on different occasions. The ability to observe pastors "in action" performing their professional duties allowed me to cross-check espoused values with enacted ones and to note such anomalies where appropriate, e.g. the case of the pastor who said he never preached from notes did so on one occasion for reasons related to the issue of pastoral authority.

The interviews and the case studies were further supplemented with a brief written questionnaire and with an analysis of 48 different sermons preached by 23 of the pastors in this study. The written questionnaires not only provided numeric data to check with the more qualitatively oriented interview, but also served to encourage pastors to raise issues and make comments that otherwise might have been missed. Some of the key data regarding the utilitarian nature of pastoral information needs that was discussed in Chapter 3 were discovered because of this very circumstance.

The Pastor as Information Professional

Chapter 2 of this study examined the extent to which the participating pastors may be considered information professionals, as that term is discussed above. This first research question was addressed from three perspectives: the professional image of the pastor, the professional authority of the pastor, and the professional knowledge of the pastor. The issue of image was raised in order to provide a conceptual framework for discussing how these pastors were similar to and different from such traditional information professionals as librarians.

Five such images were found in this study. For some pastors, the image was that of the generalist, comparable to the public librarian who is called upon to know something about almost everything. For a limited few, mostly those in larger churches, the image was that of the expert, similar to the academic librarian who has expertise in a certain subject specialty. Like the large research library, pastors in multi-staff congregations were able to call upon specialist colleagues for expert information, as well as upon their own specialized backgrounds. For most of the pastors in this study, however, the predominant image was that of the equipper. Just as a reference librarian equips patrons by directing them to the appropriate sources, so these equipping pastors helped people answer their own questions by, as one pastor put it, "steering people toward" other sources.

Another important image for these pastors as information providers was that of the wounded healer, the professional who draws deeply upon his or her own personal pilgrimage as a resource for helping others. The closest parallel in the library profession is that of the activist librarian. The point of comparison here is that some librarians display a type of activism that is very personally focused. For example, the librarian whose roots are Appalachian sometimes returns to that area to provide services to the poor with whom he or she identifies experientially. Though all information professionals probably use their own experiences in practicing their profession to some extent, the difference is that the pastors in this study typically exhibited an exceedingly high degree of personal involvement in information provision, as evidenced in everything from making "house calls" to holding the hands, literally, of those with needs.

Finally, there was the image of the pastor as interpreter. Like the special librarian, these pastors examined a variety of documents in order to explain their contents to the appropriate patrons in some concise manner. Unlike the special librarian, the interpretive pastor dealt with *sacred* text, including what some referred to as the "living Word" behind the "written words."

Besides these five professional images, the professional authority of the pastor was also a key component in analyzing how these pastors provided information. Using Wilson's (1983) concept of cognitive authority, where authority is defined as the influence that one person has over another relative to what the former tells the latter, this study looked at four bases for such authority.

The first two, educational authority and institutional authority, are very similar to the authority exercised by such traditional information professionals as librarians. Both of these kinds of authority are based, to some extent, on technical competence. For example, educational authority is based on a person's mastery over a certain range of knowledge that is usually derived from a formal degree program, and institutional authority is based on the authority that is associated with the institution itself. In the case of the latter, the issue of competence is secondary, but not absent, in that one assumes the person is employed by the institution because the institution judges him or her to be competent.

The other two kinds of authority, personal authority and divine authority, are not at all similar to the kinds of authority typically exercised by traditional information professionals. The former, though somewhat present among librarians, was more pronounced among the pastors in this study. For many of these pastors, for example, the key issue was not the accuracy of the information itself, but the "believability" of the person. One evidence of this kind of authority was noted in the case of the pastor who altered his view on information after attending a "right-wing, anti-abortion conference," where he was prepared not to listen but did so after becoming enraptured by the speaker as a person.

Divine authority has no parallel among librarians or any other types of information providers and constitutes one of the most significant differences between ministers and traditional information professionals. The most pronounced manifestation of this kind of authority was the preeminent place bestowed upon the Bible as a sacred document, a preeminence not accorded to any text in the field of library and information science.

In addition to professional image and professional authority, the professional knowledge of the pastor was another important aspect in analyzing how these ministers functioned as information professionals. Like all professionals (Mason, 1990), the pastors in this study possessed specialized knowledge and used that knowledge in the service of others. This knowledge was found to be of three types: factual (knowing answers to closed-ended questions), relational (knowing answers to open-ended questions, particularly in a counseling context), and limited (knowing what questions not to answer).

Unlike traditional information professionals, the professional knowledge of these pastors had a spiritual or religious focus, even when the ostensible information need was not so directed. The case cited in Chapter 2 of the teenage girl asking her pastor for information about Episcopalians provides a clear example of how pastors utilize their professional knowledge to provide a very "value-added" flavor to the information they provide.

In order to answer the first research question regarding the extent to which the pastor functions as an information professional, it is necessary to summarize the differences as well as the similarities between the profession of the pastorate and such traditional information professionals as librarians. Three issues were found to be of importance.

First, both are professionals who function as information providers. A significant difference is that librarians treat this as a professional "end," while the pastors in this study were more likely to view such information as a "means" to an end. For example, these pastors appeared to be more concerned with what people did with the information they provided than with the information itself. As one pastor noted regarding the information he disseminated in the pulpit, "My primary objective is not...the transference of knowledge [but rather] a changed behavior." This focus on behavioral change, not just cognitive awareness, was the purpose of much of the information being disseminated by these pastors, particularly in the pulpit and in the counseling room.

Consequently, while the ministers that were interviewed used images more closely akin to the library field than to their own field to describe their roles as information providers, they saw these images as secondary to their more primary roles as preacher, priest, and pastor.

Second, both the librarian and the minister exercise authority in their provision of information, authority that is granted to them by the public, either as patron or parishioner, at least in terms of how a professional is defined by Asheim (1978). However, it is my observation that the librarian's authority is typically based on competence that is educationally (e.g. a professional librarian has an M.L.S. degree) and, to some extent, institutionally derived (e.g. to some people, anyone who works in a library is a librarian).

The ministers in this study, though they also exercised educational and institutional authority, depended just as much, if not more so, on personal and divine authority--both of which were based more on trust than competence. The clearest example of the pastor's emphasis upon these kinds of authority was found in this minister's comment: "The only thing you see hanging in this room, although I have a doctorate..., is my ordination [certificate]. That is where I get my authority [for] I feel called of God to do what I am doing."

Third, both the librarian and the pastor claim professional knowledge, but the librarian's claim is more resource oriented while the knowledge observed during this study among pastors was more relational in direction. The librarian knows the sources that can provide the person with the information that is needed. These pastors wanted to know the person first and deal with the sources secondarily. As one minister noted, "People don't care how much you know until they know how much you care."

The Pastor as Information Gatherer

Chapter 3 of this study examined the second research question: why and how do pastors gather information as part of their professional duties? This question was addressed from two perspectives.

First, this study examined *why* pastors had information needs. It was found that these needs were not always or even mostly self-generated. Often other individuals brought their own information needs to the pastor for him or her to fulfill. Many of these needs, whether self-generated or generated by others, were utilitarian in nature. These pastors sought information because they had a specific need arising from a particular incident in which the information was used in a very instrumental manner: to prepare for a counseling case or to research a sermon topic.

Other needs, however, were much less focused and may be described as current awareness needs. The pastors in this study often gathered information for no particular reason other than to stay current in their profession and in the news of the day. The pastor whose wife "complained" because he sat around and read or watched television explained to her and to me that such practices were part of his professional duties since he had to "keep abreast of things because that's part of being a pastor." Finally, some of the pastors in this study expressed such a high degree of information need that a perception of information overload existed. These needs were typically met by means of abstracting services, such as *Current Thoughts & Trends*.

The second perspective in addressing the information-gathering behavior of the pastors in this study concerned the *how* part of this second research question: How did these pastors gather information? What were the channels that they used to acquire the information they needed? The tension over "people versus paper" noted by several of the pastors in this study summarized somewhat simplistically the distinction these ministers drew between formal and informal sources of information.

The formal sources included books, magazines, audio-visuals, computer databases, and libraries. The informal sources consisted, for these ministers, primarily of professional conferences, ministerial associations, and personal networks. Both the interview data and the results of the questionnaire indicated that informal channels were the generally preferred means of gathering information. The sole exception was the high value placed by these pastors upon their own personal libraries.

The Pastor as Information Disseminator

Chapter 4 of this study addressed the third research question: In what ways do pastors disseminate the information that they gather as part of their professional duties? The types of media used by these pastors to disseminate the information that they had gathered was also found to have an influence on the information dissemination process. Among the three major media--oral, print, and electronic--oral media were observed to be the most prominent. The two major information dissemination roles, both of which were oral, that were identified by the ministers in this community were these: the healer/counselor role and the herald/preacher role. Four less-frequently mentioned roles included the pastor as teacher, writer, media personality, and community spokesperson.

Regarding the first major role, that of the pastor as healer or counselor, several summary observations may be made about how these pastors disseminated information in that context. One observation is that the pastor's professional role and goal as caregiver/counselor appeared to exercise a controlling influence on the type and amount of information that he or she tried to disseminate.

For example, the overall emphasis by these ministers upon pastoral *care* over pastoral *counseling* tempered the type of information they gave. The pastors in this study expressed a uniform willingness to provide spiritual and routine personal advice, but many were quite reluctant to provide more sophisticated information relative to deep-seated psychological problems. Additionally, the readiness to refer that most pastors displayed--based on usually legal concerns and the time involved in more complex counseling cases--decreased the amount of information they gave. The presence of a local pastoral counseling center, which was widely used in the community, no doubt also contributed to these pastors' practice of frequently referring.

Another observation is that the media used by these pastors to disseminate counseling information impacted the information-transfer process itself. For example, the prominent use of prayer to convey information introduced aspects of divine authority and acceptability to the information just by virtue of the channel used. The frequent use of orally delivered distillations of printed information also allowed the pastor to function both as a filter in condensing and conveying "relevant" data and as a personally involved intermediary.

One pastor, for example, often bought "three or four counseling books" in order to "learn up" on a particular issue that he knew he would be addressing in an upcoming counseling case. He then condensed the information in these books and delivered it orally during counseling sessions with his counselees. In addition, the use of electronic media in counseling, most notably video programs related to premarital counseling, though relatively infrequent, further allowed the pastor to be cast in the role of "impartial judge," enabling him or her to stand above the information on video and offer "oral opinions" on its validity and usefulness, as was discussed in the first part of Chapter 4.

A final observation regarding the pastor as counselor is that the diversity and depth of the questions raised in this community relative to counseling information underscored the importance of the role that these pastors played as primary disseminators of that information. The fact that most of the questions addressed to a local information referral agency were counseling related and were often referred to pastors is one example of the prominence of these kinds of information needs in this community. Though limited by the lack of observations of specific examples of these kinds of information interchanges between counselor and counselee, the emphasis placed upon this pastoral role by clergy and community alike warranted even the limited discussion possible here.

The second major information dissemination role filled by the pastors in this study was that of herald or preacher. In looking at the pastor's role as information disseminator in the pulpit, there are also several observations that highlight significant findings in this part of the study. For example, it was observed that not everything that these pastors communicated in the sermon was intentionally informational. The "being" and "doing" aspects of the homily were just as pronounced as the "knowing." This must be kept in mind when discussing the findings related to the pastor's homiletical role in that only certain features of the sermon, those related to information, were examined in this study.

It was also observed that the role of the pastor as a person had a significant bearing on the kind of information that was communicated in the pulpit. Unlike traditional information professionals, these pastors tended to demonstrate a high degree of personal involvement with both their topics and their information sources.

For example, some pastors said they only preached on issues with which they were "personally struggling." In fact, the second most frequently used "source" in the sermons I observed was the personal experiences of the pastor. When other sources were used, they were sometimes altered slightly to suit the pastor's own purposes within the acceptable limits of oral media, as these pastors reshaped the information in the process of disseminating it. In addition, the topics on which the pastors in this study preached were predominantly of a relational nature, with counseling issues arising from needs they perceived in the church and the community accounting for more than half the topics of the 48 sermons I observed.

Finally, it was observed that the styles in which these pastors disseminated information publicly from the pulpit appeared to have some influence in the information-transfer process. The predominant use of storytelling, for example, allowed information to be disseminated in ways that appeared to encourage involvement and understanding on the part of the congregation. In addition, the stylistic image of the pastor as television news anchor appeared to reflect a possible cultural predilection for this method of information dissemination among parishioners of the television generation. However, these are rather speculative observations which require additional study.

Summary of Major Findings

In summary, this exploratory study found that the participating pastors did function in many ways as information professionals, as was evidenced in why and how they gathered information and in the ways they chose to disseminate that information. The primary point of contact between these two professions was that the pastors in this study, like traditional information professionals, used their professional knowledge to help meet others' information needs, particularly in their roles as counselors and preachers.

The distinguishing differences, however, between these pastors and such traditional information professionals as librarians were the prominent display of non-neutrality in the pastoral provision of information, the images these pastors portrayed professionally (especially those of the wounded healer and the interpreter), the differing bases of authority (pastors relied heavily on personal and divine authority), the more prominent use of informal sources by pastors, and the unique use of sacred text in both information gathering and information dissemination by these pastors.

Further research extending beyond the scope of this exploratory study is needed to determine the extent to which these findings may be true of other pastors in other communities. However, the generalizability of the findings from this study across cases is not the purpose of the present project.

Limitations

The scope of this study, as outlined in Chapter 1, has been limited to one community at one particular point in time. No claim is made that the results found here are necessarily applicable to other clergy in other communities in other times. However, this particularity is one of this study's strengths, given the complex nature of information in contemporary society. Complexity of this nature requires an in-depth examination that is set firmly in a particular context. Much is gained by the personal touch of the interview process conducted in a naturalistic framework in terms of the depth of the data to be discovered.

The particular population chosen for study in this project was, therefore, intentionally meant to be somewhat representative, not scientifically random. The choice of a university town was suggested by Porcella (1973). Its only limiting feature may have been that both the pastors and the parishioners in this community appeared to be more highly educated and perhaps more affluent than may have been the case with a non-university community, the possible effects of which have been noted in several places in this study.

Yet, the relatively high educational level also allowed me to explore a greater diversity of pastors in that clergy without advanced degrees were also adequately represented in this community and in this project. In this qualitative study, these various factors were also able to be weighed on a case-by-case basis, not merely counted as part of an aggregated sum.

My primary purpose throughout this study was to choose a community and a group of clergy that displayed sufficient depth and breadth of data to allow for a rather detailed picture to be painted of how, why, and to what extent pastors function as information professionals and providers. The diverse nature of this pastoral population certainly permitted such data to be collected. The only substantially limiting factors were the relatively low numbers of female and ethnic clergy, though nearly all of these two groups present in this community were interviewed.

The naturalistic orientation of the methods used here emphasizes more the descriptive aspect of the information needs and uses of this particular group of professionals, rather than aiming for the discovery of normative data that would allow for broad generalizations about all clergy as information users and information providers. If anything has been lost in breadth, it has, hopefully, been gained in depth of understanding. As pointed out in Chapter 1, the goal of this study has not been to prove or disprove a particular hypothesis that is context-free and applicable across cases. Analytical description, not broad generalization, has been the focal point of the present study.

In this regard, Natoli (1982), in an article entitled "Librarianship as a Human Science: Theory, Method, and Application," noted the need in library research for more studies involving detailed descriptions of humans as individuals, not merely as research variables. The theoretical basis for this study is best described by the work of Dervin and Nilan (1986) and its call for a "new paradigm" for user studies that emphasizes the "systematic individuality" of users as unique persons.

This study, therefore, attempts to advance the body of knowledge in library and information science in a way consistent with this emphasis on individuals. As Natoli also observed, "Knowledge through description--accurate detailed description-- leads to understanding and intelligent choices can only be made from clear understanding" (1982, p. 167). As an exploratory study, the focus here has been upon new findings that can enhance such understanding. These findings allow the reader to understand both the diversity and the complexities of this one group of information providers, in terms of how they individually and collectively use information.

Areas for Further Study

One of the classic definitions of communication was offered by Lasswell more than a generation ago: "Who says what in which channel to whom with what effect?" (Lasswell, 1948, p. 37). In the present study of pastors as communicators of information, one of the key components of this definition that is missing is the last one, "with what effect."

As one pastor in this study noted in this regard: "I was in campus ministry for seven years prior to coming here and I used to think there that I had little control over what students thought. Yet, sometimes I would hear them quoting back to me as their own thinking things that I had said to them. So I wonder what our impact really is?" The research design, which was focused almost exclusively on the pastors themselves, did not allow for any systematic data to be collected regarding his question about the actual "effect" that the information these pastors provided had upon the recipients.

For example, this study found that storytelling as a form of information dissemination was prominently used by these pastors, particularly in the pulpit. Though reasons were suggested for why this occurs, further studies utilizing audience analysis are needed to discover why this is actually the case and whether this practice is unique to this community or is occurring in other churches in other communities. This kind of research involving the receivers of information, which was used in the present study only in terms of the pastor as receiver (see Chapter 3), is also needed in analyzing the counseling role of the pastor as information disseminator.

In this study, to cite one example, it was found that pastors employed various strategies to disseminate counseling-related information, ranging from prayer to videocassettes. However, further study is needed to determine if any one strategy is more effective than any other in meeting these information needs or to analyze under what conditions one method may be more useful than another.

On a broader scale, further research involving the community itself would be helpful in describing in even greater detail the information-provision role of the pastorate. Based on the results of the survey conducted by The Gallup Organization and described in Chapter 1, it would be helpful to look beyond the pastoral perspective on how these professionals provide information to see what "effect" is being felt among the community at large in this regard. Though this was touched on briefly at the end of Chapter 4 under the discussion of the pastor as community spokesperson, further research involving personal interviews and case studies of community residents is needed to more accurately describe this aspect of the pastor as information professional.

Implications of This Study

One implication of this study is that the qualitatively focused, personal interview does appear to be an appropriate and feasible method for studying the informational roles of ministers. This study is the first in the field of library and information science to employ this naturalistic approach among these professionals, and there was some concern about whether ministers would be willing to share this aspect of their professional lives. The findings of this study, particularly as summarized above, suggest that research of this nature among pastors is both possible and productive.

Another implication of this study is that the research methods taught to ministers in seminary may not be properly focused. While current pedagogical practice among theological educators appears to be focused upon comprehensive, book-based search techniques carried out in institutional libraries, the findings here indicate that professional practice relies more on personal libraries and informal channels, especially professional conferences and ministerial colleagues. Perhaps more emphasis needs to be placed by theological educators, especially theological librarians, on encouraging ministerial candidates to be better book buyers, as much as borrowers, and on building informal information networks with other professionals, both inside and outside the pastorate.

The information overload that some pastors in this study felt surfaces yet another implication of this study. Given the reliance of these pastors on such abstracting services as *Current Thoughts & Trends*, it could be useful for researchers in the field of library and information science to explore more fully this type of need among these professionals. While much research and effort has been devoted to the demands for abstracting tools in the professional communities in medicine and science, the same has not been true for the pastoral profession, despite the key role that it plays in the provision of information in American society. The presence of so few abstracting services for pastors, none of which is by persons formally trained in the field of abstracting, suggests that such a need exists and that more expertly designed abstracting services would find a ready market.

A final implication arising from this study concerns the headline quoted at the beginning of this book: "Ministers rated highly as community advice and information sources." If pastors do serve as information "gatekeepers" in the community, and the findings from this study suggest that some pastors do, then this resource could be tapped by other information professionals.[36] Librarians, in particular, might develop liaisons with ministers as a means of promoting the information services that libraries provide. The pulpit could even become a "bully pulpit" for the library and other information providers in terms of the information that they can offer to assist the community.[37] The pilot study by George et al. (1989) for the American Association for the Advancement of Science among black churches and clergy is one example of how ministers can serve as information advocates to the community.

The reciprocal referral relationship found in this study between pastors and other information providers in the community, e.g. an information-referral agency and a counseling center, is another example of the possible interchanges between these groups of professionals. This study suggests that such interchanges can enhance the provision of information to community residents. What is needed, however, is further study among pastors as information professionals. Such study can expand our knowledge of how ministers fill this pivotal information role in American society and even perhaps help us understand how this role can be used to create a more informed citizenry.

APPENDIX:
A BIBLIOGRAPHIC ESSAY ON
INFORMATION USE

A Review of the Literature on "Information"

When conducting research on the use and users of information, whether those users are clergy or any other group, it seems appropriate to ask, as did Faibisoff and Ely (1976) at the beginning of their oft-cited review of information studies, "What is information?" The answers they cited range from "that which reduces uncertainty" and "that which assists in decision-making" to "symbolic representations of reality." Faibisoff and Ely themselves proposed that information be defined as "a symbol or a set of symbols which has the potential for meaning" (p. 3). Other definitions in the field include those by Bateson (1972), "the difference that makes a difference"; Rapoport (1970), "the carrier of order"; Stevens (1986), "factual data [or] ideas...used in some meaningful manner"; and Farradane (1979), "the physical surrogate of knowledge."

Indeed, the very relationship between information and knowledge has been frequently debated in the literature. Neill (1982) tried to establish a philosophical basis for information based on the third of Popper's three worlds of knowledge: the physical world, the world of conscious experiences, and the world of logical contents of books, libraries, etc. Rudd (1983), however, convincingly critiqued this line of reasoning as being an "essentially passive conception of information."

In a different vein, Nitecki (1985) argued that information and knowledge form a continuum. Boorstin (1980) divided them, however, into two opposed camps, lamenting the growth of "random, miscellaneous" information at the expense of orderly, cumulative knowledge. Machlup (1962), on the other hand, differentiated between them only slightly in defining information as "act" and knowledge as "state," preferring personally to use the term knowledge. Following Scheler's three-fold classification scheme, Machlup stressed the richness of the concept in his five-fold categorization of knowledge as practical, intellectual, past-time, spiritual, and unwanted. Commenting on these five, Miksa (1985), citing Machlup, noted that "[a]ny particular datum... may be fit into one of the five categories 'depending upon the use which the knower makes of it'" (p. 163).

This emphasis upon the user is consistent with recent research in the study of information, particularly within the emerging interpretative paradigm that is becoming common in the social sciences.[38] As Rohde (1986) argued, the problem with most all of the definitions of information cited above is that they assume a positivist paradigm. Under the assumptions of logical positivism, "information is seen as having an existence independent of thought or of sources or of receivers and as something that describes reality which can be discovered, described, and predicted" (p. 51). The image which emerges is that of information as a brick which can be transferred from one place to another. Rohde continued her critique by noting that "these assumptions are being challenged in both the information science and communications literature" (p. 51).[39]

Studies by Dervin (1976, 1977, 1980), Streatfield (1983), and Wilson (1981) suggested that in concentrating on the "product" known as information, the informing "process" has been ignored. Rohde (1986, p. 52) summarized the problems with earlier definitions of information with the following observation (citing Dervin, 1976):

> On the one hand, our research data and
> our practitioner experiences say "relativism"
> loud and clear. Meanings are in people. People
> construct their own reality. No knowledge is
> absolute. Messages sent do not equal those re-
> ceived. The same person is different across time
> and space. On the other hand... [w]e continue
> to look for normative, nonvariant rules.... We
> assume that there is "right" information--
> "objective" information.... We still ponder the
> perfect message.[40]

In an attempt to provide a more useful definition of information, Dervin (1977) delineated three kinds of information: reality or data, ideas or structures imputed to reality by people, and the behavior that selects from the first in order to create the second. In this schema there is an attempt to deal with information as not only a product but also a process, to recognize not only its objective but its subjective dimensions as well. This focus on information as process, as well as product, was also noted by Nitecki (1985). He maintained that the various definitions of the term *information* found in the literature can be classified into three basic categories: a recorded message, a process, or the content of a message.

The product-process/objective-subjective continuum also raises the issue of defining information "need," which in current research focuses on the process/subjective aspects.[41] Krikelas (1983), for example, defined information as "any stimulus that reduces uncertainty; [and] need is defined as a recognition of the existence of this uncertainty in the personal, or work-related, life of an individual" (p. 6). Such stimuli can be recorded or unrecorded and can range from documents to memory to beliefs to conversations.[42] However, a "stimulus that reduces uncertainty" is described by Krikelas (p. 7) as an inherently internalized process that cannot be observed.[43]

Consequently, a number of researchers distinguish between information need (unexpressed demands comprising unobservable cognitions) and information demand (expressed, observable behavior); see, for example, Crawford's 1978 review of this literature and the illustrative case studies by Ford (1980) and by James (1983), though the latter approach is more system, than user, oriented.

Wilson and Streatfield (1981) maintained that the "direct, objective perception of the subject's information need by another party...is not possible" (p. 174). Instead, they argued, potential information needs may be imputed to an individual on the basis of such phenomena as records of past information-seeking behavior, interviews about current information "needs" and how they are met, self-reporting of information-seeking behavior (e.g. through questionnaires), and observations of individuals in their normal settings as they perform their customary work roles (see also Wilson, 1984, for further discussion on these points).

This study attempts to examine both need and demand. The personal interviews were limited to examining what informants were willing or able to express from their internal cognitions or needs. To the extent that they did not or could not, this portion of the study was limited to an analysis of information "demands" in the technical sense.[44] However, the case studies involving participant-observation techniques allowed for the collection of data that were not limited to verbal expressions of information need and demand.

In addition, the present study breaks with many previous use studies in that the demands under study here were not limited to those that users placed upon formal information systems or services--a limitation of much previous research in this area. In recognition of this artificial restraint that is common to much of the library literature, more than a decade ago Wilson (1981) noted the need for a wider, more holistic view of the information user that would shift the focus of research from an examination of the information sources and systems used to an investigation of the role of information in users' everyday lives, work, or social settings. This is what the present research does, at least in the professional work setting of the clergy in one Midwestern community. This limitation on the work arena is not seen as overly burdensome in the present study, given that current research in this field suggests that "information needs are most closely related to the type of work one does" (Lancaster, 1990).

As the above literature indicates, the term "information" is a slippery one. As with many human phenomena that are the proper subject of social science research, information resists a simple definition.[45] What does seem to be apparent from a review of this literature is that the following three observations can be made: 1) information is an extremely complex concept that has not been totally or finally defined within the profession, but which, nevertheless, has been the subject of much research; 2) information is not merely an "objective" phenomenon or product that can be transferred from one source to another with no accompanying changes; and 3) information is integrally related to the user of that information.

With these observations in mind, it is important to provide some kind of definition of the concept of information in this study. Operationally, there is a need to provide some sense of what is being studied, but without delimiting its nature to the extent that individual nuances and informant observations during field research are precluded. On the other hand, it seems legitimate not only to recognize the full range of what the concept of information may be, but also to choose deliberately--given the focus of this study--to examine only certain aspects of that concept, at least in terms of providing some reasonable limits to the kinds of questions asked in this study.

Between the Scylla and Charybdis of these twin concerns, this study was conducted on the basis of the following definition of information: "any statement made by a minister within the context of his or her professional duties which can be attributed, either directly or indirectly, to an external source, whether that source be written or oral, named or unnamed." This definition allowed the study to focus not only on information sources (the subject of Chapter 3), but also on how these sources were used by ministers as they disseminated the information they found (the subject of Chapter 4). The emphasis here is more on information as process than product.

A Review of User Studies in General

User studies, suggested Krikelas (1983), "probably form the largest single body of research literature in librarianship" (p. 5). According to Bisco (1967), cited by Brittain (1970), "the first known empirical studies of the needs and uses of information, in contrast to the recorded uses of stored materials, were reported by Bernal ... and Urquhart ... at the Royal Society Scientific Information Conference during June and July of 1948" (p. 13). Within three decades of these British beginnings, Crawford (1978) estimated that more than 1,000 such studies had appeared in print. In the last decade alone more than 500 information-need and user studies have been published (Dervin and Nilan, 1986; Hewins, 1990). Rohde's (1986) recent research yielded more than 2,000 potentially relevant documents in one database alone. Reviews of this literature in the *Annual Review of Information Science and Technology* volumes (hereafter *ARIST*), which began in 1966, now number eleven.[46]

Menzel (1966) wrote the first review of user studies for *ARIST*, which concentrated, as did most of the later *ARIST* reviews, on information use and needs among scientists and technologists. Preceding Menzel's study were reviews by Davis and Bailey (1964), who examined 438 user studies relevant to engineering, and by the Auerbach Corporation (1965), who reviewed 676 items related to Department of Defense user needs. The second *ARIST* review was compiled by the Herners (1967) and dealt with the various methods used in user studies.

Paisley's 1968 *ARIST* review is one of the most cited, with its call for more theory. He suggested a need for what Merton (1967) called "theories of the middle range."[47] Paisley also outlined a ten-point conceptual framework of how scientists function as users. These ten "concentric circles" of the various systems within which information users (at least scientific information users) operate are culture, politics, discipline, specialization, invisible college, formal organization, work team, economy, formal information system, and--the most foundational system of all--what Paisley called "the scientist within his own head." This latter is a recognition of the internal cognitions and process orientation of the information concept.

Allen's 1969 *ARIST* review of information needs and uses reduced Paisley's list of ten to six by collapsing several categories. Lipetz (1970) in his *ARIST* review examined the measurement instruments and methodologies common to user studies, noting the proliferation of questionnaires in particular. He, too, noted the absence of theory in the field of user studies. The 1971 *ARIST* review of user studies by Crane and the 1972 review by Lin and Garvey looked at models of information-seeking behavior, based primarily on general communication models.

Martyn, in his 1974 *ARIST* review, suggested that the study of users fell into three basic periods: during the 1950s and early 1960s the chief area of concern was the broadly based information needs and uses of scientists and technologists, during the mid 1960s the emphasis shifted to better methods on the one hand and fewer studies on the other, and during the late 1960s and early 1970s the study of the economic benefit of information and its effects became prominent. Martyn (1974, p. 5) argued that "the age of the dinosaur, the period of the broadly based, discipline-wide user study, is over," anticipating some of the concerns for more individually based, situationally focused studies that Dervin and Nilan (1986) were to call for. Crawford (1978) also conveniently summarized earlier *ARIST* reviews and noted the trend toward more studies of a wide variety of users.

One of the more comprehensive reviews of the literature of user studies in general is that by Dervin and Nilan in the 1986 *ARIST* volume. Their review focused on "the conceptualizations that drive the research" (p. 3) in this field and is especially pertinent to the present study. They categorized the corpus of this literature into two distinct genres: the majority of studies which observe users in terms of systems and the minority of studies that look at users in terms of users.

The bulk of the studies in this area, Dervin and Nilan argued, are system oriented and fall into one of six broad approaches: 1) the demand on systems/resources approach (measuring the extent to which users use different services), 2) the awareness approach (focusing on respondent awareness of current services), 3) the likes-dislikes approach (examining user satisfaction with various services), 4) the priorities approach (generating library wish lists), 5) the community profile approach (doing demographic surveys of users), and 6) the interests, activities, and group membership approach (assessing user interests and involvement).

Dervin and Nilan criticized these "traditional" approaches for focusing on the system, not the user. In particular, the majority of the studies done to date, in their view, concentrated on only objective, not subjective information; viewed users as passive recipients rather than as active constructors of information; sought broad generalizations that tended to ignore situation-specific contexts; looked atomistically at only one encounter between a user and a system rather than holistically at users' broader information needs; focused on easily observable external behavior rather than pursuing the internal cognitions of users; and concentrated so much on finding predictable group behavior that "systematic individuality" was overlooked. Based on these observations, the reviewers called for a shift to "an alternative paradigm," one that focuses on the user and how he or she seeks information concerning situations about which their knowledge is incomplete (cf. the ASK model of Belkin, 1980).[48]

In the most recent *ARIST* review of user studies, Hewins (1990) noted that much of the current research in this area does follow the alternative paradigm and is much more user focused. She pointed to the critical-incident technique popularized by Allen (1966) as an increasingly popular and productive method for researching users' information needs and behaviors. This new paradigm and approach are particularly prevalent in studying professionals as users. She cited as one example the growing body of literature in medical informatics, which studies the information needs and uses of the medical profession, a literature that has been reviewed recently by Elayyan (1988).

Unfortunately, similar research among other professionals is not as prolific. In many ways Faibisoff and Ely's statement from the 1970s is still true: "The literature regarding information needs of educators, clergymen, lawyers, doctors, social workers, and other professionals is scanty" (1976, p. 7). While a few professions have been researched at some length, for example, physicians (Elayyan, 1988), engineers (Kremer, 1980), and scientists (Martyn, 1987), a number of groups-- particularly in the humanities--have been left unexplored (though see Wiberley and Jones, 1989, and Vale, 1988).[49] One such professional group whose information needs and uses have been little studied is the clergy, despite the fact that there are as many ministers in America as there are physicians (537,000 in medicine and 541,000 in ministry) and considerably more clergy than scientists (541,000 versus 395,000).[50]

A Review of User Studies Among the Clergy

What little literature that exists concerning the clergy as information users can be divided into two general categories: 1) studies of ministerial reading habits, and 2) broader examinations of ministerial information needs and uses.[51] Though the present study is concerned with the full spectrum of information sources that ministers use--both formal and informal, almost all of the prior studies on this topic concentrated on formal information channels, especially reading habits. These studies will be reviewed first, followed by a review of the few studies that encompassed a broader look at ministerial information sources.

Since the first published study of ministerial reading habits by Lancour in 1944, there have been few other such studies, and only two of these have been published in the library literature (Lancour, 1944, and Huseman, 1970). Convenient reviews of most of these studies are given by Tanner (1989) in an unpublished paper and by Erdel (1982) in the ministerial journal *Reformed Review*. As Erdel observed, this paucity of research "is particularly glaring in view of the minister's traditional dependence on books for teaching, preaching, counseling, and writing, the recent emphasis on continuing education for ministers, the widespread distribution of theological libraries, and the tremendous upsurge in religious publishing over the last several years" (p. 141).

Lancour's 1944 study, "The Reading Interests and Habits of the Graduates of the Union Theological Seminary," was based on a 1937 survey of 252 Union alumni serving as ministers. The 122 respondents (48%) to his brief survey represented eighteen denominations distributed across the country. He concluded that ministers read widely, though religion, fiction, and biography accounted for nearly two-thirds of ministers' reading interests; that most books which ministers read were bought rather than borrowed; that they read magazines regularly, chief among which were *Christian Century, Reader's Digest, Harper's,* and *Atlantic*; and that most ministers read on average 18.5 hours per week, though half did most of their reading in the summer or while on vacation. Lancour concluded that "the reading tastes of this group of clergymen...are of comparatively good quality; though falling short of the standard one would expect of a group with such high educational background and so rich an opportunity for intellectual leadership" (p. 35).

The next major study on ministerial reading patterns was conducted by Hawkins in 1954. In her unpublished master's thesis, "An Investigation of the Reading Habits of Students and Graduates of the School of Medicine and the Candler School of Theology at Emory University," Hawkins surveyed 640 students and professionals in the fields of medicine and ministry. Of the 184 respondents (28%), only 50 were ministers. She concluded that although pastors spent more time reading than physicians did, physicians read more widely. She also found that professional interests influenced most reading preferences, a finding in keeping with Strang (1942) and suggested by Porcella (1973).

In 1961 *Christianity Today,* one of the most widely circulated magazines among ministers, surveyed "a random sampling of 100 Protestant ministers" ("How Much Do Ministers Read?" p. 647) in observance of National Library Week. The results indicated that half the respondents read less than ten books per year and that only six in a hundred used their local library regularly. A study was done in 1968 by De Klerk at Emory University in the form of a paper entitled "A Study of Reading Interests of Ministers of the Christian Reformed Church," but it is unavailable except for a brief summary in Erdel's review (1982, p. 142).

Besides Lancour's 1944 article in *Library Quarterly*, the only other study published in the professional library literature is Huseman's "Books, Periodicals, and the Pastor" in the January 1970 issue of *Drexel Library Quarterly* (the whole issue was devoted to "Books, Librarians, and the Clergy"). Huseman surveyed 117 pastors of the Lutheran Church of America in Pennsylvania, asking more than 100 questions, but he focused primarily upon whether churches provided book allowances for their pastors (only 15% did so). Like Lancour, Huseman concluded that the "typical" minister spent some twenty hours per week reading, but mostly in theological subjects (p. 7).

In 1974 the American Theological Library Association published in its annual *Proceedings* a condensation of a paper read by Brockway on "The Reading and Library Habits of Connecticut Pastors." Unfortunately, the reported results were very skimpy, being based on a partial survey of 1,500 Connecticut pastors found in the yellow pages (only 17% responded).

A much more thorough study was done by Levitt (1976) as a student at Trinity Evangelical Divinity School in Deerfield, Illinois, and published in that seminary's *Trinity Journal*. His survey of 835 Evangelical Free Church pastors yielded a 25% response rate. He focused, however, mostly on book-buying rather than book-reading patterns. He did find that more than 90% of the ministers responding thought they "should" read books that were popular among their congregations and that they "should" recommend books from the pulpit. No attempt was made to determine actual ministerial practice.

Tanner (1989) sent a self-administered written questionnaire to a random sample of 700 ministers serving in the religious heritage known as the Christian Churches and Churches of Christ, a Protestant religious group that exercises local congregational autonomy. His hypothesis was that ministerial reading habits were rather narrowly focused in terms of both volume and variety and that this focus was associated with the minister's perceived professional role--a research area suggested by Porcella (1973). The responses from 325 (46%) of these ministers supported the first part of this hypothesis, but not the second part. Ministerial reading interests cannot be tied simply to professional role. These professionals appeared to display much more subtlety in their reading habits than a written questionnaire was able to uncover.

Other findings in the study by Tanner (1989) indicated that these particular ministers owned a median of 600 books (size of library correlated only slightly [r = .23] with number of books read), purchased 20 books per year, and read more now than when they first entered the profession. Some 16% of the books and half of the magazines they read were in subject areas outside of the formal ministry. The plurality (37%) of their reading time, which averaged 14.5 hours per week, was spent in sermon preparation. The one question related to less formal channels of information sources (listening to audiotapes) indicated that about half used this source and half did not. Some 53% of these ministers borrowed books from a library at least once in the last six months. The mean number of books borrowed was 6.8 per six months, compared to 14.3 for American adult book readers, who comprise roughly half of the adult population in this country (Book Industry Study Group, 1984).

Tanner (1989, p. 40) concluded his study with these words:

> Finally, it must be admitted that the present study--based as it is on a self-administered survey instrument--can only begin to crack the cover of reading interests among ministers. Further and different study is needed to get behind the mere mechanical numbers. In-depth interviews with a variety of ministers, conducted on

the field in their offices, is needed to probe the
reading patterns and psyches of preaching ministers. While this kind of study may not lead to
easy generalizations, that is as it should be.

In addition to these studies that looked at the more
formal channels of information used by modern ministers, two
much more broadly focused research projects have also been
conducted, both in the form of doctoral dissertations--Allen
(1987) and Porcella (1973). Allen dealt with foreign clergy, and
while the data are not directly applicable to American ministers,
the results are worth noting briefly here.

Allen (1987) mailed a self-administered questionnaire to
a sample of 606 Baptist church leaders in Costa Rica, Guate-
mala, and Honduras; she received responses from 56.7 percent.
Her purpose was "to gain an understanding of how people in
developing countries obtain needed information and what patterns
of use might be discovered to aid in predicting such use" (p. iii).
She looked at both general and theological information use patterns in order to "test some of the theories regarding information
seeking" (p. 2).

Although Allen found no evidence in the literature for a
"consensually agreed upon theory of information seeking and
source utilization" (p. 40), she did identify five components that
such a theory might contain. First, information needs impinge
on all people's lives. Second, the human activities produced by
the life situations of individuals contribute to a recognition of
information needs. Third, people use various types of information resources to meet their information needs, with prior studies
indicating that the overwhelming choice for information sources
is interpersonal. Fourth, people satisfy their information needs
with varying degrees of success, with such success related to
certain demographic variables (e.g. age, education, income) and
to the presence or absence of various barriers--personal, institu-

tional, and societal (cf. Wilkin, 1977). And finally, the level of satisfaction may determine whether an information resource is used again.

Allen found that increased church leadership responsibility was the greatest factor in predicting use of printed information sources and mass media, but that there was no correlation between leadership responsibility and the use of informal information sources. She did find that the ministers in her study with lower incomes used radio and television more, while urban ministers with higher incomes used libraries and printed sources more frequently. Education, not age or sex, was the strongest predictor of all types of information sources used. While interesting, these results are limited to information-seeking behavior and shed little light on how or why ministers use information.

The other doctoral study of clergy, in addition to Allen, was conducted by Porcella (1973) regarding "The Information Gathering Habits of the Protestant Ministers of Cedar Rapids, Iowa," and it remains the standard study in this area. Porcella surveyed 113 of the 117 Protestant clergymen preaching in Cedar Rapids, Iowa, in order to test his hypothesis that theologically conservative ministers relied primarily upon the Bible and aids to Biblical interpretation, while more liberally oriented ministers used a broader range of information sources, e.g. books, magazines, television, radio, and movies. His particular focus was upon the preaching task of these ministers.

Porcella found, ironically, that doctrinal viewpoint was strongly correlated with exposure to information sources, but that his hypothesis was not supported with respect to the use of information sources for sermon preparation--the focus of his study. As he summarized his own findings, "the data revealed an overall tendency among both conservatives and liberals towards rather limited levels of sermon preparation in terms of total time spent reading and searching in all types of information sources" (abstract). He did find, however, that the predominantly "rural" community under study had a higher percentage (59.3%) of "conservative" clergy than might otherwise be "typical." Only 18.6% of the ministerial respondents identified themselves as "liberal" on the basis of a set of questions that Porcella had included in the questionnaire as a means of identifying doctrinal orientation.

Porcella's main methodological approach was the self-administered questionnaire, which in his study consisted of 57 questions covering 19 pages. The first part of the survey instrument dealt with the use of libraries and asked for information regarding how and how often respondents had used institutional libraries. He did not include questions relative to the reasons for which these libraries were or were not used, nor what degrees of success ministers had in this area of seeking information. Consequently, the raw data gathered in this (and other) areas by Porcella does not admit to easy interpretations about ministerial motives or analysis of much more than surface behavior.

The second part of the questionnaire dealt with ministers' own personal libraries, asking questions about size, content, and use. In an attempt to devise a more objective, comparative standard, Porcella listed more than 30 specific books (theological "classics") and asked respondents to indicate which ones they owned. For some of these titles, he also asked how often they were used. Though the list he compiled at the time was undoubtedly reflective of the "best" of current scholarship, one wonders if the ownership of such a limited list of books is the best reflection of ministerial reading depth.

The third part of Porcella's questionnaire asked about ministers' reading habits relative to books, magazines, and newspapers. He employed variations of the critical-incident technique to elicit more current, and more accurate, responses. As in the second part, Porcella also asked if they had read specific titles, which in this case were books that had either been best sellers or widely reviewed during the past year. He took a similar approach with magazines--listing both ministerial and non-ministerial titles.

The fourth part of the survey instrument dealt with ministers' "use" of radio, television, and movies. Here Porcella found that conservative clergy used such media significantly less often than did clergy with a more liberal theological orientation.

The fifth part of the questionnaire examined the particular focus of Porcella's study, the "use of information sources for preaching ministry." The responses to this set of questions suggested that more conservative ministers tended to value more highly the Bible and aids to Biblical interpretation while more liberal ministers used a broader range of information resources. However, further analysis of these data by Porcella indicated that these valuations were less apparent in the actual practices of these two groups. The implications of this observation for the current study are that espoused and enacted values may vary and that it is important not only to ask ministers what sources they say they use or value, but also to observe what they actually use in practicing their profession, for example, in their preaching.

The sixth and final part of the questionnaire covered demographic and doctrinal variables. An examination of all 57 questions asked in Porcella's survey shows how heavily quantitative his approach was, only three questions being open-ended and most calling for numeric responses. He did, however, supplement these closed-ended questions with brief interviews, but their major purpose was to test the reliability of the printed questionnaire. Most of his analysis was based on statistical tests such as the Pearson correlation coefficient and multiple regression analysis.

While the unusually high response rate and the extremely comprehensive questionnaire from Porcella's study provided a wealth of data on this particular sample of Protestant clergy, the heavy quantitative emphasis did not allow for a full picture to be painted of the information needs and uses of this group of professionals--at least in terms of the kinds of newer user studies called for by Dervin and Nilan (1986). Also his focus on only the preaching role necessarily limited his research into the larger information needs and uses of this community of professionals. Indeed, Porcella concluded his dissertation by noting that future studies should examine the broader roles of the modern minister that extend beyond the single task of preaching. He suggested that such a study be conducted "in a major center of intellectual activity, such as a university community" (p. 104).

Consequently, the goal of the present study has been to explore the pastor as an information professional in this larger professional context of multiple roles for the contemporary clergy, using a university community as the research site. While the pulpit's role in ministerial information needs and uses is one focus, the present study also considers a wide range of the information needs and uses of the clergy.

ENDNOTES

1. The specific question asked during the telephone survey was this: "In any community there are certain types of people you can go to for information or advice. I would like your opinion concerning the importance of having these people available as sources of advice, regardless of whether or not you personally use them for advice." The exact wording of this question means that the results from this survey technically only indicate the potential role that ministers occupy as sources of information and advice, not necessarily the actual role that they occupy as information sources.

2. It should be pointed out that the survey discussed here was conducted by The Gallup Organization for the National Association of Chain Drug Stores. That may explain one reason why pharmacists were rated so highly, but there is no indication that the question was biased (other than the fact that surveyors included pharmacists among the six professionals named).

3. These figures have remained fairly stable during the last decade, according to Gallup and Castelli, *The People's Religion: American Faith in the '90's* (1989), pp. 29-35.

4. These statistics were compiled by The Gallup Organization for the Princeton Religion Research Center and reported in their 1990 annual publication, *Religion in America: 1990*, edited by Bezilla (1990). Like the membership and attendance figures (see n. 3 above), these numbers have remained rather constant for the last ten years.

5. The results of these library surveys of citizens of California and New England were reported conveniently in King and Palmour (1981). The California study indicated that 7% of the respondents used "religious leaders" and an equal percentage (7%) used "a library" as information sources. The New England study listed the former at 10% and the latter at 17%. Somewhat skewing these results was the inclusion of a separate category described as "a professional (like a doctor or lawyer or social worker)," a category certainly open to the profession of "religious leaders."

6. The source of this quotation was an AAAS conference brochure, "Your Guide to AAAS 1990." This reference was provided by Dr. Linda Smith, professor in the Graduate School of Library and Information Science at the University of Illinois at Urbana-Champaign, who attended the 1990 AAAS annual conference.

7. See George et al. (1989), who published the initial results of the first two phases of this project in the AAAS publication *Saving Minds: Black Churches and Education*. While the survey efforts did yield 380 responses, this number reflected a response rate of only 7.9% of the 4,800 sampled, and most of these (176) were from black churches in the South. The focus of the AAAS project to date has been more upon educational programs for children in the church than it has been upon the specific role of the minister as a direct provider of information.

8. Note also the research by Clarke (1985), who looked at the informational role that ministers can occupy in providing preventative education on the topic of battered women.

9. Though otherwise unsubstantiated, Bell (1990) in a newsletter published by the American Association of Bible Colleges stated that in the 1970s only 170 such suits were filed

in this country. In the 1980s the number rose to 12,000. The article noted that a recent conference of the American Bar Association declared religious litigation as a new frontier in American law and focused on techniques for bringing suit against pastors and churches. An interesting variation on this theme is the suggestion cited by Huth (1989) that physicians who can ensure regular use of the professional medical literature should have their malpractice premiums reduced.

10. This quotation is taken from "New Englands [sic] First Fruits" (1643), a document amounting "almost to an official statement of the founding fathers" of Harvard, according to Morrison (1935, p. 247), from which this citation is taken.

11. As further evidence of the widespread impact that clergy had upon colonial America, Fant (1987), citing research by Martin (1964), noted that 40% of the entries in Evans' *American Bibliography* are sermons.

12. A rather thorough analysis and evaluation of the Doctor of Ministry degree program offered by American seminaries is found in Carroll and Wheeler (1987).

13. The census data for this community were provided by a social science professor specializing in demographic studies who taught at a local university.

14. These examples of information professionals are not meant to be exhaustive, but rather illustrative. The focus here is on persons who are associated most closely with the field of library and information science. However, information professionals may be found in other fields as well. Mason (1990), for example, listed such diverse occupations as accountants, records managers, and museum curators--in addition to librarians and archivists--in his article "What Is an Information Professional?"

Mason's definition of information professionals is that they are persons who "possess specialized knowledge about knowledge itself which they use to improve the intellectual state of people" (pp. 123-24). Obviously, pastors differ in two key components of this definition: their specialized knowledge is not primarily "about knowledge itself" and they are concerned with more than just the "intellectual state" of their parishioners. The point of my comparison between traditional information professionals and pastors is that both are professionals engaged substantively in the practice of providing information to others. To bypass the differences, I could have used the term "information provider" instead of "information professional," but I did not for three reasons.

First, the term "provider" ignores the professional aspects of what pastors do in disseminating information, and those are important since ministry is not just an occupation. Second, the term "provider" also unduly stresses the dissemination of information over its acquisition, and both are at issue in this study. Third, the use of the term "information professional" allows me to show not only how these two professions are similar, but how they differ. The next endnote suggests further evidence on this point.

15. The discussion in this chapter on what constitutes a professional, including an information professional, is limited in scope. Certainly other criteria besides Asheim's (1978) have been suggested in the literature. Mason (1990), for example, focused on only two criteria: professionals possess specialized knowledge, and they use this knowledge in the service of others. Both of these criteria also apply to pastors as professionals, though also see the endnote above for two key ways in which pastors differ from traditional information professionals, as defined by him. Mason also included in his discussion of information professionals, however, such characteristics as "intellectual empathy" and "fiduciary relationship." The first is

closely akin to my description of the pastor as wounded healer, and the second is similar to my observations about the pastor's personal authority built on trust.

Abbott's (1988) analysis of professionals is more task oriented than either Asheim or Mason. He defined professionals as "exclusive occupational groups applying somewhat abstract knowledge to particular cases" (p. 8), giving particular attention to the "jurisdictions" that professionals have. However, pastors also qualify as professionals under his definition. In fact, he described clergy as professionals who had "personal problems jurisdiction." This focus on answering personal problems is a key aspect of information provision highlighted in such citizen-oriented library studies as Chen and Hernon (1982), King and Palmour (1981), and Warner, Murray and Palmour (1973).

To be sure, Abbott did not include pastors in his discussion of information professionals, which he defined as persons who "help clients overburdened with material from which thay [sic] cannot retrieve usable information" (p. 216). However, even he admitted the difficulty in defining "information," preferring instead to describe (not define) those professionals concerned with qualitative information (e.g. librarians) and those professionals concerned with quantitative information (e.g. accountants). The point is that pastors certainly qualify as professionals under any of these arguments. Furthermore, I contend, as I argue in Chapter 2, that pastors also display some of the characteristics of information professionals suggested by Asheim (1978), Abbott (1988), and Mason (1990), though I am careful as well to note the points at which I believe they differ.

16. A recent overview of contemporary clergy, for example, by Messer (1989), a seminary president, suggested five dominant pastoral images: wounded healer, servant leader,

political mystic, enslaved liberator, and practical theologian. Since the present study focuses on the pastor as information professional, not on all that the pastor does or is, the lack of overlap between images is to be expected.

17. For a critical overview of current homiletical theory, see Eslinger (1987).

18. Note also Bellah's (et al.) most recent social critique, *The Good Society* (1991), and its chapter on "The Public Church," where he traced the loss of the church's institutional authority in America, with the notable exception of the black church.

19. The discussion of authority is limited in this study to only one kind of authority--cognitive. Such forms as political, military, parental, and administrative authority are not under discussion here. Nor is the issue of authority versus power being examined. For a useful summary of this issue, as well as how authority may be exercised in other religious circles, see Sutton (1983), pp. 338-349. Wilson (1983) also provides a helpful bibliography for looking at some of the larger concerns outside the scope of this study.

20. In his book *The Religious Order: A Study of Virtuoso Religion and Its Legitimation in the Nineteenth-Century Church of England*, Hill (1973) expanded upon Weber's discussion of charismatic authority to differentiate between charismatic and virtuoso religious leaders. Wrote Hill (p. 2):

> The religious virtuoso follows what he takes to be a pure and rigorous interpretation of normative obligations which already exist in a religious tradition, [while the charismatic] represents a shattering of what exists already and the articulation of an entirely new basis of normative

obligation.... While the typical statement of a charismatic leader can be given as, "It is written, but I say unto you ...," the character- istic statement of a virtuoso is, "It is written, and I insist...."

In commenting on this distinction, Marty (1989) made the point in American preaching that many of the so-called charismatic authorities, most notably Martin Luther King, Jr., were really virtuoso authorities who did not offer new interpretations of sacred text as would a charismatic, but merely insisted by virtue of their rhetorical and personal power that the principles of Scripture be followed.

21. In fact, at the close of one interview with this pastor, I told him, as we were stepping out into the hall, how much I had appreciated the previous Sunday's sermon that he had preached. He called me back into his office and with tears in his eyes acknowledged that I had been the first one in that congregation to do so--after several years of ministry there.

22. Innis (1951), for example, noted the monopoly that each of these three media has exercised in turn historically and that to argue against the use of electronic media is to fight a historically losing battle. Carey (1967) pointed out that monop- oly, however, does not mean exclusivity and that even the rise of print media in the 16th century did not mean the loss of orality. The monopoly of electronic media in popular society only means that print and oral media have become residual, not absent.

23. The British New Testament scholar F.F. Bruce (1988), for example, introduced his treatise on the Biblical canon in the history of the Christian church with a section entitled, "People of the Book." He did note, however, that this designation has also been applied to Jews and to Muslims, in

addition to Christians. Relevant here as well is the principle of *sola Scriptura* promulgated by Martin Luther as a means of combatting the Catholic church's use of oral tradition to interpret the Bible (cf. Wood, 1969, pp. 69 ff.). I owe these references to Dr. Robert Lowery, professor of New Testament at Lincoln Christian Seminary in Lincoln, Illinois. For a library-oriented view of Martin Luther's position on books in general, see Montgomery (1962).

24. Note, however, the increasing use of the image for preaching in more recent homiletical theory; see, for example, Buttrick (1987), Long (1989), and especially Troeger (1990).

25. Even in the literate world of Puritan New England, the "aural sermon" was dominant, as Stout (1986) has shown.

26. A research interest in ministerial roles was noted by one of the pastors in this community. He had recently written an article, which had been accepted for publication in a refereed theological journal, based on research conducted for his Doctor of Ministry degree. His focus was on the various roles filled by modern ministers, using the ministerial roles suggested by Blizzard (1958), as did Porcella (1973) in his dissertation. His finding was that many modern ministers lacked an overall "master role" that provided a unifying and solidifying center to their professional tasks. He further speculated that the lack of such a master role might be a contributing factor to the number of ministers who drop out of the ministry.

27. Compare a similar review of preaching by Shelley (1986) who also remarked that "the pulpit has become a counseling tool" (p. 22).

28. Not included here are those pastors who did not counsel because of lack of opportunity. As noted in Chapter 3, there were some churches whose members did not ask the pastor

counseling-related questions. These pastors surmised that their parishioners were either not having such problems, not seeking counseling if they were, or not willing to talk to their pastor about such issues.

29. A less-frequently mentioned reason for not doing counseling was some pastors' concern for church growth. Several pastors of newly started congregations and of very large congregations noted that the time demands of the counseling role limited the number of people to whom the pastor could minister. In one situation, the pastor of a fairly new church who had a master's degree in counseling from a major university refused to do counseling because it would "limit this church to about 120 people and I want us to grow to over a thousand."

30. It should be pointed out that 16 (26%) of the 62 pastors interviewed in this study delivered Sunday evening messages in addition to the Sunday morning sermon. These Sunday evening addresses are not included in this study for three reasons. First, the great majority of ministers did not have such messages. Second, most of the ministers who had Sunday evening services did not regularly preach, relying instead on "lay members" or guest pastors to make presentations. Third, those ministers who did deliver Sunday evening messages usually described them as being quite different from the Sunday morning sermon, often being more of an informal Bible study directed to those few "core" members of the church who attended such services. Therefore, this study concentrated on Sunday morning sermons.

31. It is possible that the need for involvement and integrity on the part of the preacher could have had some filtering effect upon the topics that were chosen and the nature of the information communicated on those topics. It may be that the topics not preached on and the information not delivered was just as significant as what was said during the course of this study. However, the limited timeframe of this research project does not

allow for much more than theoretical speculation on this point. Still, in considering the role of the pastor as information disseminator in the pulpit, it would make an interesting future study to look at what was not being said in the sermon.

32. This statement is not meant to imply that every piece of information used by a pastor in a sermon was intended or considered to be of divine origin or of ultimate significance. The point to be made here is that even when a pastor quoted routine statistics from the newspaper, they were used in a "religious" context for spiritual purposes that were quite apart from their original setting. It was not the secular story, but the sacred moral of the story that was at issue in these pastors' dissemination of information.

33. Compare also the concept of "voice merging" described by Miller (1991), whereby multiple sources tend to become merged orally into the pastor's sole voice.

34. Crites (1971) made this relevant observation regarding the importance of storytelling for Christianity: "It is significant that the early Christian preaching was largely a storytelling mission, offering people a new story, the Christian kerygma, to reorient their sense of the meaning both of historical time and of their own personal life-time" (p. 308). His article provides a convenient point of entry into the literature on the religious implications of storytelling.

35. Abrahams (1969) discussed the issue of personal involvement in terms of the capability or tendency of various genres to produce such interaction between performer and audience. He even provided a chart (p. 112) showing the level of interaction from one end of an "interpersonal involvement scale" to the other that each genre displays. He placed storytelling (the various forms of which he grouped under "fictive genres") in the middle of his involvement scale.

36. Note the study by Bissonette (1977) in the *Community Mental Health Journal*. He concluded that not only ministers occupy a strategic gatekeeper role in the community, but also such groups as policemen, hairdressers, and bartenders (the latter role being the primary focus of his study).

37. Some evidence of the church's influence on library use is suggested by results of a national survey conducted by the Harris polling organization and reported by Westin and Finger (1991). A comparison of nonusers, users, and heavy users of libraries in terms of cultural activities and civic involvement indicated that 62% of those who claimed to be heavy library users were members of religious congregations, far more than professed membership in labor unions (of which only 12% were heavy users), voluntary associations (only 21%), or charitable or educational organizations (50%). Only those who said they visited art galleries or museums accounted for a higher percentage (73%) of heavy library users. Darkening this otherwise sunny scenario, however, was the finding that the highest percentage (57%) of library nonusers were also members of religious congregations (Westin and Finger, 1991, p. 25). Noteworthy also in this regard are the findings reported by Warner, Murray, and Palmour (1973) based on a survey of Baltimore adults. When asked to rate the helpfulness of a number of informal information sources, more respondents rated religious institutions as very helpful than they did any other of the seven groups listed, though libraries were not included (p. 156).

38. See, for example, the comparison of these two paradigms in Guba and Lincoln (1988) and the critique of the positivist paradigm by Streatfield (1983). In library and information science, one of the most recent treatments of the paradigm shift that is occurring was by Hale (1991). Grover and Greer (1991) and Altman (1991) also discussed this shift.

39. One implication of the new view of information is

that it suggests that such traditional terms as *information gap* and *information rich/poor* may be inaccurate models for describing what is actually happening. Third World researchers, for example, are more prone to look at issues such as power and the quality of information rather than stressing a positivist emphasis upon information as an object. This issue was discussed briefly by Rohde (1986).

40. This line of reasoning is consistent with arguments first laid down by sociologists such as Mead, Berger and Luckman, Schutz, and Blumer, whose positions were summarized by Bradley (1990, pp. 11-15). In the religious realm of meaning, Berger (1969) later applied the same arguments in his book *The Sacred Canopy*. One of the primary functions of religious groups and their leaders, he contended, is to construct and maintain an "objective knowledge" that imposes a "common order of interpretation" upon experience, thereby establishing a "sacred cosmos." Part of what pastors do in the pulpit is to maintain a sacred canopy of meaning for their parishioners. While the present study did not attempt to analyze the particular philosophical foundations upon which ministers' use of information is built, this larger view should be kept in mind as part of the context within which ministers, either knowingly or unknowingly, function in their use of information.

41. Rohde (1986) observed that "the association of the word 'information' with 'need' implies a basic need similar to other basic human needs, divided by psychologists into three categories: physiological, affective, and cognitive" (p. 53), categories which are interrelated, even when examining information needs.

42. Studies of information use among American adults indicate, for example, that a somewhat nebulous, non-document-oriented "own experience" is the most common source for meeting information needs (Chen and Hernon, 1982).

43. As Krikelas admitted, however, information can not only reduce uncertainty, it can also create uncertainty. Consequently, in a later footnote Krikelas (1983, p. 18, fn. 10) changed his definition to "information is a stimulus that creates a change in one's level (degree) of certainty."

44. What is important to understand here is that, in the words of Korzybski (cited by Bateson, 1972), "the map is not the territory." Of course, it is also assumed that most ministers will have information needs/demands, though Krikelas's (1983, p. 10) observation in this regard is worth remembering: "There is no known natural law that requires everyone to have an information need at the time of a given study."

45. Note, for example, the case for understanding complexity that Peshkin (1988) made in the study of ethnicity by interpretive methods. See also Benge's (1984) controversial review of information studies, entitled "Where Are the Emperor's Clothes?"

46. These eleven *ARIST* reviews are found in the volumes covering 1966 to 1972, 1974, 1978, 1986, and 1990.

47. Poole (1985) provided an example of what Paisley called for in 1968. In his book *Theories of the Middle Range*, Poole suggested a theory of "avoidance-least effort," a "theory which perhaps guides all behavior of the scientist or engineer in the formal information setting" (p. 95). The basic assumptions underlying this theory are that humans seek to solve their problems primarily by avoiding pain and by exerting the least effort. The theory is limited in its application only to formal information systems of scientists and engineers.

48. Belkin's (1980) somewhat controversial ASK model stands for a user's Anomalous State of Knowledge, which examines how people seek information concerning situations

about which their knowledge is incomplete.

49. Even the use of information among janitors has been the subject of recent research (Chatman, 1990). Her study explored the information needs among this low-income group within the framework of alienation theory.

50. These figures are taken from the U.S. Census Bureau's *Current Population Survey*, as cited in *Statistical Abstracts of the United States, 1990* (p. 389). The figures for the clergy have been adjusted upward by more recent data compiled by Jacquet (1990, p. 255).

51. A review of representative literature published recently in the field of homiletics was also conducted as background research for the case study of sermons. Some of the key works (identified by two professors of homiletics) that were reviewed for this study included: Robinson (1980), Stott (1982), Cox (1985), Craddock (1985), Markquart (1985), Buttrick (1987), Eslinger (1987), Fant (1987), Long (1989), and Troeger (1990). Fant (1987), in particular, had a helpful chapter, entitled "Out of the Gutenberg Galaxy." Craddock (1981) also had a useful case study that analyzed how and why a minister researches and delivers a sermon.

LIST OF SOURCES CITED

Abbott, Andrew. *The System of Professions: An Essay on the Division of Labor*. Chicago: University of Chicago Press, 1988.

Abrahams, Roger. "The Complex Relations of Simple Forms." *Oeuvre* 2 (1969): 104-128.

Allen, Jean Short. "Information-Seeking Patterns and Resource Use by Baptist Leaders in Three Central American Countries." Ph.D. dissertation, The University of North Carolina at Chapel Hill, 1987.

Allen, Thomas. "Information Needs and Uses." *Annual Review of Information Science and Technology* 4 (1969): 3-29.

_____. "Managing the Flow of Scientific and Technical Information." Ph.D. dissertation, MIT Sloan School of Management, 1966.

Altman, Ellen. "Whither LIS Research: Ideology, Funding, and Educational Standards." In *Library and Information Science Research: Perspectives and Strategies for Improvement*, pp. 114-127. Ed. by C. McClure and P. Hernon. Norwood, NJ: Ablex, 1991.

Anderson, A. "A Call for Interprofessional Ecumenism." *Journal of Religion and Health* 14 (July 1975): 177-188.

Anderson, A.J. "How Do You Manage? Case Study: Rewriting the Classics." *Library Journal* 117 (April 1, 1992): 90-92.

Asheim, Lester. "Librarians as Professionals." *Library Trends* 27 (Winter 1978): 225-257.

Askey, D. et al. "Clergy as Intermediary--An Approach to Cancer Control." *Progress in Cancer Control IV: Research in the Cancer Center* 4 (1983): 417-424.

ATS Factbook, 1990-91. Compiled by the Association of Theological Schools in the United States and Canada. Vandalia, OH: ATS, 1991.

Auerbach Corporation. *DOD User Needs Study, Phase I: Final Technical Reports.* 2 vols. Philadelphia: Auerbach Corporation, 1965.

Averill, Lloyd. "The Art of Saying Something." *Christianity Today* 32 (October 21, 1988): 29-32.

Barna, George. *Sources of Information for Ministry and Business.* Glendale, CA: The Barna Research Group, 1990.

Bateson, Gregory. "Form, Substance, and Difference." In his *Steps to an Ecology of Mind*, pp. 448-466. New York: Ballantine, 1972.

Belkin, Nicholas. "Anomalous States of Knowledge as a Basis for Information Retrieval." *Canadian Journal of Information Science* 5 (1980): 133-143.

Bell, Randall. "A Word from the Executive Director." *American Association of Bible Colleges Newsletter* (September 1990): 2.

Bellah, Robert et al. *The Good Society*. New York: Knopf, 1991.

_____. *Habits of the Heart: Individualism and Commitment in American Life*. New York: Knopf, 1986.

Benge, Ronald. "Where Are the Emperor's Clothes?" *Journal of Librarianship* 16 (1984): 211-219.

Berger, Peter. *The Sacred Canopy: Elements of a Sociology of Religion*. New York: Anchor Books, 1969.

Berkley, James. "What Pastors Are Paid." *Leadership: A Practical Journal for Church Leaders* 13 (Spring 1992): 84-89.

Bezilla, Robert, ed. *Religion in America: 1990*. Princeton: The Princeton Religion Research Center, 1990.

Bissonette, Raymond. "The Bartender as a Mental Health Service Gatekeeper: A Role Analysis." *Community Mental Health Journal* 13 (1977): 92-99.

Blizzard, Samuel. "The Parish Minister's Self Image of His Master Role." *Pastoral Psychology* 9 (December 1958): 25-32.

Book Industry Study Group. *1983 Consumer Research Study on Reading and Book Purchasing*. 3 vols. New York: Book Industry Study Group, 1984.

Boorstin, Daniel. *Gresham's Law of Knowledge or Information*. Washington, DC: Library of Congress, 1980.

Bradley, Johanna Rediger. "Bureaucratic and Individual Knowledge and Action in the Public Services

Departments of an Academic Library." Ph.D. dissertation, University of Illinois, 1990.

Brandeis, Louis. *Business--A Profession.* Boston: Small, Maynard, and Company, 1914.

Bratcher-Porter, Shelvy. "Cancer Knowledge and Cancer Education Among Black Clergy." Ph.D. dissertation, Texas Woman's University, 1987.

Brittain, J. M. *Information and Its Users.* Bath, England: Bath University Press, 1970.

Brockway, Duncan. "The Reading and Library Habits of Connecticut Pastors." *American Theological Library Association Proceedings* (1974): 125-127.

Bruce, F. F. *The Canon of Scripture.* Downers Grove, IL: InterVarsity Press, 1988.

Bruder, E. "The Clergyman's Contribution to Community Mental Health." *Hospital and Community Psychiatry* 22 (1971): 207-210.

Buttrick, David. *Homiletic: Moves and Structures.* Philadelphia: Fortress Press, 1987.

Carey, James. "Marshall McLuhan and Harold Adams Innis." *Antioch Review* 27 (1967): 5-39.

Carroll, Jackson and Wheeler, Barbara. *Study of Doctor of Ministry Programs Summary.* Hartford, CT: Auburn Theological Seminary and Hartford Seminary's Center for Social and Religious Research, 1987.

Case, Donald. "The Collection and Use of Information by Some American Historians: A Study of Motives and Methods." *Library Quarterly* 61 (January 1991): 61-82.

Chatman, Elfreda. "Alienation Theory: Application of a Conceptual Framework to a Study of Information Among Janitors." *RQ* 29 (Spring 1990): 355-368.

Chen, C. and Hernon, P. *Information Seeking: Assessing and Anticipating User Needs.* New York: Neal-Schuman, 1982.

Clarke, Rita-Lou. "Pastoral Care of Battered Women." D.Min. project, School of Theology at Claremont, 1985.

Cox, James. *Preaching.* San Francisco: Jossey-Bass, 1985.

Craddock, Fred. *As One Without Authority.* Nashville: Abingdon Press, 1979.

_____. "Occasion-Text-Sermon." *Interpretation* 35 (January 1981): 59-71.

_____. *Preaching.* Nashville: Abingdon Press, 1985.

Crane, Diana. "Information Needs and Uses." *Annual Review of Information Science and Technology* 6 (1971): 3-39.

Crawford, Susan. "Informal Communication Among Scientists in Sleep Research." *Journal of the American Society for Information Science* 22 (1971): 301-310.

_____. "Information Needs and Uses." *Annual Review of Information Science and Technology* 13 (1978): 61-81.

Cressy, David. "Books as Totems in Seventeenth Century

England and New England." *Journal of Library History* 21 (1986): 92-107.

Crites, Stephen. "The Narrative Quality of Experience." *Journal of the American Academy of Religion* 39 (1971): 291-311.

Davis, R. and Bailey, C. "Bibliography of Use Studies." Unpublished paper, Graduate School of Library Science, Drexel Institute of Technology, Philadelphia, 1964.

Dervin, Brenda. "Communication Gaps and Inequities: Moving Toward a Reconceptualization." In *Progress in Communication Sciences*, 2:73-112. Ed. by B. Dervin and M. Voigt. Norwood, NJ: Ablex, 1980.

_____. "Strategies for Dealing with Human Information Needs: Information or Communication?" *Journal of Broadcasting* 20 (1976): 324-333.

_____. "Useful Theory for Librarianship: Communication, Not Information." *Drexel Library Quarterly* 13 (1977): 16-32.

Dervin, Brenda and Dewdney, Patricia. "Neutral Questioning: A New Approach to the Reference Interview." *RQ* 25 (Summer 1986): 506-513.

Dervin, Brenda and Nilan, Michael. "Information Needs and Uses." *Annual Review of Information Science and Technology* 21 (1986): 3-33.

Durkheim, Emile. *The Rules of Sociological Method.* 8th ed. Trans. by S. Solovay and J. Mueller. Ed. by George Catlin. New York: Free Press, 1964.

Eisenstein, Elizabeth. *The Printing Press as an Agent of Change*. 2 vols. Oxford: Oxford University Press, 1979.

Elayyan, Ribhi. "The Use of Information by Physicians." *International Library Review* 20 (1988): 247-265.

Ellul, Jacques. *The Humiliation of the Word*. Trans. by J. M. Hanks. Grand Rapids, MI: William B. Eerdmans Publishing Company, 1985.

English, Stephen and Dibert, Nickolas. "Punishing the Preacher: Casting Light on Clergy Malpractice." *The Brief* (Summer 1988): 7-11, 28-29.

Erdel, Timothy. "Bring Also the Books: Studies of Ministers as Readers." *Reformed Review* (Spring 1982): 136-151.

Eslinger, Richard. *A New Hearing: Living Options in Homiletic Method*. Nashville: Abingdon Press, 1987.

Estabrook, Leigh and Horak, Chris. "Public vs. Professional Opinion on Libraries: The Great Divide?" *Library Journal* 117 (April 1, 1992): 52-55.

Faibisoff, Sylvia and Ely, Donald. "Information and Information Needs." *Information Reports and Bibliographies* 5, No. 5 (1976): 2-16.

Fant, Clyde. "Out of the Gutenberg Galaxy." In his *Preaching for Today*, pp. 159-173. San Francisco: Harper and Row, 1987.

———. *Preaching for Today*. San Francisco: Harper and Row, 1987.

Farradane, Jason. "The Nature of Information." *Journal of Information Science* 1 (1979): 13-17.

Flexner, Abraham. *Medical Education in the United States and Canada: A Report.* New York: Carnegie Foundation for the Advancement of Teaching, 1910.

Ford, N. "Relating 'Information Needs' to Learner Characteristics in Higher Education." *Journal of Documentation* 36 (June 1980): 99-114.

Gadamer, Hans-Georg. *Dialogue and Dialectic: Eight Hermeneutical Studies on Plato.* New Haven, CT: Yale University Press, 1980.

_____. *Truth and Method.* New York: Seabury Press, 1975.

Gallup, George, Jr. and Castelli, Jim. *The People's Religion: American Faith in the '90's.* New York: Macmillan, 1989.

Geertz, Clifford. *The Interpretation of Cultures.* New York: Basic Books, 1973.

George, Yolanda et al. *Saving Minds: Black Churches and Education.* Washington, DC: American Association for the Advancement of Science, 1989.

Goody, Jack. *The Domestication of the Savage Mind.* Cambridge: Cambridge University Press, 1977.

_____. *The Logic of Writing and the Organization of Society.* New York: Cambridge University Press, 1987.

Greeley, Andrew. "Challenges Facing U.S. Catholics: The Next Ten Years." *Commonweal* (Nov. 17, 1989): 617-623.

Grover, Robert and Greer, Roger. "The Cross-Disciplinary Imperative of LIS Research." In *Library and Information Science Research: Perspectives and Strategies for Improvement*, pp. 101-113. Ed. by C. McClure and P. Hernon. Norwood, NJ: Ablex, 1991.

Guba, E. G. and Lincoln, Y. S. "Naturalistic and Rationalistic Enquiry." In *Educational Research, Methodology, and Measurement: An International Handbook*, pp. 81-85. Ed. by John Keeves. Oxford: Pergamon Press, 1988.

Hale, Martha. "Paradigmatic Shift in Library and Information Science." In *Library and Information Science Research: Perspectives and Strategies for Improvement*, pp. 336-346. Ed. by C. McClure and P. Hernon. Norwood, NJ: Ablex, 1991.

Hawkins, Miriam. "An Investigation of the Reading Habits of Students and Graduates of the School of Medicine and the Candler School of Theology at Emory University." Master's thesis, Emory University, 1954.

Healy, John. "Reclaiming the Good News." *America* 159 (November 26, 1988): 437-439.

Herner, Saul and Herner, Mary. "Information Needs and Uses in Science and Technology." *Annual Review of Information Science and Technology* 2 (1967): 1-34.

Hewins, Elizabeth. "Information Need and Use Studies." *Annual Review of Information Science and Technology* 25 (1990): 145-172.

Hill, Michael. *The Religious Order: A Study of Virtuoso Religion and Its Legitimation in the Nineteenth-Century Church of England*. London: Heinemann, 1973.

Holland, Dewitte, ed. *Preaching in American History: Selected Issues in the American Pulpit, 1630-1967.* Nashville: Abingdon Press, 1969.

Holt, Grace. "Stylin' Outta the Black Pulpit." In *Rappin' and Stylin' Out*, pp. 189-204. Ed. by Thomas Kochman. Urbana, IL: University of Illinois Press, 1972.

"How Much Do Ministers Read?" *Christianity Today* 5 (April 24, 1961): 647.

Huseman, Dwight. "Books, Periodicals, and the Pastor." *Drexel Library Quarterly* 6 (January 1970): 4-26.

Huth, Edward. "The Underused Medical Literature." *Annals of Internal Medicine* 110 (1989): 99-100.

Innis, Harold. *The Bias of Communication.* Toronto: University of Toronto Press, 1951.

Intellectual Freedom Manual. 3rd ed. Compiled by the Office for Intellectual Freedom of the American Library Association. Chicago: American Library Association, 1989.

The Interpreter's Dictionary of the Bible. Ed. by G. A. Buttrick. 4 vols. Nashville: Abingdon Press, 1962.

Jacquet, Constant, ed. *Yearbook of American and Canadian Churches, 1990.* Nashville: Abingdon Press, 1990.

James, Robert. "Libraries in the Mind: How Can We See Users' Perceptions of Libraries?" *Journal of Librarianship* 15 (January 1983): 19-28.

King, Donald and Palmour, Vernon. "How Needs Are Generated; What We Have Found Out About Them." In *The

Nationwide Provision and Use of Information, pp. 68-79. ASLIB/IIS/LA Joint Conference Proceedings, September 15-19, 1980. London: The Library Association, 1981.

Kremer, Jeannette. "Information Flow Among Engineers in a Design Company." Ph.D. dissertation, University of Illinois, 1980.

Krikelas, James. "Information-Seeking Behavior: Patterns and Concepts." *Drexel Library Quarterly* 19 (Spring 1983): 5-20.

Lancaster, F. Wilfrid. "Needs, Demands, and Motivation in the Use of Sources of Information." Unpublished preprint of a paper delivered at the International Symposium on the Future of Scientific, Technological and Industrial Information Services. Leningrad, USSR, May, 28-31, 1990.

Lancaster, F. W. and Smith, Linda C. "Science, Scholarship and the Communication of Knowledge." *Library Trends* 27 (Winter 1978): 367-388.

Lancour, Harold. "The Reading Interests and Habits of the Graduates of the Union Theological Seminary." *Library Quarterly* 14 (January 1944): 28-35.

Lasswell, Harold. "The Structure and Function of Communication in Society." In *The Communication of Ideas: A Series of Addresses*, pp. 37-51. Ed. by Lyman Bryson. New York: Harper and Brothers, 1948.

Lawless, Elaine. "Oral 'Character' and 'Literary' Art." *Western Folklore* 44 (April 1985): 77-96.

Levitt, Jim. "A Survey of Evangelical Free Church Pastors on the Minister's Library." *Trinity Journal* 5 (Spring 1976): 126-134.

Lin, Nan and Garvey, William. "Information Needs and Uses." *Annual Review of Information Science and Technology* 7 (1972): 5-37.

Lindvall, Terry. "Preaching: The Language of the Age." *Christianity Today* 30 (October 18, 1986): 23.

Lipetz, Ben-Ami. "Information Needs and Uses." *Annual Review of Information Science and Technology* 5 (1970): 3-32.

Lischer, Richard. "The Limits of Story." *Interpretation* 38 (January 1984): 26-38.

Long, Thomas G. *The Witness of Preaching.* Louisville: Westminster Press, 1989.

Lynch, Mary Jo. "Librarian Salaries in 1990." In *The Whole Library Handbook*, pp. 71-72. Compiled by George Eberhart. Chicago: American Library Association, 1991.

Machlup, Fritz. *The Branches of Learning.* Vol. 2 of *Knowledge: Its Creation, Distribution, and Economic Significance.* Princeton: Princeton University Press, 1982.

_____. *The Production and Distribution of Knowledge in the United States.* Princeton: Princeton University Press, 1962.

Malony, H. Newton; Needham, Thomas; and Southard, Samuel. *Clergy Malpractice.* Philadelphia: Westminster, 1986.

Markquart, Edward. *Quest for Better Preaching: Resources for Renewal in the Pulpit.* Minneapolis: Augsburg, 1985.

Martin, Howard. "Puritan Preachers on Preaching: Notes on American Colonial Rhetoric." *Quarterly Journal of Speech* 50 (October 1964): 285.

Marty, Martin. "Martin Luther King: The Preacher as Virtuoso." *Christian Century* 106 (April 5, 1989): 348-350.

Martyn, John. "Information Needs and Uses." *Annual Review of Information Science and Technology* 9 (1974): 3-23.

_____. *Literature Searching Habits and Attitudes of Research Scientists.* Boston Spa: British Library, 1987.

Mason, Richard. "What Is an Information Professional?" *Journal of Education for Library and Information Science* 31 (Fall 1990): 122-138.

Mathews, Anne. "The Role of the U.S. Department of Education in Library and Information Science Research." In *Library and Information Science Research: Perspectives and Strategies for Improvement,* pp. 45-62. Ed. by C. McClure and P. Hernon. Norwood, NJ: Ablex, 1991.

May, Mark. *The Education of American Ministers.* Vol. 2 of *The Profession of the Ministry.* New York: Institute of Social and Religious Research, 1934.

McGrath, Eileen. "Don't Get Off the Reference Track." *Library Journal* 117 (April 1, 1992): 92-94.

McLuhan, Marshall. *The Gutenberg Galaxy.* New York: New American Library, 1962.

_____. *Understanding Media*. New York: McGraw-Hill, 1964.

McNeill, John. *A History of the Cure of Souls*. New York: Harper and Brothers, 1951.

Menzel, Herbert. "Information Needs and Uses in Science and Technology." *Annual Review of Information Science and Technology* 1 (1966): 41-69.

Merton, Robert. *Social Theory and Social Structure*. Glencoe, IL: Free Press, 1967.

Messer, Donald. *Contemporary Images of Christian Ministry*. Nashville: Abingdon Press, 1989.

Miksa, Francis. "Machlup's Categories of Knowledge as a Framework for Viewing Library and Information Science History." *Journal of Library History* 20 (Spring 1985): 157-172.

Miller, Keith. "Martin Luther King, Jr., and the Black Folk Pulpit." *Journal of American History* 78 (June 1991): 120-123.

"Ministers Rated Highly as Community Advice and Information Sources." *Emerging Trends* 12 (May 1990): 3.

Moberg, David. *The Church as a Social Institution: The Sociology of American Religion*. 2nd ed. Grand Rapids, MI: Baker Book House, 1984.

Montgomery, John. "Luther and Libraries." *Library Quarterly* 32 (April 1962): 133-147.

Morrison, Samuel. *The Founding of Harvard College*. Cambridge, MA: Harvard University Press, 1935.

Natoli, Joseph. "Librarianship as a Human Science: Theory, Method, and Application." *Library Research* 4 (1982): 163-174.

Neill, S. D. "Brookes, Popper, and Objective Knowledge." *Journal of Information Science* 4 (1982): 33-39.

The New Westminster Dictionary of Liturgy and Worship. Ed. by J.G. Davies. Philadelphia: Westminster Press, 1986.

Niebuhr, H. Richard. *Christ and Culture.* New York: Harper and Row, 1951.

Niles, Lyndrey. "Rhetorical Characteristics of Traditional Black Preaching." *Journal of Black Studies* 15 (September 1984): 41-52.

Nitecki, Joseph. "The Concept of Information-Knowledge Continuum: Implications for Librarianship." *Journal of Library History* 20 (Fall 1985): 387-407.

Nouwen, Henri. *The Wounded Healer: Ministry in Contemporary Society.* Garden City, NY: Doubleday, 1972.

Olson, D. R. "From Utterance to Text: The Bias of Language in Speech and Writing." *Harvard Educational Review* 47 (1977): 257-281.

Ong, Walter. *Orality and Literacy: The Technologizing of the Word.* London: Methuen, 1982.

_____. *The Presence of the Word: Some Prolegomena for Cultural and Religious History.* New Haven: Yale University Press, 1967.

Ortega, Jose y Gasset. *The Mission of the Librarian*. Boston: G.K. Hall, 1961.

Oswald, Roy and Kroeger, Otto. *Personality Type and Religious Leadership*. Washington, DC: The Alban Institute, 1988.

Paisley, William. "Information Needs and Uses." *Annual Review of Information Science and Technology* 3 (1968): 1-30.

Pandit, Idrisa. "Informal Communication in the Humanities: A Qualitative Inquiry." Ph.D. dissertation, University of Illinois, 1992.

Patton, Michael. *Qualitative Research Methods*. Beverly Hills, CA: Sage Publications, 1980.

Peshkin, Alan. "Understanding Complexity: A Gift of Qualitative Inquiry." *Anthropology & Education Quarterly* 19 (1988): 416-424.

Poole, Herbert. *Theories of the Middle Range*. Norwood, NJ: Ablex, 1985.

Porcella, Brewster. "The Information Gathering Habits of the Protestant Ministers of Cedar Rapids, Iowa." Ph.D. dissertation, University of Illinois, 1973.

Postell, Claudia. "Trends--Clergy Malpractice: An Emerging Field of Law." *Trial* 21 (1985): 91-93.

Postman, Neil. *Amusing Ourselves to Death: Public Discourse in the Age of Show Business*. New York: Viking, 1985.

Price, Derek de Solla. "Networks of Scientific Papers." *Science* 149 (July 30, 1965): 510-515.

_____. *Science Since Babylon.* New Haven, CT: Yale University Press, 1961.

Rapoport, Anatol. "The Promise and Pitfalls of Information Theory." In *Introduction to Information Science*, pp. 13-17. Ed. by T. Saracevic. New York: Bowker, 1970.

Roberson, M. "The Influence of Religious Beliefs on Health Choices of Afro-Americans." *Topics in Clinical Nursing* 7 (October 1985): 57-63.

Robinson, Haddon. *Biblical Preaching.* Grand Rapids: Baker Book House, 1980.

Rogers, E. M. *Diffusion of Innovations.* 3rd ed. New York: The Free Press, 1983.

Rohde, Nancy Freeman. "Information Needs." In *Advances in Librarianship*, 14: 49-73. Ed. by W. Simonton. New York: Academic Press, 1986.

Rubin, Michael and Huber, Mary. *The Knowledge Industry in the United States: 1960-1980.* Princeton, NJ: Princeton University Press, 1986.

Rudd, David. "Do We Really Need World III? Information Science With or Without Popper." *Journal of Information Science* 7 (1983): 99-105.

Scarlett, W. "The Clergyman's Role and Community Mental Health." *Mental Hygiene* 54 (1970): 378-381.

Schuller, David; Strommen, Merton; and Brekke, Milo, eds. *Ministry in America*. San Francisco: Harper and Row, 1980.

Shelley, Marshall. "Matter-of-Fact Intensity: Preaching." *Christianity Today* 30 (October 17, 1986): 22.

Shepherd, William, Jr. "A Second Look at Inductive Preaching." *Christian Century* 107 (September 19-26, 1990): 822-823.

Shields, Suzette Larae. "Black Ministers' Self-Perceived Role in the AIDS Crisis." Master's thesis, California State University at Long Beach, 1988.

Soper, Mary Ellen. "Characteristics and Use of Personal Collections." *Library Quarterly* 46 (1976): 397-415.

Statistical Abstracts of the United States, 1990. Washington, DC: U.S. Department of Commerce, Bureau of the Census, 1990.

Stevens, Norman. "The History of Information." In *Advances in Librarianship*, 14:1-48. Ed. by W. Simonton. New York: Academic Press, 1986.

Stott, John. *Between Two Worlds: The Art of Preaching in the Twentieth Century*. Grand Rapids: Eerdmans, 1982.

Stout, Harry. *The New England Soul: Preaching and Religious Culture in Colonial New England*. New York: Oxford University Press, 1986.

Strang, Ruth. *Exploration in Reading Patterns*. Chicago: University of Chicago Press, 1942.

Streatfield, D. "Moving Towards the Information User: Some Research and Its Implications." *Social Science Information Studies* 3 (1983): 223-240.

Sutton, Brett. "Literacy and Dissent." *Libraries and Culture* 26 (Winter 1991): 183-198.

_____. "Spirit and Polity in a Black Primitive Church." Ph.D. dissertation, University of North Carolina at Chapel Hill, 1983.

Tanner, Thomas M. "'Bring the Books': A Study of Ministerial Reading Habits Among Christian Church Ministers." Unpublished paper, University of Illinois Graduate School of Library and Information Science, 1989. [An adapted version was published in *Journal of Religious & Theological Information* 1 (1993): 53-76.]

_____. "Ministers of Information: The Flow of Information Among the Clergy of a Small Community, An Exploratory Study." Unpublished paper, University of Illinois Graduate School of Library and Information Science, 1991.

Taylor, Robert. "Questions-Negotiation and Information Seeking in Libraries." *College and Research Libraries* 29 (May 1968): 178-194.

Taylor, Steven and Bogdan, Robert. "In-Depth Interviewing." In their *Introduction to Qualitative Research Methods: The Search for Meanings*, pp. 76-105. 2nd ed. New York: John Wiley and Sons, 1984.

Theiss, Norman. "Preaching for Public Life." *Interpretation* 45 (July 1991): 253-266.

Troeger, Thomas. *Imagining a Sermon.* Nashville: Abingdon Press, 1990.

Vale, Mark. "Information Structure and the Information-Seeking Behavior of Lawyers." Ph.D. dissertation, Stanford University, 1988.

Wall, James. "Beyond Blandness in Preaching." *Christian Century* 105 (May 11, 1988): 467-468.

Warner, E.; Murray, A.; and Palmour, V. *Information Needs of Urban Residents: Final Report.* Washington, DC: Office of Education, 1973.

Watson, Patricia. "The Angelical Conjunction: The Preacher-Physicians of Colonial New England." Ph.D. dissertation, Johns Hopkins University, 1987.

Weber, Max. *The Theory of Social and Economic Organization.* Trans. by A. M. Henderson and Talcott Parsons. New York: Free Press, 1964.

Weedman, Judith. "Communication Patterns Among Cultural Gatekeepers: A Sociometric Analysis of Interactions Among Editors, Reviewers, and Critics of Children's Literature." Ph.D. dissertation, University of Michigan, 1989.

Westin, Alan and Finger, Anne. *Using the Public Library in the Computer Age: Present Patterns and Future Possibilities.* Chicago: American Library Association, 1991.

Wiberley, S. E., Jr. and Jones, W. G. "Patterns of Information Seeking in the Humanities." *College and Research Libraries* 50 (1989): 638-645.

Wilkin, Anne. "Personal Roles and Barriers in Information Transfer." In *Advances in Librarianship*, 7: 257-297. Ed. by M. J. Voigt and M. H. Harris. New York: Academic Press, 1977.

Williamson, Charles. *Training for Library Service: A Report Prepared for the Carnegie Corporation of New York*. Boston: The Merrymount Press, 1923.

Willimon, William. "Preaching: Entertainment or Exposition?" *Christian Century* 107 (February 28, 1990): 204-206.

Wilson, Patrick. *Second-Hand Knowledge: An Inquiry into Cognitive Authority*. Westport, CT: Greenwood Press, 1983.

Wilson, T.D. "A Case Study in Qualitative Research?" *Social Science Information Studies* 1 (1981): 241-246.

_____. "The Cognitive Approach to Information-Seeking Behavior and Information Use." *Social Science Information Studies* 4 (1984): 197-204.

Wilson, T.D. and Streatfield, D. "Structured Observation in the Investigation of Information Needs." *Social Science Information Studies* 1 (1981): 173-184.

Wood, A. S. *Captive to the Word, Martin Luther: Doctor of Sacred Scripture*. Exeter: Paternoster Press, 1969.

INDEX

abortion 276
abstracting services 164-167, 290-292, 327
access to information 276
AIDS 3, 99, 100, 102, 105, 239, 244
Annual Review of Information Science and Technology 334-337
audiotapes 169-170
audiovisuals 168-175
authority 65-70, 228, 314-317

Barna, George 125, 149
Bible 55-65, 91-92, 130-141, 179-180, 212, 226, 280-286
Biblical literacy 284-285
black churches 2-3, 328
black clergy 17
black preaching 59, 226
books 141-154, 292-293

case study 15-16, 260 (*see also* methodology)
channels *see* information channels
charisma 86-87, 352-353
church
    growth 148, 355
    information provider 21-22
    membership 1
clergy
    as information professional 21-109
    as librarian 33-65
    malpractice 4, 242-243, 252-256
    in this study 16-17

communications 208, 246, 325
    bias 220, 223
community
    information referral center 239-240
    spokesperson 1, 307-308, 326
    in this study 18-19
computers 176-182, 219, 280-281
conferences 78, 193-197
counseling 148, 203, 231-258, 271-275, 319-320
    center 254-255
critical incident technique 337
current awareness needs 121-123
current events 293-295
Current Thoughts & Trends 124-125, 143, 165-166, 180-181,
        318, 327

divine authority 90-98, 314-315

education of clergy
    continuing education 77-78
    current practice 327
    history in the United States 5-6
    overview 70-71
    sociological study 6-8
    in this study 72-74
educational authority 70-79, 314
Eisenstein, Elizabeth 211, 230
electronic media 216-225, 281, 295, 304-307, 353
Ellul, Jacques 209
equipper 43-48
expert 38-43

Gallup Poll 1
gatekeeper 1, 327
Greek 138-141, 286-287

Hebrew   138-141, 286-287

illustrations *see* sermon: illustrations
image of the clergy   23-25, 31-65, 313-314
information
    access   276
    channels   127-129
        formal channels   130-191
        informal channels   191-206
    definition   329-334
    dissemination   208-308, 318-322
    gatekeeper *see* gatekeeper
    gatherer   110-207, 317-318
    needs   110-124, 317-318, 332, 342-343
    overload   124-127, 327
    professional   21-109, 309-317, 322, 349-351
    referral *see* referrals
        referral center   239-240
    sources   128-129, 277-296, 327
    transfer   321
    use   2 (*see also* user studies)
InfoSearch   180
institutional authority   79-85, 314
interpreter   54-65
interpretive paradigm *see* naturalistic paradigm
interview questions   13-14

journals *see* periodicals

knowledge
    factual   101, 105
    limited   106-108
    professional   98
    relational   101-106
    spiritual   99-100
    versus information   329-330

lectionary 133-138
legal issues *see* clergy: malpractice
librarian
    academic 38-43
    activist 48-54
    public 33-37
    reference 43-48
    special 54-65
library
    church 185-186
    institutional 181, 186-191, 357
    personal 141-143, 182-186
    research 2-3, 324, 334

malpractice *see* clergy: malpractice
media 208-211, 304-307, 319-320
men's movement 153-154
mentoring 204-206
methodology 11-16, 260-261, 311-312, 323-326, 332-333
minister *see* clergy
ministerial associations 198-201
ministry *see* clergy
Ministry Currents 125-126
Ministry in America 7
movies 174-175, 295-296

naturalistic paradigm 12, 324-326, 330, 357
networks 201-206
newspapers 154-157

Ong, Walter 208-209
oral media 225-230, 247-250, 279-280
orality *see* oral media

pastor *see* clergy
pastoral care *see* counseling

pastoral counseling *see* counseling
periodicals 154-167, 292-293
personal authority 85-89, 314-315
personal experiences 287-290, 321, 356 (*see also* wounded
            healer)
personal networks 201-206
plagiarism 279
Porcella, Brewster 343-346
Postman, Neil 209-210
prayer 267-269
preaching 58-62, 87-89, 148, 244-245, 258-299, 320-322
            (*see also* sermon)
print media 211-216, 303-304
professional authority 65-70, 314-315
professional competence 253-255

questionnaire 15

radio 170-171, 304-305
reading groups 145
reading habits of clergy 338-341
referrals 251-257, 328
relationships 243-244
Religion Index 181
religious authority 84

seminars *see* conferences
seminary education 76 (*see also* education of clergy)
sermon
    Bible, use of 280-286
    deliverer 264-269
    delivery 296-299
    illustrations 287-299
    pastoral 271-275
    purpose 262-264
    sources 277-296

sermon (continued)
   televised 305-307
   topics, choice of 269-277
   see also preaching
storytelling 296-298, 325, 356

teaching 300-302
television 171-173, 216-225, 295-296, 305-307
"theories of the middle range" 335

user studies
   general 334-338
   clergy 338-346

value-added information 25-30
video 221
videocassettes 175, 250-251

wounded healer 48-54, 265
writing 213-214, 302-304

ABOUT THE AUTHOR

THOMAS M. TANNER is a graduate of Lincoln Christian College (A.B.) and Lincoln Christian Seminary (M.Div.). He also holds three degrees from the University of Illinois: the M.A. in Classical Philology, the M.S. in Library Science, and the Ph.D. in Library and Information Science. Dr. Tanner is Library Director and Director of Strategic Planning at Lincoln Christian College and Seminary in Lincoln, Illinois. In addition, he has served as a preaching minister, a library consultant, an evaluator for the American Association of Bible Colleges, and as a seminary professor. He has published several articles in professional journals, as well as *A Manual of Style for Bible College and Seminary Students*, 4th ed. (Lincoln Christian College and Seminary Press, 1994).